Persuading the Supreme Court

Persuading the Supreme Court

The Significance of Briefs in Judicial Decision-Making

Morgan L. W. Hazelton

and

Rachael K. Hinkle

University Press of Kansas

Published by the University Press of Kansas (Lawrence, Kansas 66045), which was organized by the Kansas Board of Regents and is operated and funded by Emporia State University, Fort Hays State University, Kansas State University, Pittsburg State University, the University of Kansas, and Wichita State University.

Library of Congress Cataloging-in-Publication Data

Names: Hazelton, Morgan L. W., author. | Hinkle, Rachael K., author.
Title: Persuading the Supreme Court : the significance of briefs in judicial
    decision-making / Morgan L. W. Hazelton and Rachael K. Hinkle.
Description: Lawrence, Kansas : University Press of Kansas, 2022. |
    Includes bibliographical references and index.
Identifiers: LCCN 2021061605
    ISBN 9780700633630 (paperback)
    ISBN 9780700633647 (ebook)
Subjects: LCSH: United States. Supreme Court. | Judicial process–United
    States. | Legal briefs–United States.
Classification: LCC KF8742 .H39 2022 | DDC 347.73/26–dc23/eng/20220608
LC record available at https://lccn.loc.gov/2021061605.

British Library Cataloguing-in-Publication Data is available.

Printed in the United States of America

10 9 8 7 6 5 4 3 2

The paper used in this publication is acid free and meets the minimum requirements of the American National Standard for Permanence of Paper for Printed Library Materials Z39.48–1992.

For my mother, Trica, and my mother-in-law, Katie.
   —MLWH

For my mother, Julie, and Pat Hoose, who sends hilarious
birthday cards.
   —RKH

Contents

Figures and Tables

Figures

Tables

Preface

On the first day of graduate school in political science at Washington University in St. Louis, Missouri, we discovered we were kindred intellectual spirits. We both had attended law school and were leaving legal careers—Rachael as a judicial clerk and Morgan as an attorney working in civil defense. More than that, we both had a love of text, be it literary, judicial, or academic. Finally, we were keenly interested in learning and using quantitative tools to garner new insights into issues of law and politics. These shared experiences and interests form the backbone of the research we undertook for this book.

Years later, as part of an exploration of a joint project about Supreme Court decision-making, Jim Spriggs suggested that we obtain the text of Supreme Court briefs. That suggestion led us on a long and winding road that has culminated in this book. Although Jim had to withdraw from the project after a few years, we are very grateful to him for that important suggestion and his insights from prior work on briefs. We are also grateful to him for the overall guidance to us both in and after graduate school.

Since we both came to political science with backgrounds as attorneys, we approached this project with the suspicion that the arguments lawyers make matter in ways that are likely to be interesting. Much ink has been spilled on the role of ideology in judicial decision-making. However, we felt there was much more to be learned about the mediating role of how lawyers provide information to the justices to help them assess which policies are likely to meet their goals. Since both of us were also interested in developing and using computational methods for textual analysis, this project formed a perfect opportunity to blend our theoretical expectations with nuanced empirical examination.

We began by collecting the briefs available on Westlaw from 1970 to 2005. Further investigation revealed gaps in the data, which we sought to fill by obtaining all briefs available from Lexis. Since the two services create their unique identifiers for briefs, even a seemingly simple task such as eliminating the overlapping documents present in both data sets was a headache. Rather than stop with electronically available briefs, we took to the sub-sub-basement of the Cornell Law Library to track down and scan hard copies of missing briefs. While both of us contributed to the data collection, Rachael bore more of the brunt of this grueling work. After years of data collection and processing, Lee Epstein invited us to submit a piece on Supreme Court briefs to a special issue of the *Washington University Journal of Law and Policy* devoted to exploring the Supreme Court under the leadership of Chief Justice Roberts. This invitation spurred us to extend our data collection an additional ten years.

Over the years, we remained doggedly persistent through all the challenges posed by the data collection because we had questions we wanted to answer. Morgan further expanded this already ambitious project by conducting interviews of practitioners and former Supreme Court clerks to provide an authentic, experience-based foundation to our theoretical arguments. We are indebted to these fascinating interviewees who generously shared their experiences and understanding of Supreme Court litigation. Morgan identified themes and points of contention across the interviews and integrated those insights throughout the book. After years of hard work on data collection and interviews, we are excited about all the interesting questions we can raise and explore in this book. Our data allows us to weave together multiple lines of research and firsthand accounts to present a more unified picture of Supreme Court practice. For example, we extend theoretical expectations about litigant resources to amici and incorporate insights from work on amicus briefs to examine litigant briefs. Our work also considers the complex interactions among briefers and how that coordination speaks to theories regarding lobbying. Relatedly, we take on the task of understanding how briefs can signal policy coalescence and how the Court interprets such communications.

This project is an heir to Paul Collins's *Friends of the Supreme Court* in both substance and form. That excellent book set the bar in our understanding of amicus briefs. Tackling the task of moving forward our knowledge of the Supreme Court in a comparable way has been both intimidating and inspiring. Not only have we built on the excellent insights in his book to build our theory but we also seek to follow his example in making data readily available to the research community and supporting research in this area in a variety of ways. His comments on various parts of this project over the years have been very useful and are greatly appreciated.

Additionally, we owe a sizeable intellectual debt to the work of Pam Corley (including her work with Paul Collins and others), whose path-breaking articles regarding using quantitative tools to examine the text of briefs and opinions opened the door to this work. In addition to this invaluable foundation, she has been generous with her insights and feedback over the years. Pam has also provided clearheaded encouragement and mentorship. We are fortunate to be in the same field as her.

The list of others to whom we are also grateful for their thoughts on this work is quite extensive. We have received incisive and insightful comments from audiences at a range of academic gatherings, including workshops at Saint Louis University School of Law, the Baldy Center for Law and Policy at the University at Buffalo, and Washington University in St. Louis, as well as the Political Economy and Public Law Conference, the Conference on Empirical Legal Studies, the Political Economy of the American Judiciary Conference hosted by Kellogg's Ford Motor Company Center for Global Citizenship and Northwestern Pritzker Law School, and annual conferences of the American, Midwest, and Southern Political Science Associations. We are especially grateful for the helpful advice provided by Alyx Mark, Claire Wofford, John Scheb, Kevin Quinn, Lee Epstein, Michael J. Nelson, Paul Collins, Paul Gardner, Rich Pacelle, Ryan Black, Steve Puro, and Tracey George. We are also grateful to David Congdon for being a consistently excellent editor throughout this process. Working with him has truly been a pleasure.

The extensive data collection and interviews required for this project would not have been possible without a variety of important help and resources. We appreciate the funding provided by the Baldy Center for Law and Social Policy at the University at Buffalo, which supported our efforts to obtain the text of hard copies of briefs missing from electronic databases. We would also like to thank the Cornell Law Library staff, who was very helpful in facilitating that aspect of the project, especially Margaret Jane Ambrose. Finally, we are grateful for the assistance of many diligent research assistants over the years, including Abigail Szidon, Jaime Vandenover, John Whitlock, Joseph Williams, Joshua Boston, Joshua Turner, Oliver Clarke, Rachael Behling, Ramisa Hassan, Robert Topping, Sophia Crain, and Samilia Oluwatope Adelaiye.

Acknowledgments

Morgan

The amount of support I receive for my work from my husband, James Brookes, has made me the envy of many of my friends. He has also helped raise our son, Jaxon, to be my cheerleader in my many endeavors. I owe them both a debt of gratitude for all the ways they have contributed to the creation of this book. Furthermore, they complete my life and are a great source of joy and comfort. I am also grateful to my parents, James and Trica Hazelton, who taught me to be interested, aware, and diligent. They also both provided excellent examples of interest in a wide range of intellectual traditions and how such approaches can complement each other. I have also been blessed with smart and interesting in-laws. My mother-in-law, Katie Brookes, has an insatiable interest in the world around her that has extended to my research. It has been very gratifying.

I have also been exceedingly lucky to have generous and brilliant colleagues in many settings. The second legal education that I received working at Scott & Hulse has been invaluable to my research. My graduate education was greatly enhanced by being a part of the Center for Empirical Research in the Law and exposed to its faculty, students, and staff. Moreover, Saint Louis University has provided me with fantastic colleagues, both present and past. I have enjoyed a wealth of tangible and intangible resources flowing from many corners of the university. Both the Department of Political Science and the School of Law contributed significantly to this interdisciplinary work.

I could not have asked for a better partner in research, writing, and crime than Rachael. On that first day of graduate school, I could have never guessed what a central role she would play in my life.

Rachael

My mother is fond of telling people that I have her brain—a comment that is invariably followed by her stating that she really wishes I would give it back. Joking aside, my parents have provided me with a tremendous amount for which I am grateful. For purposes of these pages, the most relevant gift my parents have bestowed on me is the ability to write. I was homeschooled from third through twelfth grade, so the entire foundation of my not inconsiderable education was laid by my parents. In the wake of the COVID-19 pandemic, parents everywhere have a pretty good idea about exactly how much of a sacrifice that entailed. The years of diagramming sentences, writing paper after paper, and revising draft after draft were not exactly a cakewalk for me either. But that hard work has paid off, both mine and theirs. My first book would not be complete without acknowledging the debt I owe my parents (and especially my mother) for preparing me to be the writer I am today.

A large number and variety of people have supported me in a zillion ways as I have navigated life while working on a book project. There is no way to mention them all. I am grateful to my colleagues at the University at Buffalo for creating an environment that is conducive to getting research done (especially in my years as an assistant professor). I appreciate all the emails that were actually emails (instead of meetings) and the chair finding extra room in the budget when I needed to get to conferences to present work from this project. One couldn't ask for a more supportive department. I would also like to thank my AP family for support and camaraderie beyond academia. A group of people who make you laugh, tell you you're funny, discuss the best place to buy donuts, and pick you up when you feel your worst is truly invaluable.

Last, but far from least, I am daily thankful for Morgan. She is the best of coauthors and the best of friends.

Persuading the Supreme Court

Introduction

In February 2013, the Supreme Court released a unanimous opinion in the case of *Florida v. Harris*,[1] overturning a decision by the Florida Supreme Court. This fourteen-page opinion represented the culmination of more than five years of legal proceedings in four courts with twenty judges, all focused on the question of what is required to establish probable cause based on an alert from a drug-sniffing dog. Specifically, the justices had resolved how the reliability of a dog should be established in such cases. Is training enough? Certification? Should we consider how the dog performs in controlled settings, in the field, or both? In the absence of probable cause, any evidence that police discover because of the alert is not admissible. Thus, the standard announced by the Supreme Court of the United States was an important one. It helped determine what evidence is allowed in criminal trials, which can be the difference between whether a defendant goes to prison or a prosecutor fails to convict. In understanding the question at hand and resolving it, the justices were able to rely on a wealth of information flowing to the Court, with the most crucial stream coming from briefs from the defendant, the state, and interested groups and individuals. It is but one example of how attorneys communicate information to the Court via written filings and how such information is used by the justices to decide cases. Despite the importance of the Court and the information it receives, many questions remain unanswered regarding the production of such information and its relationship to the Court's decisions. In this book, we leverage the multitude of written submissions to the Court over the course of more than three decades to shed light on both their construction and impact.

Sniffs, Drugs, and Criminal Justice

On June 24, 2006, Clayton Harris was driving his pickup truck on State Road 20 in Bristol, Florida.[2] In the words of the state of Florida, "It was not going to be his day."[3] At that same time, Officer William Wheetley was patrolling the road with his K-9 partner Aldo. Officer Wheetley noticed that the tags on Harris's truck were expired and pulled Harris over. While speaking to Harris, he observed that Harris was shaking and breathing heavily. He also spotted an open can of beer in the truck. The officer asked to search the truck, but Harris refused.

Upon this refusal, Wheetley brought Aldo around the vehicle to sniff for contraband. Officer Wheetley reported that during the search, Aldo alerted him that something might be awry in the vehicle, specifically around the driver's side door. The Florida Department of Law Enforcement had certified Aldo regarding detecting various controlled substances, but that certification had lapsed. Such certification was not required for the work Aldo was performing. Additionally, while Officer Wheetley had trained with the dog, the officer had not been certified as part of a team with Aldo.

A search of the truck revealed a long list of items used to make methamphetamines: pseudoephedrine pills, matches, muriatic acid, antifreeze, iodine crystals, and more. Aldo had been trained to detect methamphetamines but received no training regarding the pseudoephedrine, the precursor, or any of the other ingredients that were found. Upon these discoveries, Harris confessed that he had been "cooking methamphetamine for about a year."[4] Wheetley arrested Harris for illegal possession of the pseudoephedrine.

A few weeks later, Harris and Wheetley met again when Wheetley pulled Harris over for a broken taillight. Again, Wheetley deployed Aldo, who alerted the officer that he detected something near the driver's-side door. This time, Wheetley did not find any controlled substances in the truck. He did, however, find an open bottle of liquor.

In the trial court, public defenders representing Harris attempted to suppress the evidence from the first of these two searches on the basis that there was no probable cause for the warrantless search. Specifically, they argued the search resulted from a false alert from a dog with a potentially expired certification and for whom the prosecution would need to produce evidence of field performance. At the suppression hearing, the focus was on evidence regarding the extent to which there was evidence of sufficient training and ability on the part of Aldo and his handler to justify the search. Officer Wheetley testified regarding the training that both he and Aldo had received. He also explained that he kept records of when Aldo alerted him and he found contraband but not for when Aldo alerted him but he did not find anything illegal. In his estimation, Aldo likely responded to a residual smell of methamphetamines on the driver's-side door handle. Wheetley was, however, unable to estimate how long Aldo might respond to residual odors. The trial judge denied the motion without issuing findings of fact. Harris ultimately pled no contest to the charges and was sentenced to two years in prison and five years of probation. As part of that deal, he reserved his right to appeal the denial of his motion to suppress, which he pursued.

With the continued assistance of public defenders, Harris appealed the resulting conviction. The intermediate appellate court affirmed the trial court's decision in the fall of 2008 in a very short per curiam opinion that consisted of a list of citations. With the continued assistance of public defenders, Harris then petitioned the Florida Supreme Court for discretionary review on the basis that the appellate court's decision conflicted with the ruling of another appellate court in the state. *Police K-9 Magazine,* the Canine Development Group, and the National Police Canine Association filed amicus curiae briefs (or so-called friend-of-the-court briefs, called amicus for short) supporting the state of Florida's position that the search was constitutional.

On September 22, 2011, the Florida Supreme Court held that Aldo's alert was insufficient to establish probable cause as required by the Fourth and Fourteenth Amendments of the US Constitution based on the totality-of-the-circumstances test. In doing so, the court set out a list of evidence that the State must present regarding the reliability of the dog alerts, including training and certification records pertaining to the dog and officer, field performance records with information about false alerts, and any other objective evidence of the dog's reliability. In the decision, the Florida Supreme Court noted that the applicable totality-of-the-circumstances test required a court to consider the extent to which dogs are alerting to residual odors.

Unhappy with the Florida Supreme Court ruling, the state of Florida filed a writ of certiorari with the Supreme Court of the United States in late 2011. Florida asserted that the state high-court ruling was not in keeping with the federal circuit's interpretation of the Fourth Amendment and should be reviewed. Harris, still represented by public defenders, opposed the review on the basis that the Florida Supreme Court's opinion did not conflict with the US Supreme Court's Fourth Amendment jurisprudence and that consideration of field performance did not destroy the ability of law enforcement to use detector dogs. Finally,

Harris asserted that the Court should avoid review so that it would not become embroiled in setting the standards for canine training and certification. The Supreme Court granted certiorari in March of 2012.

Learning about the Big Show

With the Supreme Court granting certiorari, Harris and the state of Florida were now litigating the merits of the case in the highest court in the United States on a constitutional matter with implications for federal, state, and local governments. How should the parties and their attorneys proceed? How might this practice look different than what came before? What other groups and individuals might become involved? How will the justices respond?

We use a multifaceted approach to learning about Supreme Court practice and the central role of briefing. It is one that pulls from an abundance of sources and methodological traditions. The foundations include legal sources in the form of formal rules, practice guides, and published interviews and articles regarding the perspectives of former clerks and justices in conjunction with social science research regarding Supreme Court litigation. We use these sources, original interviews with former Supreme Court clerks and attorneys with experience before the Court, and quantitative analyses of a rich original data set of tens of thousands of briefs, with measures built using sophisticated natural language processing tools. To begin, we discuss the various sources and their contributions and illustrate their benefits and limitations. We then weave these ideas together in setting forth our theories regarding the role of information and resources in Supreme Court litigation and a preview of the book that follows.

The Formal Rules

One way we could learn about the contours of such merits litigation would be to consult the US Supreme Court's formal rules and related publications. *The Rules of the Supreme Court of the United States* (US Supreme Court 2019) and preceding versions lay out details regarding the formal procedures and requirements, much of which centers on briefs. The rules provide guidance on the mechanics of practice. For example, we learn about the timing of briefs. Petitioners are to file their briefs on the merits within forty-five days of when the Court granted certiorari, followed by the respondents' briefs on the merits thirty days after the petitioners file their briefs, and the petitioners' reply briefs are due thirty days after that (Rule 25). An outside group of individuals wishing to file an amicus brief must obtain the consent of all parties or file a motion for leave to file. As described by the clerk of the Court in Harris (2019, 2):

> The deadline to file an amicus brief in support of a petitioner or appellant is thirty days after the case is placed on the docket or the Court calls for a response, whichever is later. The deadline to file an amicus brief in support of a motion for leave to file a bill of complaint in an original action is sixty days after the case is placed on the docket. Neither of these deadlines may be extended. The deadline to file an amicus brief in support of a respondent, defendant or appellee is the same as the deadline to file a brief in opposition or motion to dismiss or affirm; this amicus deadline is therefore extended when the deadline to file the brief in opposition or motion to dismiss or affirm is extended. Rule 37.2(a).

In addition to the hard and fast procedural rules, they also give standards guiding filings. Rule 37 directs that amicus briefs should provide new information to the Court rather than being repetitive of other briefs. But, of course, actual practice is not exactly captured by the formal rules and guidance.

Practice Guides

Another obvious source would be guides about appellate practice, with a special eye toward advice regarding Supreme Court litigation.[5] Much of the advice regarding Supreme Court practice overlaps with appellate practice generally (Kole 2013), such as highlighting the importance of briefs.[6] The central role of briefs has been highlighted by justices, including Roberts, Thomas, and Ginsburg (Garner 2010). The general writing advice includes discussions of brevity, "good, clear English," and avoiding exaggeration (Shapiro et al. 2019, 13.11). However, the guides also highlight a number of ways in which such practice is unique (e.g., Mayer Brown n.d.; Shapiro et al. 2019). First, there is the position of the Court at the apex of the judicial hierarchy:

> The first and most important factor to remember is that counsel is writing for a supreme court whose decisions are not reviewable by any higher tribunal. Consequently, the Court is not bound by authorities to any greater extent than it wishes to be and is much freer to reach what it regards as the correct or sensible decision than any subordinate tribunal. This means that, although prior authority is not to be ignored, counsel should place greater emphasis on convincing the court on grounds of reason and principle, apart from authority. (Shapiro et al. 2019, 13.11[F]).

There is also the ambiguous role of facts outside the record, where such facts are both discouraged generally and often allowed in the form of briefs that address "published material containing facts that bear upon the reasonableness of legislation" or so-called Brandeis briefs (Shapiro et al. 2019, section K). Additionally, the "sophisticated" nature of the practice makes it "a more demanding undertaking then preparing briefs in other courts" (13.12).

Furthermore, the robust nature of amicus practice in the Supreme Court leads to more attention on such briefs (Mayer Brown n.d.; Shapiro et al. 2019). Guide authors highlight technical aspects, such as deadlines and the requirement to identify sponsors (Shapiro et al. 2019, 13.14). They also discuss stylistic issues, including that briefs should be as short as possible and objective in tone (e.g., Ebner 2017; Mayer Brown n.d.). There are often also less technical types of advice, specifically the need to avoid repetition and the risk that clerks and justices won't read "me too" briefs (Mayer Brown n.d.; Simpson and Vasaly 2015; Shapiro et al. 2019). Some guides provide more nuance; for example, Ebner (2017) advises that amicus briefs should not venture outside of the questions presented in the party briefs.

Practice guides often go beyond further articulation of the rules and general writing advice to provide guidance regarding the how and why of such briefs. First, descriptions of the role of amicus briefs highlight the informational, political, and policy-related functions of such briefs. For example, in defining the functions of amicus briefs, Simpson and Vasaly (2015, 24) include "examining policy issues," "providing a more attractive advocate," "supplementing a party's brief," and "providing technical expertise." Additionally, well-written amicus briefs can act to replace poorly written party briefs (Mayer Brown n.d.). Some also highlight prior work that paints a mixed picture as to the likelihood that clerks and justices will engage amicus briefs, especially repetitive ones, in depth (Simpson and Vasaly 2015; Mayer Brown n.d.). Moreover, many include advice regarding the logistics and importance of recruiting amici based on these functions while also highlighting the importance and limits of coordination among parties and amici (Kollross 2021; Mayer Brown n.d.; Shapiro et al. 2019; McGimsey 2016). Furthermore, they describe the influence of reputable attorneys and the powerful role of the solicitor general (Mayer Brown n.d.).

Directly Consulting Experienced Individuals

Another approach, which we engage, is to speak directly to individuals who have acted as attorneys before and clerks for the Court. We conducted eighteen original interviews with individuals who have experience with Supreme Court litigation.[7] Of those participants, fifteen had experience as an attorney who filed a party and/or amicus brief with the Supreme Court and eight were former clerks (five individuals had overlapping experience). Attorney and Former Clerk H noted that clerking and practicing before the Court are "different experiences." Thus, learning from individuals with both types of experience is important. Furthermore, these interviews allow us to add the perspectives of attorneys and former clerks who aren't publishing guides and are not subject to the desirability biases that may come from "speaking on the record."

While we discuss the interviews in much more detail in the chapters to come, some interesting themes emerge from them. Often interviewees reinforced and expanded on the perspectives of guides. For example, they accentuated the importance of briefs. In one instance, Attorney R stated that briefs represent "the chance to win the case" and "persuade" the Court. They also offered contextualized advice regarding the content of briefs. Multiple interviewees advised that amicus briefs should only be as long as needed. As described by Attorney Q, they attempt to be "as short and concise as possible . . . the shorter, the better." Attorney J explained this approach in terms of the "capacity" of clerks and justices to digest information.

Furthermore, the interviewees were sensitive to the special aspects of practice in front of the Supreme Court, especially regarding its policymaking functions. An attorney with experience as a clerk (B) noted that it is "unique" to the Supreme Court that "justices are always thinking beyond the participants in the case." Several interviewees explicitly described the Court as "a policy-making body," with even more implying it. This understanding of the Court influences how litigators approach it. For example, in one interview, an attorney (P) explained that it is a "classic mistake" to tell the Court, "Don't worry regarding the consequences" because the Court is "really concerned regarding the floodgates and future cases."

Moreover, the interviewees did not always reflect the dominant advice from the guides but rather expressed a wide range of approaches, sometimes influenced by their specific perspectives. There were disagreements on various topics, including the importance of experience, targeting briefs to specific justices, and aspects of coordination. In one example, interviewees varied in their views of repetition in amicus briefs. While many participants criticized repetitive briefs, others thought they had the potential to help. On one end, Former Supreme Court Clerk N described repetitive amici as "distinctly not helpful." At the other end of the spectrum, another interviewee with experience as a clerk and litigator in the Court (I) said that bringing up central ideas across multiple briefs was "like voting," meaning it should be done "early and often." Additionally, they explained that repetition can be the difference between an idea seeming "crazy" and getting "five votes."

Social Science Theory and Research

It is also very important to borrow from the wealth of scholarly theories and rigorous quantitative research in the social sciences to help understand the bigger picture of Supreme Court litigation. Theoretical frameworks from fields such as political science, economics, and psychology dovetail with the study of law to help us understand why litigants and justices behave in the ways they do. The plural of anecdote is famously not data, and empirical studies can help us understand the extent to which more individualized accounts represent general phenomenons. The practice guide authors themselves are often relying on these types of studies (e.g., Shapiro et al. 2019). Thus, we engage a number of important areas of thought and inquiry in developing our theories of Supreme Court litigation. Specifically, we engage a rich literature regarding the role of information in decision-making and how that relates to Supreme Court litigation. In doing so, we dive into the central role of briefs in communicating information to the justices.

INFORMATION AND DECISION-MAKING

In *Florida v. Harris*, the US Supreme Court was called upon to make a decision that would shape policy regarding alerts from drug-sniffing dogs for the entire country. Crafting policy is a tricky business. Policy makers of all types must contend with competing interests and political pressures and the inherent difficulties of designing policy. In each of these areas, officials must deal with uncertainty (Hazelton, Hinkle, and Spriggs 2019; Krehbiel 1992; Szmer and Ginn 2014; Yackee and Yackee 2006): What is the issue? What are appropriate goals in this policy area? Which policy will best carry out the policy maker's intentions in creating the course of action? What will the political ramifications of a given policy be for the person deciding? Thus, policy makers need and want information to reduce the uncertainties surrounding planning. Furthermore, affected parties and groups naturally want to provide information in an attempt to sway them (Downs 1957). Therefore, it should be of no surprise that information is central to a wealth of theories regarding the creation of policy (Hazelton, Hinkle, and Spriggs 2019; Austen-Smith 1996; Krehbiel 1992).

The extent to which groups will invest resources in a policy area is also vital information for policy makers. The resources dedicated to information provision itself can act as such information (Hazelton, Hinkle, and Spriggs 2019). It provides them with an indication of the extent to which groups care about a topic and the resources they are able and willing to dedicate to pursuing policy in that area. In part, this information is very useful because it informs policy makers regarding the extent to which groups are likely and able to respond to decisions with which they don't agree or promote ones with which they do (Hazelton, Hinkle, and Spriggs 2019; Abramowicz and Colby 2009; Arnold 1992; Leyden 1995; Moe 1988).

THE SUPREME COURT, POLICY, AND INFORMATION

The Supreme Court acts as a powerful policy-making body in the US system: "Court decisions announce policy in much the same way that legislation and agency rules do. For example, such decisions state the new rules and define who is bound by them" (Hazelton, Hinkle, and Spriggs 2019, 129). For example, in *Florida v. Harris*, the Court's opinion set forth the policy for determining when a dog alert should be considered reliable in terms of ascertaining whether there was probable cause for a search. As such, the members of the Court and their staff also need information over a wide array of topics, including facts, technical information, legal arguments, public opinion, and more (Hazelton, Hinkle, and Spriggs 2019; Collins 2008; Corley 2008; Epstein and Knight 1999; Johnson 2001; Johnson, Wahlbeck, and Spriggs 2006).

Despite the lack of an electoral connection, the justices should care about how the public and the elected branches, who are beholden to the public, will receive their decisions (Epstein and Knight 1998). The Court famously lacks both a purse and sword: it controls neither a revenue stream to support the institution nor a means of force to ensure adherence with its edicts. Compliance rests on the general acceptance of the Court's legitimacy and enforcement by other branches (Hazelton, Hinkle, and Spriggs 2019; Spriggs and Wahlbeck 1997; Friedman 2009; Hall 2014). Both legitimacy and enforcement by the other branches are, of course, tied with public opinion. First, unpopular decisions can endanger support from groups with a stake in those decisions (Hazelton, Hinkle, and Spriggs 2019; Ura and Merrill 2017; Clawson and Waltenburg 2008; Gibson and Caldeira 1992; Hoekstra 2000, 2003). Noncompliance itself can weaken the Court's ability to inspire adherence in the future (Hazelton, Hinkle, and Spriggs 2019; Friedman 2009; Hall 2010, 2014; Spriggs 1996; Spriggs and Wahlbeck 1997, 368). Second, the other branches are more likely to adhere to decisions they dislike where the public supports the Court (Friedman 2009; Hall 2010; Hall 2014; Spriggs 1996; Spriggs and Wahlbeck 1997). In these ways, one can understand the Court to have constituents upon whose support it "relies. . . against its political opposition" (Gibson and Caldeira 1992, 1140).

Relatedly, the Court has reason to care about popular support because much of its structure and power are dependent on the elected branches, particularly Congress. The Constitution provides little in the way of requirements regarding the structure of the federal courts. Per Article III, there will be a Supreme Court, and its justices will have life tenure and nonreducible salaries. According to the terms of the Constitution, Congress may decide the number of justices and structure of the lower federal courts upon which the Supreme Court sits at the apex. Additionally, while Article III lists the types of cases and controversies over which the Court will have jurisdiction, Section 2 allows Congress to make exceptions and restrictions to the Court's appellate jurisdiction. This appellate jurisdiction represents the overwhelming bulk of the Court's docket. While there is dispute over how far Congress can go in restricting appellate jurisdiction, there are indications that it is quite a bit (Monaghan 2019). Thus, the Court has reason to want to keep Congress relatively happy or have enough popular support to weather moments of conflict. For example, public support for the institution helped protect the Court from Franklin Roosevelt's plan to pack the Court in light of unfavorable rulings (Caldeira 1987). Certainly, commentators express doubt that the Court would survive if it were consistently against public opinion (Hazelton, Hinkle, and Spriggs 2019; Friedman 2009; McCloskey and Levinson 2016; Ura and Merrill 2017; Kramer 2004; Levin 2006).

While the Court needs information regarding public opinion on the issues before it, such information is often not readily available (Hazelton, Hinkle, and Spriggs 2019; Friedman 2009, 379; Rosen 2006, 9; Caldeira 1991; Ura and Merrill 2017). Additionally, public opinion on a related topic may be nascent, and the salience of issues to the public may be difficult to discern (Hazelton, Hinkle, and Spriggs 2019; Friedman 2009; Rosen 2006; Pildes 2011). This vacuum creates a need for a conduit of information to the Court. A system that privileges party briefs and encourages vigorous amicus participation from outside parties fulfills this need (Barker 1967; Black, Owens, et al. 2016; Collins, Corley, and Hamner 2015; Hazelton, Hinkle, and Spriggs 2019). These briefs provide the Court with the views of interested groups and individuals from diverse perspectives (Perkins and Collins 2017). Such information acts as a rough proxy for public opinion. More importantly, it provides the views of the subpopulations that are most likely to become aware of an opinion and respond to it (Barker 1967; Hazelton, Hinkle, and Spriggs 2019; Rice 2020): the briefs come from the parties and amici who have sufficient interest and resources to make their voices heard in the country's highest court. This system reflects informational lobbying more generally (Epstein and Knight 1999; Collins 2008, 2018; Hazelton, Hinkle, and Spriggs 2019).

THE FLOW OF INFORMATION TO THE COURT AND THE CENTRAL ROLE OF BRIEFS

Due to the Supreme Court's influential position in American government and its ability to set policy, it should be no surprise that the Court enjoys an environment rich in information. The American judicial system is an adversarial system in which parties compete to establish facts and legal arguments (Hazelton, Hinkle, and Spriggs 2019; Kim 2014). Moreover, the Court's position in the judicial hierarchy and its procedures and norms ensure a steady flow of information to the justices and their clerks. These structural factors encourage both parties and interested observers to provide relevant information to the Court primarily through carefully crafted and coordinated written briefs.

The design of US courts ultimately encourages information flowing to the Court (Hazelton, Hinkle, and Spriggs 2019; Black, Hall, et al. 2016; Feldman 2017a, 2017b; Collins, Corley, and Hamner 2015; Corley 2008). Litigants are highly motivated to provide information to the courts because the US system places this burden on them: the system puts litigants in the driver's seat regarding raising issues and seeking and providing information. It also creates competition between the parties to provide information, thereby increasing the overall provision of facts, arguments, etc. (Hazelton, Hinkle, and Spriggs 2019; Kim 2014).

The vast majority of this information flows to courts through written filings. In appellate courts, briefs are the primary vehicle for such information (Black, Hall, et al. 2016; Collins, Corley, and Hamner 2015; Hazelton, Hinkle, and Spriggs 2019). The justices themselves tout their importance (Corley 2008; Feldman 2017b). In addition to being a primary source of information, briefs "contextualize the lower court opinions that the justices must assess and define the conflicts over those opinions" (Hazelton, Hinkle, and Spriggs 2019, 130 [citations omitted]). Furthermore, briefs set the stage for oral arguments, another means by which the justices can collect information (Collins and Solowiej 2007).

The adversarial nature of the process increases the importance of the attorneys who litigants hire to represent them: the better the attorneys they hire, the more likely they are to be able to produce quality briefs with essential information (Haire, Hartley, and Lindquist 1999; Feldman 2016; Hanretty 2014; Larsen and Devins 2016; Szmer, Songer, and Bowie 2016; Szmer and Ginn 2014; Wheeler et al. 1987). The behavior of legal educators, clients, lawyers, and justices indicates that briefs are important (Hazelton, Hinkle, and Spriggs 2019). Law schools target curriculum around teaching students how to write briefs (Corley 2008; Hazelton, Hinkle, and Spriggs 2019). In recent decades, bar examiners have changed bar exams to test drafting skills (Preparing for the MPT 2022). Clients who have reached the Supreme Court invest large amounts of money in legal representation, sometimes in the millions of dollars (Belz 2017). Attorneys often charge in the $400 to $800 per hour range for representation at the high court. Paul Clement, an elite veteran Supreme Court litigator, costs a staggering $1,350 per hour (Lat 2015; Belz 2017). Another star in the Supreme Court bar, Theodore Olson, charges $1,800 (Lat 2015).

In addition to the competition to provide information to the Court, the Supreme Court benefits from its position atop the judicial hierarchy regarding the quantity and quality of information to which it has access. The Supreme Court is generally the last stop in a long line of courts and decisions. The vast majority of cases that are heard by it have been litigated for years. The benefit of this work by parties, lawyers, and judges in the lower court proceedings flows to the Court in a multitude of ways: the justices and their clerks can peruse well-developed factual records, the prior decisions and accompanying reasoning of lower court judges, and briefs containing well-defined issues and arguments that have developed usually over multiple iterations (Feldman 2017b; Hazelton, Hinkle, and Spriggs 2019). Justices themselves comment on this fact (Garner 2010, 116 and 152).

Litigant briefs play the primary role in defining the questions and issues before the Court (Epstein, Segal, and Johnson 1996), a task assisted by experience in the lower courts. In defining such features of the case, they often bring important factual, technical, and legal information to the justices based on years of the exchange of information, argument, and research (Feldman 2017b; Hazelton, Hinkle, and Spriggs 2019). Moreover, the Supreme Court's placement at the apex of the judicial hierarchy means that the stakes for a case heard by the Court are huge: the Court's decisions are the final resolution in the immediate disputes, and the pronouncements will become the law of the land. Additionally, Supreme Court decisions can act as a catalyst for the development of policy in the other branches (Rice 2020). Thus, parties and interested groups are highly motivated to expend resources in securing favorable outcomes and rules. Such expenditures often include hiring elite attorneys who have experience with the Court and high-level briefing (Belz 2017).

Of course, the importance of briefs is far from limited to those provided by parties to the suit. Today, interested groups and individuals file amicus curiae briefs in almost all Supreme Court cases (Collins 2007). Such participation has grown over time. The Court itself determines the rules around briefing. The modern Court has fostered rules that encourage broad amicus support, including liberal rules regarding amicus participation (Collins 2008; Hazelton, Hinkle, and Spriggs 2019). It also sometimes requests additional briefing on an issue from parties or participation from amici (Collins 2004; Hazelton, Hinkle, and Spriggs 2019; Johnson, Wahlbeck, and Spriggs 2006).

Parties themselves are highly motivated to encourage participation from such individuals and groups, as their input may assist in a multitude of ways (McGuire 1994; Larsen and Devins 2016; Hazelton, Hinkle, and Spriggs 2019): it allows for the provision of more information in light of word limits, promotes new types of information, and signals support for outcomes and arguments from relevant stakeholders or broad coalitions. Individuals and groups are often well incentivized to take on the costs of providing such briefs themselves based on the potential to influence policy that will likely affect them (Canelo 2022; McGuire 1994). In the case of membership groups, it also allows an organization to illustrate their worth to actual and potential members (Hansford 2004). Third parties spend an estimated $25,000 to $50,000 per amicus brief (Totenberg 2015). Despite these high costs, amicus participation has risen dramatically over time to the point where it is present in nearly every case before the Court (Hansford and Johnson 2014).

Beyond merely encouraging amicus participation, there is evidence that well-trained attorneys help coordinate the overall flow of information to the Court on behalf of their side. This type of coordination is common in other kinds of informational lobbying (Hula 1999; Hojnacki et al. 2012; Mahoney and Baumgartner 2015; Junk 2019). Such cooperation means that a large body of information received by the Court is part of a campaign. There are also many potential benefits to the groups and parties that come together to provide such information in terms of pooled resources in an increasingly complex space (Hula 1999). While the Court provides rules limiting the contours of such collaboration, it maintains rules and procedures in which such coordination thrives (Larsen and Devins 2016). The Court likely allows such coordination because it is, overall, beneficial to the justices. It allows the Court to receive information regarding aspects of policy making such as the extent to which there is policy coalescence (Hazelton, Hinkle, and Spriggs 2019). Thus, theory and existing empirical evidence indicate that litigants and their attorneys are working hard to provide the Court with a wide array of types of information to influence outcomes and legal rules.

Roadmap

Finally, to learn about Supreme Court litigation, we could integrate aspects of what we learn from the interviews, existing theory and research, the formal rules, and practice guides and use those insights to carry out original quantitative research. Here, we do just that. In this book, we investigate both the causes and consequences of information provision at the Supreme Court. Specifically, we look at the conditions influencing the production of information to the Court and how clerks and justices use the information they receive in deciding cases and crafting the decisions that apply to future cases, touching back with the case of *Florida v. Harris* for context. In considering the creation of the information that reaches the Court via briefs, we consider the features of litigants, parties, briefs, and their relationships. We use both qualitative and quantitative methods in our inquiries. First, in developing our theories, we draw from our eighteen original interviews. We test our theories with statistical analyses fueled by an original data set drawn from the full text of over twenty-six thousand litigant and amicus merit briefs filed in the Supreme Court between 1984 and 2015, the text of the majority opinion in those cases, and the text of the lower court opinion under consideration. We use computational linguistic tools to extract information from the briefs to help in our assessment, including information regarding the parties, attorneys, and their arguments. While the effects we uncover are often small in size, as is common when dealing with textual data, they help us learn about decision-making and, in the aggregate, can be quite meaningful.

In chapter 1, we assess the lay of the land by looking at the characteristics of the Supreme Court, briefs, parties, and attorneys and how they have changed over time. This examination lays the groundwork for the subsequent chapters that go on to explore the complex relationships among the characteristics we describe in this chapter. However, even simple descriptive analyses reveal interesting patterns. We show the well-known pattern that the quantity of amicus briefs has increased over time. We provide new insight into this pattern, however, by showing that the increase in amicus briefs is driven by individuals and interest groups. Business and governments have not seen a significant increase in the number of amicus briefs they have filed over time. The average number of participants in each individual amicus brief has also remained relatively steady over time. The number of attorneys employed to draft each amicus brief has remained fairly consistent, but it has increased for litigant briefs. The contents of the briefs themselves show interesting patterns as well.

There is substantial variation in brief length, including above the Court-imposed word limits. Compared to amicus briefs, the litigants' briefs contain more citations to Supreme Court precedent, less complex syntactic structure, and less emotional language. Finally, we look at the nature of filers and attorneys who participate in briefing the Court. Interest groups file the most amicus briefs while individuals are most likely to be litigants. Over forty-thousand attorneys signed a brief and 45 percent of those only signed a single brief. Seventy-three of the attorneys signed one hundred or more briefs. Consistent with accounts from interviewees about an increasingly elite Supreme Court bar, we also found that the average experience of the attorneys who draft both party and amicus briefs has been increasing over time.

Next, in chapter 2, we investigate how attorney and litigant characteristics influence the types of information they provide in submissions. We theorize that greater resources, experience, and expertise all contribute to crafting higher-quality briefs. In this chapter, the exploration of a wide variety of hypotheses reveals four broad patterns. First, there is evidence that attorneys with more experience and those who clerked for a justice produce better briefs in terms of quantity and type of information. Second, once we account for other aspects of litigant resources, the classic variable reflecting filer type (individual, interest group, government, etc.) shows little evidence of the expected patterns. Third, both former and current solicitors general act in some unexpected ways, such as writing litigant briefs with less information than other attorneys. The fourth, and final, pattern we observe is that our theory that resources, experience, and expertise lead to higher-quality briefs has more descriptive power with respect to amicus briefs than it does for litigant briefs.

We then explore issues surrounding coordination among parties and supporting amici in producing information, with particular attention paid to how attorney and litigant characteristics influence the extent to which briefs assembled for a side provide new or reinforcing information in chapter 3. We find evidence that briefs in party-amicus dyads are more similar when attorneys for either the party or amicus have more experience. Additionally, filer experience exhibits similar effects regarding amicus briefs. Thus, experience seems to lend itself to at least certain types of repetition despite the widespread statements against repetition in amicus briefs. This finding supplements the social science literature indicating that repetition is helpful by illustrating its relationship with experience. In this vein, former Supreme Court clerks and solicitors general produce amicus briefs that are more like the party briefs they write to support. Not all experience leads to more similar briefs; more experienced filers produce less similar dyads when they act as parties, indicating that complex goals may be at play. Additionally, other factors, such as interest-group participation, increase dissimilarity in party and amicus briefs.

Once we consider these aspects of the causes of information, we turn to the consequences of such information. Specifically, we examine how such information translates into who wins the cases before the Court and the resulting legal rules and policy that it announces. In chapter 4, we look into how the information provided via briefs affects the disposition of the case in favor of one side over another as well as how individual justices vote. Both information and people matter. The side that presents more overall content in briefs, more briefs, and more strategic citations to the current median justice has a significantly higher likelihood of winning a case. Even after controlling for the information in the briefs, there are attorney characteristics that matter too. An advantage in terms of attorney experience and the participation of the current solicitor general confer an advantage in securing both votes and victories.

We then pivot to consider how such briefing influences the actual decisions that will become the law of the land: we probe how the information in individual briefs translates into the language of opinions in chapter 5. Our results further the view that shared information across briefs is reflected in the Court's opinions that define legal policy. These effects have important implications. The results suggest that both issues of policy coalescence and psychological effects are afoot. The benefits of providing new information likely exist but not in shaping the opinions of the immediate case. We also find evidence that the resource advantage stems from the knowledge and skill of the attorney involved, as well as individuals and groups filing amici.

Then in chapter 6, we assess how the collective information assembled for a side translates into these written opinions. We do so based on both theory and firsthand accounts of how briefs are consumed. Our results both reinforce our findings in chapter 5 and offer new insights. We continue to find evidence of the influence of shared information. We also find evidence that collective resources and attorney quality matter greatly in which side has greater influence over the opinion text. Interestingly, at the case-side and case level, the influence of clerkship experience is not apparent. This lack of finding raises questions about and ties to existing work regarding the contours of former clerk advantages. We also find that at the collective level, emotional language is detrimental.

Finally, in the conclusion, we discuss what we have learned about the production of information by litigants and their attorneys, its consumption by justices and their clerks, and the relationship between them. We also highlight how such information helps us understand decision-making and informational lobbying generally. Among our many findings, four overall takeaways stand out as particularly important contributions to how we understand the process of influencing the Supreme Court and policy makers broadly. First, filer and attorney resources and experience influence how briefs are produced and the results they achieve. Second, the information in briefs is more influential in shaping the majority opinions of the Court rather than who wins or loses. Third, we find that resource advantages stem from the ability of parties to hire attorneys who produce better briefs and engender greater trust with the Court. Fourth, we find that policy coalescence across briefs coupled with the psychological influence of repetition influence the majority opinions the Court produces.

1 | Briefs and the People Who Produce Them

In *Florida v. Harris*, the Supreme Court had a considerable amount of information presented to them to help determine "when a sniff is up to snuff." In addition to the lower court record, including transcripts and opinions, they had eleven briefs on the merits to assist them: Florida's petition and reply briefs, Harris's response, and eight amicus briefs, including one filed by the United States. These briefs helped contextualize the lower court record and opinions and highlight the potential policy implications of possible decisions.

But what does that body of information look like when we step back to look at the forest of the entire Supreme Court docket rather than focusing on individual trees? Are there objective characteristics of the briefs and people who produce them that can help us understand the process of both how briefs are produced and how they impact the Court? We think there are. Some of the numbers behind the *Florida v. Harris* briefing are illustrative. First, we can look at the overall quantity of information presented to the Court to see the big picture of how the Court obtains information from the briefs. In this case, there were a total of over eighty-eight thousand words in the compiled briefs. This is quite close to the length of George Orwell's novel *1984* or Jane Austen's *Persuasion*.[1] Of course, the content of the briefs is very different than Orwell's alarming prognostications or Austen's incisive character exposition. The briefs are focused on the legal and policy implications of government searches in general and dog sniffs in particular. One key feature of the type of legal analysis often found in briefs is citation to past opinions of the Supreme Court (Manz 2002). While the justices are not technically bound by those precedents, they do tend to give them a considerable amount of deference (Hansford and Spriggs 2006; Hazelton, Hinkle, and Spriggs 2019; Schauer 2007). The collected briefs include 297 citations to Supreme Court precedent.

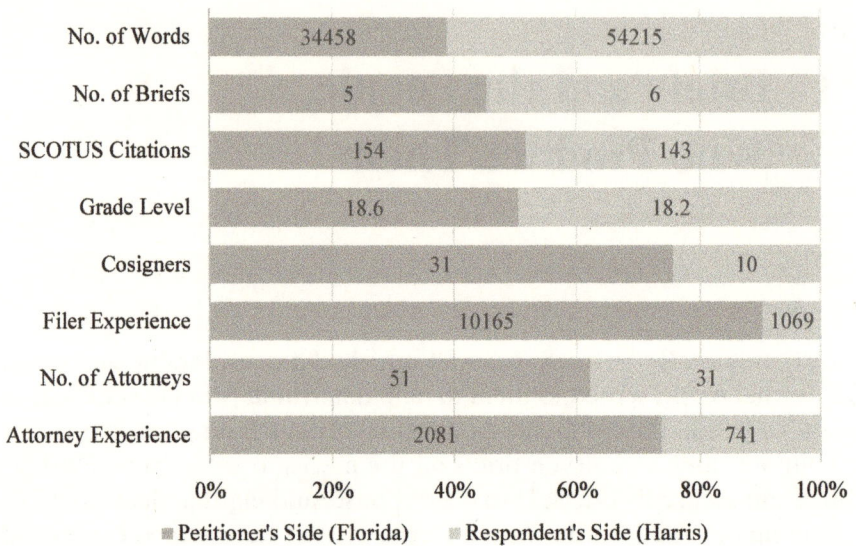

	Petitioner's Side (Florida)	Respondent's Side (Harris)
No. of Words	34458	54215
No. of Briefs	5	6
SCOTUS Citations	154	143
Grade Level	18.6	18.2
Cosigners	31	10
Filer Experience	10165	1069
No. of Attorneys	51	31
Attorney Experience	2081	741

Figure 1.1. *Florida v. Harris* by the numbers.

Even more interesting than the case totals, we can break down the briefs into the two sides of the case to explore some of the features of the information and resources marshaled on behalf of the petitioner and respondent in turn. A look at the scope of the information (which we illustrate in figure 1.1) shows that the briefs filed by the respondent and by amici on his behalf were nearly twenty thousand words longer than the briefs filed by the petitioner and amici for the petitioner. This is not surprising since there are six briefs on the respondent side compared to five on the other side. However, in spite of this difference in the number of briefs and overall length, the total cumulative citations to the Supreme Court were rather similar, with the petitioner briefs actually enjoying a slight, eleven citation, advantage.

Such raw counts only begin to probe the content and nature of the information provided to the Court. Throughout the course of this book, we will look at a wide variety of measures designed to quantify a variety of informational characteristics. For now, we only examine one further aspect of the briefs in our example case: the complexity of the text. To assess this, we use the average reading grade level across all briefs for each side.[2] The briefs for both sides are pitched at quite similar levels. Both are fairly complex, with reading grade levels that correspond to about two years into graduate study. While the respondent briefs are somewhat more readable, the difference from the briefs on the petitioner's side is less than one-half of a grade level. This corresponds to the advancement in reading comprehension that happens among second-year law students from their first semester to their second semester.

So far, the broad numeric summaries in *Florida v. Harris* appear, if anything, to favor Harris. But we can look beyond the content of the briefs to further investigate both the people who commissioned and created those briefs and their respective experience with submitting briefs to the Supreme Court. Existing research shows the number of briefs submitted by each side can have an impact (Collins 2008) and suggests that the number, power, and experience of the entities that sign each brief also matter (Box-Steffensmeier, Christenson, and Hitt 2013). While there was one fewer brief filed on Florida's side, there were twenty-one more cosigners compared to Harris's side. An even larger discrepancy in favor of Florida emerges when we look at the previous experience of the filers. The thirty-one filers on the petitioner's side had a total cumulative experience submitting over ten thousand briefs compared to the ten filers on the respondent's side having experience with just over one thousand previous briefs. In other words, Florida's side enjoyed a three-to-one advantage in terms of the number of filers and a ten-to-one advantage in terms of experience. Lastly, we look at the attorneys who signed the briefs. Fifty-one attorneys were employed on the petitioner's side and thirty-one on the respondent's side. When we look at the brief-writing experience of those attorneys, an even larger petitioner advantage emerges. Altogether, the petitioner's attorneys had signed 1,340 *more* previous briefs than the respondent's attorneys.

While *Florida v. Harris* is only one case, the raw numbers are suggestive. It may well be that the substantial experience brought to bear on behalf of the petitioner helped convince the Court that this particular sniff was up to snuff. More importantly, we can extract these, and other, objective quantities from thousands of briefs at a time. In subsequent chapters, we will use such measures to test a variety of hypotheses about the production and consumption of briefs. But in this chapter, we begin by presenting a broad overview of a wide variety of key features of briefs stretching over multiple decades. This guided tour through a large swath of briefs will serve to both paint a picture of briefing activity in the Supreme Court and introduce many of the quantities of interest we will utilize in later chapters. We begin with an overview of the number and content of briefs over time. Next, we proceed to explore the number and variety of filers. Finally, we conclude with an examination of attorney participation over time.

Supreme Court Briefs from 1984 to 2015: An Overview

In order to tackle questions about how resources shape the information in briefs and how both resources and information shape Court outputs, this book explores merits briefs for orally argued cases from 1984 to 2015.[3] We collected the text of more than twenty-five thousand briefs filed during this time frame. Next, we extracted the type of brief, the names of all filers and attorneys who signed the brief, and a wealth of other characteristics. The resulting rich data set allows us to do the type of exploration we illustrated previously with the briefs from *Florida v. Harris.*

We begin by considering different types of briefs. Our primary focus is on two types of briefs—those filed by parties and amicus curiae. The distinction is important, as the two types of briefs carry out different functions (discussed in greater detail in chapter 3). They are identified in practice guides as distinct in their nature, scope, and purpose (Mayer Brown n.d.; Shapiro et al. 2019). Furthermore, interviewees described them in very different terms, for the most part attributing more significance to party briefs. Attorney and Former Clerk M noted that party briefs are "critical" in crafting opinions. They describe them as "overwhelmingly" helpful as they define the specific questions and scope of the case: the "starting point is [party] briefs." While clerks conduct some of their own research, the briefs "by and large" define the case. "Scoping" is a major contribution of party briefs. This is due to the "case and controversy requirement" of Article III. Likewise, Former Clerk N said that party briefs are "clearly" important.

The interviewees were less convinced that most amicus briefs are influential, though they often discussed the potential for important amicus briefs. Attorney C went so far as to say that they should have asked if amicus briefs matter at all. They believed that "most don't." An amicus brief needs to "give something new." And, the attorney added, amicus briefs "don't usually sway" the Court. Former Clerk N similarly said that the "bottom line is that occasionally [amicus] briefs matter." In this vein, Attorney and Former Clerk H noted that they didn't "recall relying on green briefs" when drafting opinions.[4] They said they may have pulled unique citations from amicus briefs. Former Clerk N stated that amici "usually don't matter, but can." Amici can matter in "particular cases" where "specific information is needed" and there is a "lack of space in the party briefs." For example, an amicus brief could include originalist arguments that didn't fit in the party briefs. The former clerk remembered specific cases where amici were "important." They noted an instance in which a justice asked about a specific amicus brief during oral arguments.

Furthermore, the interviewees described differences in the manner in which party and amicus briefs are consumed by clerks and justices. Attorney and Former Clerk H reported that clerks read every brief and engage in "screening and summarizing" for the justices. They would look at the table of contents of amicus briefs to see if the brief differed from other amici. If not, they would pay it "less attention." This approach to amicus briefs was also echoed by Attorney and Former Clerk B, who stated that party briefs would certainly be read with care by clerks and justices. However, more variable care would apply with amicus briefs; if an amicus brief signaled "new issues," it would get the same type of care from the clerks. Similarly, Attorney and Former Clerk L said that when reading amicus briefs, one could "quickly see what helps" in a brief. Along the same lines, Attorney and Former Clerk I remembered the "mechanics" of reading briefs. They also described being confronted with "huge piles of green" (another reference to the color-coded brief covers). In such cases, they would "flip through" to see if the brief had something "new." If not, they would cross it off and "move on." In keeping with that approach, Former Clerk K said they would stop reading an amicus brief if it became apparent that it was just repetitive information while Former Clerk N said they would "skim to see if [the amicus brief] was useful." Former Clerk G went so far as to assert that "not all clerks read all amicus briefs."

Table 1.1 shows the distribution of briefs by these key types. Briefs filed by the litigants make up 35 percent of our data while the remaining 65 percent are filed by amici. In addition to the well-recognized distinction between party and amicus briefs, we also break these categories down further as well. Petitioner reply briefs are quite distinct from the main party briefs as they are short, limited in scope, and filed by the same filers and attorneys as the main petitioner brief. As such, we exclude them from our analyses in this chapter to avoid their

Table 1.1. Distribution of Briefs by Type, 1984–2015

Brief Type	Number	Percentage
Petitioner	3,070	11.8
Respondent	3,182	12.2
Petitioner Reply	2,870	11.0
Amicus for Petitioner	8,206	31.5
Amicus for Respondent	8,301	31.8
Amicus for Neither Party	455	1.7
Total	26,084	100

short length or repetition of participants from skewing the patterns we examine. However, we do include amicus briefs filed on behalf of neither party. Attorney C noted that briefs that are in support of neither side by academics can be effective. While we necessarily exclude such briefs from analyses in subsequent chapters (where the position being advocated is a critical variable), we include them here to provide the full picture of participation in lobbying the Supreme Court.

One trend in Supreme Court briefing that is frequently noted by scholars is the increasing number of amicus briefs being filed (Collins 2008; Kearney and Merrill 2000). Figure 1.2 illustrates this well-known trend. The dashed line shows the number of amicus briefs filed per term, and it reveals notable increases. Nearly one thousand amicus briefs were filed in 2012 while fewer than five hundred were filed in 2001. Meanwhile, the number of litigant briefs has gradually declined over time, a trend that is directly linked to the Court's decreasing caseload. The increase in amicus briefs from 1994 forward is considerably more dramatic than the gradual decrease in party briefs. In fact, over this time period, there is an increase of twenty amicus briefs per term ($p < 0.001$) and a decrease of 1.9 party briefs per term ($p = 0.001$).[5]

Exploration over time is useful, as attorneys and former clerks suggested in interviews that practice may have changed in multiple and sometimes competing ways. Attorney and Former Clerk M noted that there are "fewer cases taken" by the Court, and there has been an increase in the "volume of information" that is provided. This raises questions regarding "what can be processed." In their estimation, the current state of the Court and the cases it takes "raises the stakes in any given case." Furthermore, the increase in information provided to the Court and its effect on cases creates a "feedback" loop. Thus,

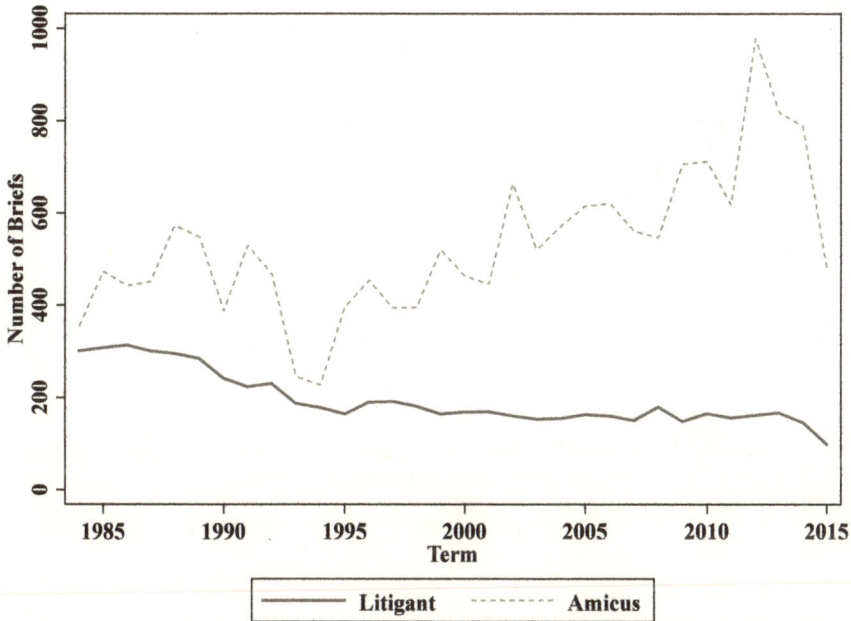

Figure 1.2. Merits briefs over time. The number of merits briefs per term from 1984–2015. The solid line tracks the number of main party briefs, and the dashed line shows the number of amicus briefs.

we see continual increases in information, which stands in "sharp contrast" to "other courts." This is an interesting point in relationship to a comment by Attorney O that in their general practice, they see judges "getting blitzed with information" and that such things "matter to decisionmakers" across the board. According to Attorney and Former Clerk M, the advancement of technology has likely influenced the increase in briefs because one "can get information so much more easily." It is now "harder and more important" to separate "the wheat from the chaff," especially when considering "second-order arguments."

The depth of information we collected allows us to look beyond this often-discussed pattern to probe nuances of participation trends in more depth. First, we examine the change in the number of filers who sign each brief. A brief may be signed by a single person or group or by several. As amicus participation has increased over time in terms of the number of briefs filed, it is also possible that overall participation of groups has increased by dint of more groups signing on to individual

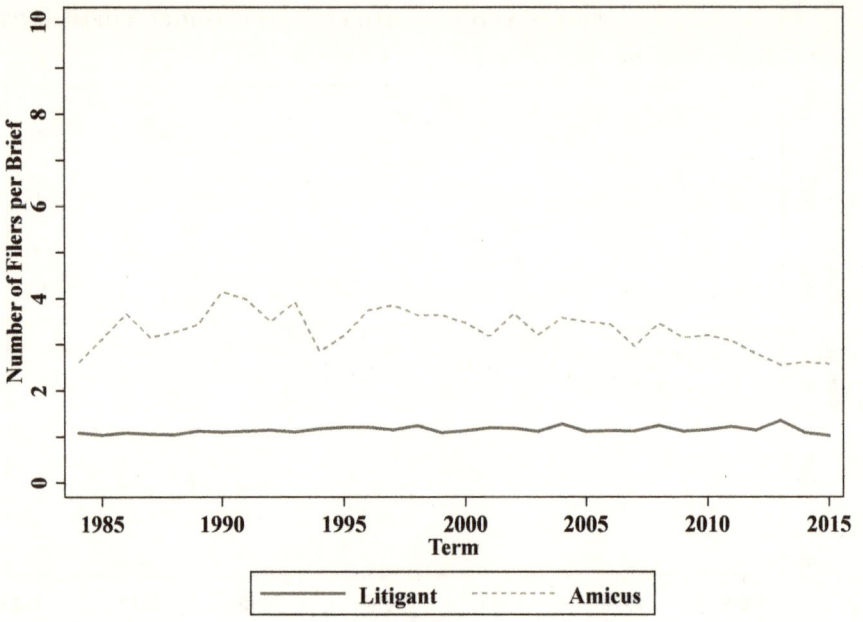

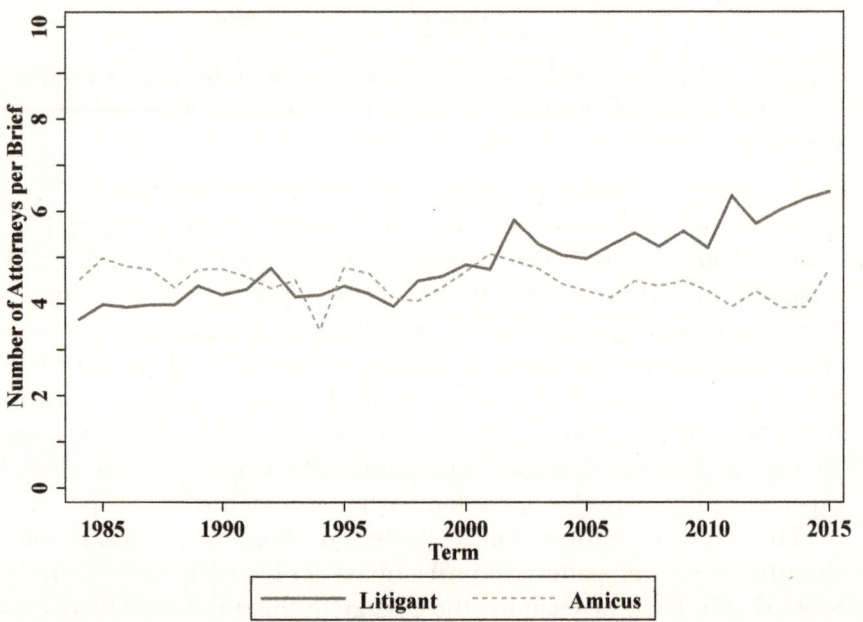

Figure 1.3. Filers and attorneys per brief over time. The average number of filers per brief (top panel) and attorneys per brief (bottom panel) that signed a merits brief each term. The solid line tracks the number in litigant briefs, and the dashed line shows the number for amicus briefs.

briefs. Along similar lines, attorney participation may have shifted as well. Scholarly commentary has noted that the Supreme Court bar is becoming increasingly elite (Larsen and Devins 2016; Lazarus 2007). Attorney R described the same pattern in their interview. This might manifest as a greater number of attorneys participating in creating the briefs submitted to the Court. To explore these possibilities, figure 1.3 shows the number of filers and attorneys per brief each term. Both filer and attorney participation are normalized by the number of briefs each term so that we can examine whether there are any interesting patterns above and beyond those regarding the raw number of briefs displayed in figure 1.2.

The top panel in figure 1.3 shows that the average number of filers per brief has remained relatively steady over time. There is a slight increase over time for litigant briefs ($p = 0.045$) and a slight decrease over time for amicus briefs ($p = 0.018$). However, both trends are very small in substantive terms. Throughout the time span, the yearly averages are close to one filer per party brief and three filers per amicus brief. The trend for attorney participation in amicus briefing is similarly stable across time, with most annual averages near four attorneys per brief. However, the number of attorneys per litigant brief has grown a noticeable amount over time ($p < 0.001$). From 1984 to 2015, the average number of attorneys per party brief shifted from 3.7 to 6.4.

The Contents of Briefs

Knowing how many briefs are filed only begins to scratch the surface. Next, we go under the hood to see what the contents of those briefs look like. While we extract a wide range of measures of the information in briefs throughout the book, here we provide a synopsis of a handful of intuitive measures that give an overview of the body of information provided to the Court. We begin by looking simply at how long briefs are.[6]

When it comes to drafting briefs, more is not always better. Many practice guides direct attorneys to draft briefs that are as short as possible (Ebner 2017; Shapiro et al. 2019). This sentiment was also echoed by multiple interviewees. Attorney and Former Clerk M accentuated the importance of clarity, persuasiveness, and the idea that for an amicus brief "sometimes less is more." Briefs should be "fairly succinct." It is better to respect the page and word limits and engage in "radical triage." This involves "boiling down a big record," and the importance of abstract concepts makes the task "difficult." Former Clerk G also promoted this view—a brief should be "clear and simple." Attorney R likewise said that the goal is to be "as pithy as possible" and write in a "powerful and succinct" way. In this vein, Attorney E wanted to be as short as possible and avoid being "long-winded."

Multiple interviewees noted the importance of brevity for amicus briefs in particular. Attorney and Former Clerk H noted that "amicus don't need to use all the space." Attorney Q, who works on amicus briefs, relayed that they try to just brief "the issue [they are] primarily concerned with and not others." Thus, they attempt to be "as short and concise as possible. . . the shorter, the better." Attorney J shared this sentiment, saying they want briefs to be as "short as possible" and "concise," noting the limits regarding "capacity" for a reader.

Furthermore, this is an area where justices and clerks have been quite vocal: they prefer that briefs are as short as possible (Lynch 2004; Garner 2010). Chief Justice Roberts remarked, "I have yet to put down a brief and say, 'I wish that had been longer'" (Garner 2010, 35). Similarly, Justice Scalia noted that "prolixity" was a "major shortcoming" that he saw in briefs. Justice Thomas has explained, "So I think, for example, if you have a clear argument that's 20 pages rather than the full 50, that's an easy brief to read: 'Boy, I'm going to pick this one up because it's only 20 pages' [laughter], as opposed to, 'Look, this person has crammed every square centimeter or millimeter he could find on this page.' That's when you say, 'My goodness' [laughter]" (102). Such sentiments were also echoed by Justices Stevens (50), Kennedy (79), and Ginsburg (137, 141–142).

Our data indicate that being concise is often easier said than done. Figure 1.4 shows the distribution for party briefs (on the top) and amicus briefs (on the bottom). The vertical line in each panel denotes the word limit for each type of brief set forth in Supreme Court Rule 33.[7] Somewhat surprisingly, a substantial portion of briefs exceed the word limits even though we excluded all ancillary materials such as appendices and preliminary matter. Twenty-six percent of party briefs are longer than the applicable fifteen-thousand word limit. Moreover, this doesn't reflect a lot of close misses. Twenty-five percent of party briefs are longer than 15,100 words. Seventeen percent of amicus briefs are longer than the nine-thousand word limit and 16 percent are longer than 9,100 words. The Supreme Court rules do provide a mechanism for requesting permission to exceed the word limits. Although data regarding requests is not readily available, even assuming all over-length briefs were granted such permission, there is no evidence of favoritism by the Court in granting these requests. In fact, briefs that exceed the word limit have a slightly lower chance of both being on the winning side and having their language appear in the majority opinion.[8] There is also a significant amount of variation in briefs that do not use the entire word limit. In short, there is substantial variation in word count.[9] Words are necessary to convey information to the Court. They are the building blocks of arguments and a lawyer's most basic tool. The substantial variation in word counts reflects a fundamental heterogeneity in the information each brief provides the Court.

Next, we examine the number of citations to Supreme Court precedent contained within party and amicus briefs. Due to the importance of reasoning by analogy in legal analysis, references to previous case law carry particular significance (Manz 2002; Schauer 2007). While words are the building blocks of arguments, citations are the mortar that holds legal arguments together and gives them strength. Furthermore, the Supreme Court's own previous rulings are the most prestigious resources available for brief writers to cite (Hansford and Spriggs 2006; Hazelton, Hinkle, and Spriggs 2019).[10] Figure 1.5 shows that a single brief can contain anywhere from zero to two hundred and fifty citations. In general, litigant briefs contain more citations overall, which is unsurprising considering their higher word limit. Figure 1.6 shows the average number of citations per brief over time. While there is some general fluctuation, no dramatic patterns appear, although it does appear that the usage of Supreme Court citations is decreasing a bit since the turn of the century.[11]

We now turn to an examination of the writing style in briefs. A wide variety of measures have been developed to summarize the level of education needed to understand a document (Black, Owens, et al. 2016; Nelson and Hinkle 2018). While there is no doubt the justices can understand the briefs submitted to them, grade level is an indicator of the textual complexity in briefs. Various scholars note that simpler writing can be more effective (Black, Owens, et al. 2016; Feldman 2016; Nelson and Hinkle 2018). Attorney P echoed this point, stating that when writing briefs, one should simply "write first and cut out half the footnotes." Along similar lines, Attorney E built a brief around a specific focus and main issue without "throwing up a bunch" of ideas. They dislike the

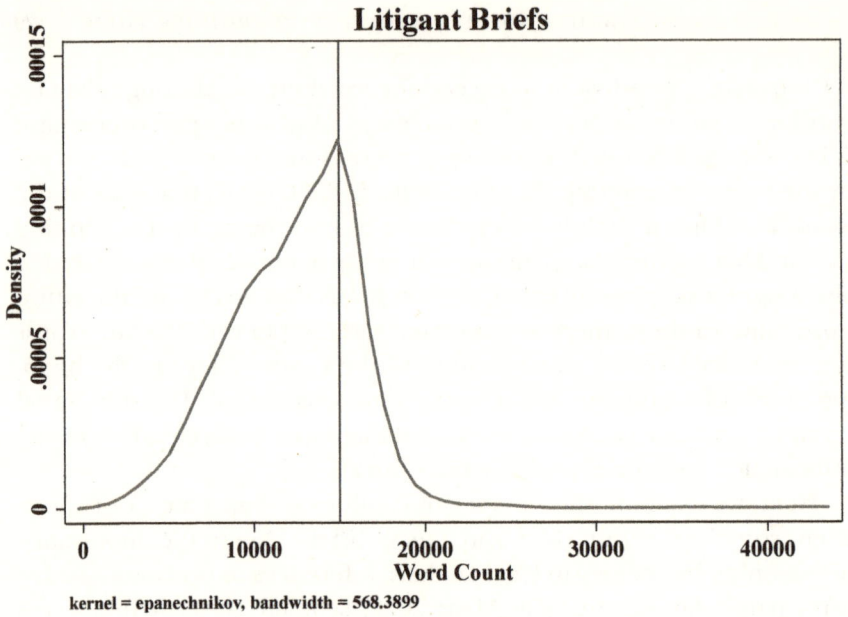

Litigant Briefs

kernel = epanechnikov, bandwidth = 568.3899

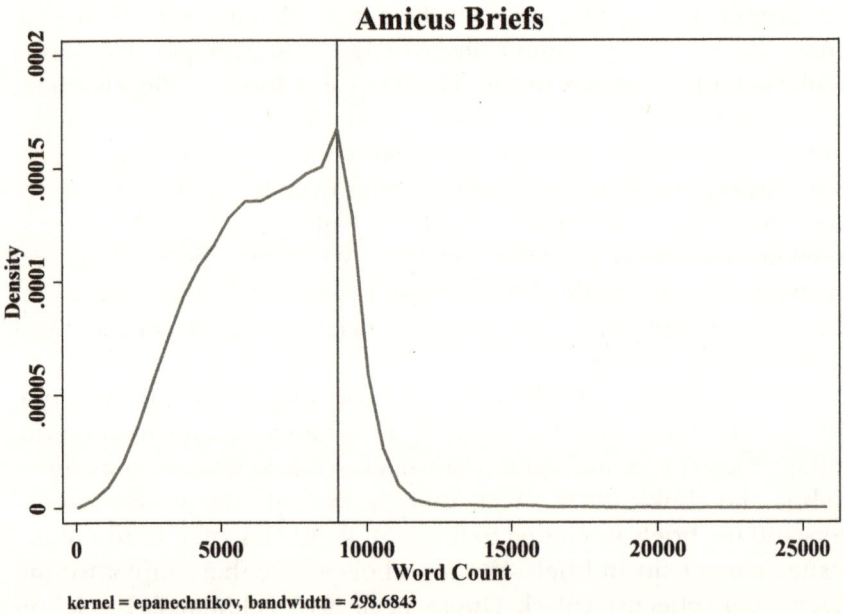

Amicus Briefs

kernel = epanechnikov, bandwidth = 298.6843

Figure 1.4. Distribution of word count. The panel on the top shows the distribution of word count in main party briefs. The panel on the bottom shows the distribution of word count within amicus briefs. The vertical line in each panel illustrates the word limit for each type of brief as stated in Supreme Court Rule 33.

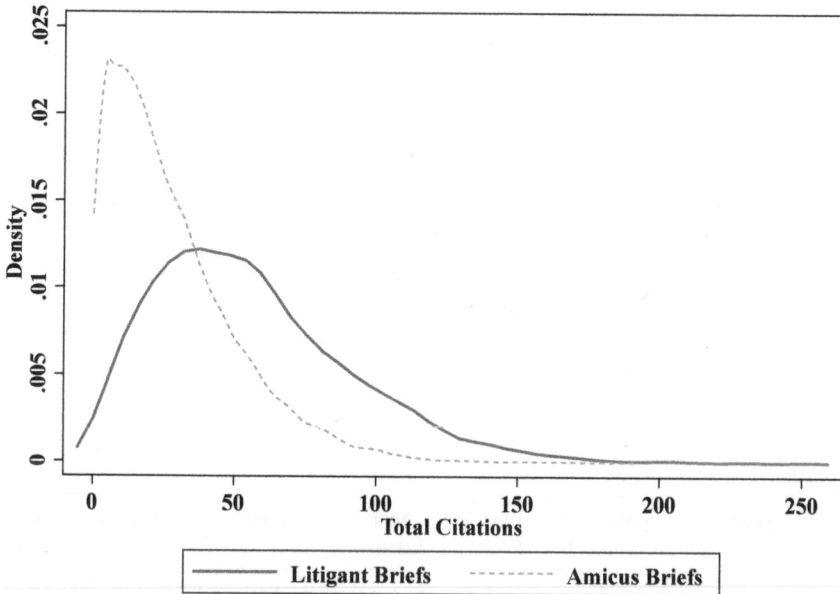

kernel = epanechnikov, bandwidth = 5.3430

Figure 1.5. Distribution of citation count. The distribution of the total number of citations to Supreme Court precedents in main party briefs (solid black line) and amicus briefs (dashed gray line).

approach of bringing up lots of issues because it "corrupts other arguments" and you can be "attacked for weak arguments." Rather, they like to be "direct and to the point" and approach Supreme Court briefs in a "pithy" manner and try to avoid "cutesy briefs." Many justices have also highlighted the importance of clarity and accessibility in brief writing (Garner 2010).

We look at the simplicity of briefs by examining the reading grade level at which they are written. There are several measures available that provide results on the intuitive grade level scale. As DuBay (2004) illustrates, these measures can provide different estimates. We find some variation in our data set, although they all lead to very similar substantive conclusions in the various analyses we conduct throughout the book. Since the choice of metric makes very little substantive difference, we use the grade-level metric that provides the median estimate in our data among five commonly used measures.[12] Figure 1.7 shows how average reading grade level has changed over time. Two notable things emerge.

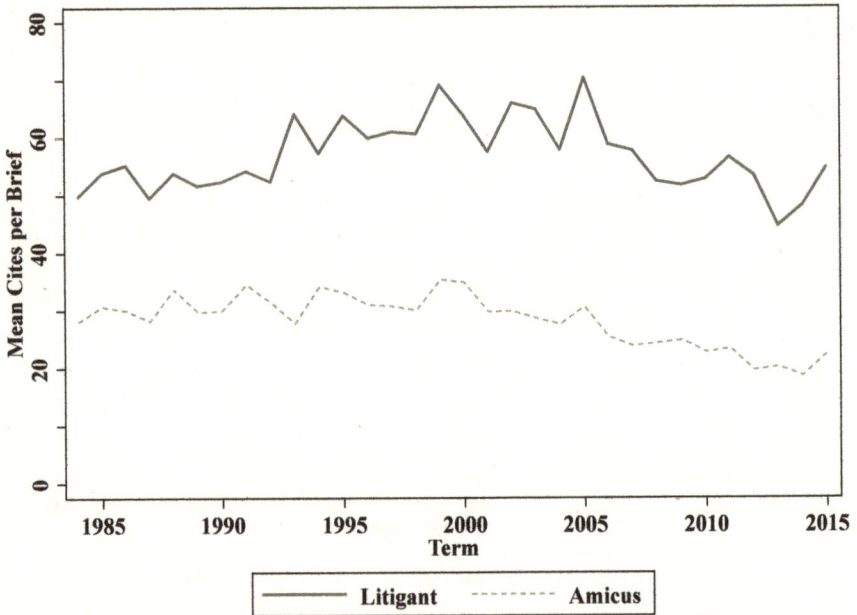

Figure 1.6. Citation usage over time. The average number of total citations to Supreme Court precedents per brief for each term, separated by amicus and party briefs.

The first is that consistently across time, amicus briefs appear to be at least a bit more textually complex than litigant briefs. The second is that while grade level is generally fairly stable across time, there are exceptions. Most notably, around 2005, the average grade level for both kinds of briefs jumped from around sixteen to around eighteen and stayed at the new higher level. While the mechanism behind this jump is not clear, it does correspond temporally with substantial personnel changes on the Court. Around this time the Court saw both turnover in leadership with the passing of Chief Justice Rehnquist and a shake-up in the Court median with the retirement of Justice O'Connor.

As a final example, we look at the usage of emotional language in briefs. Attorneys are often discouraged from resorting to such language in their arguments (Scalia and Garner 2008). Several of our interviewees discussed the downside of emotional language. According to Former Clerk N, "In my view, briefs that take an 'impassioned' tone are not effective. The most effective briefs strike a reasonable tone even as they

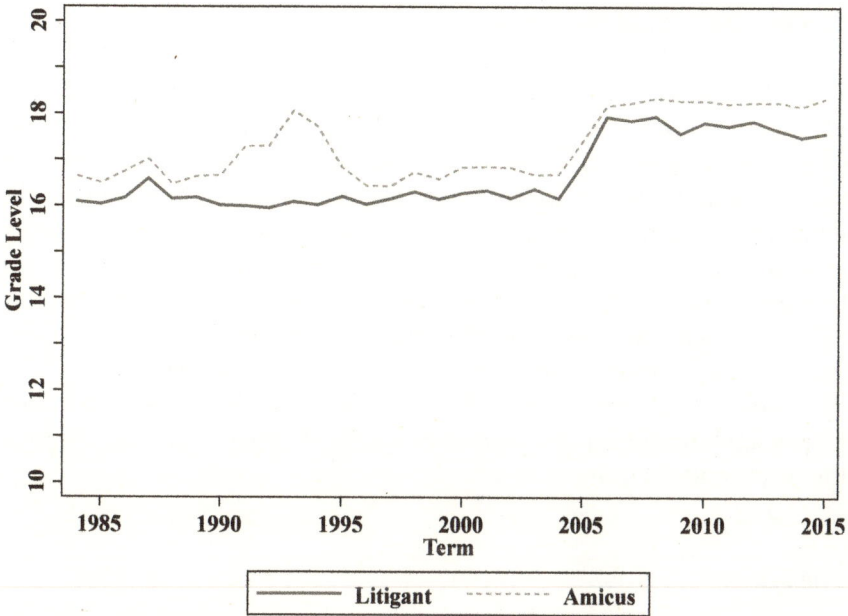

Figure 1.7. Reading grade level over time. The distribution of the average grade level for all briefs in a given term, separated by amicus and party briefs.

try to present the facts or law in the way most favorable to their position." Similarly, Attorney R believed it was among the biggest mistakes to not treat a case as a "legal issue" but instead to be too "emotional." Bad briefs are "overly verbose, exaggerated, and hyperbolic" according to Attorney and Former Clerk L. Such language "can hurt," and one can write briefs "without adjectives." Justice Ginsburg has spoken against using such language (Garner 2010, 142). This advice is borne out in empirical findings that Supreme Court justices are less likely to vote for a litigant the more emotional language their brief contains (Black, Hall, et al. 2016). Yet such language is still used. Figure 1.8 shows the average percentage of a brief that constitutes either positive or negative emotional words over time.[13] There is little notable temporal variation with the averages hovering in the general vicinity of 3 percent emotional language. However, throughout the time frame, the average amicus brief is more emotional than the average litigant brief.

The People Behind the Briefs

The forgoing analysis reveals interesting patterns regarding the nuances of briefs filed over multiple decades. In this section, we explore the range and distribution of resources that have been devoted to lobbying the Supreme Court via briefs. Since Galanter's groundbreaking work, scholars have long noted that resources play a role in Court outcomes (Galanter 1974). Here, we investigate variation in the level of resources brought to bear in Supreme Court briefing. Do have-nots seek out the Supreme Court as a haven for lobbying for favorable policies? Do powerful and experienced actors dominate this playing field? How have these dynamics changed over time? We examine resources from a variety of angles, including both the characteristics and experience of those who file briefs and their attorneys.

The Filers

The long line of work building on Galanter (1974) typically distinguishes between "repeat player" and "one-shot" litigants by using broad categories as a proxy for litigant resources. In order to track this work, we classify each brief filer into one of five categories: national government, subnational government, interest group, business, or individual.[14] This idea that the identity and nature of filers can be significant in Supreme Court litigation was also present in the interviews. With respect to amicus briefs in particular, Attorney P thinks that the content doesn't matter but rather the "names on the brief matter . . . . If [the brief is] from someone they respect, they will pay attention." So, one should "assemble as many and varied amici to sign onto the brief as possible," with a focus on "prestigious" additions.

While measuring the prestige of each filer is challenging, we extend our analysis beyond the five categories listed to also consider which filers are actually repeat players or one-shotters within the context of Supreme Court briefing. Figure 1.9 shows the breakdown of every unique filing entity that signed a brief from 1984 to 2015. Overall, the two most common types of filers are interest groups and individuals. In fact, those two types make up nearly 70 percent of all filers that have filed one or more briefs in the Supreme Court over three decades. The typical understanding of these categories is that individuals have the least resources and

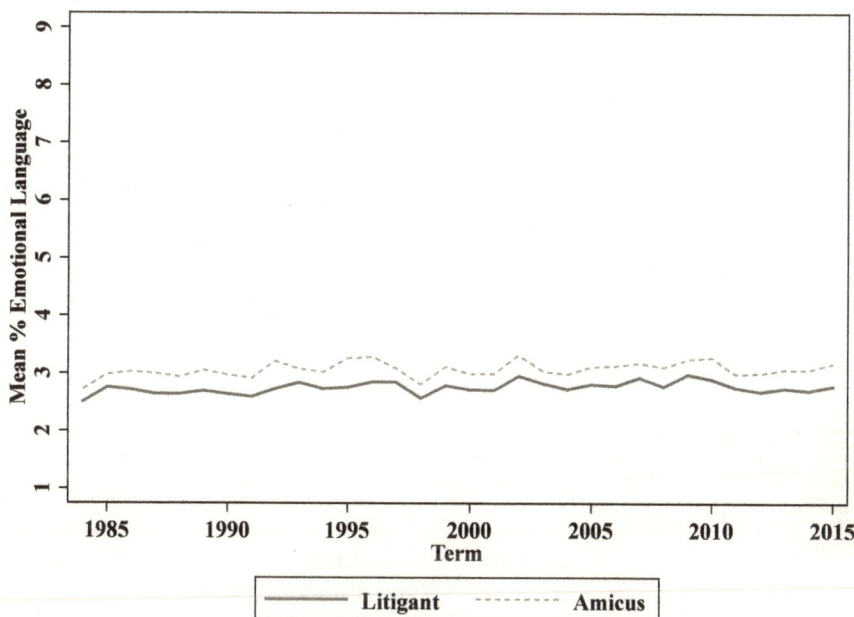

Figure 1.8. Use of emotional language over time. The distribution of emotional language for all briefs in a given term, separated by amicus and party briefs.

the national government has the most resources (Black and Boyd 2010; Collins 2008; Szmer and Ginn 2014). The distribution of repeat players across categories offers some further support for this assumption. Only 25 percent of individual filers are repeat players who have submitted briefs to the Supreme Court on more than one occasion. At the other end of the scale, 72 percent of interest group and subnational government filers are repeat players. That percentage is closer to half for both businesses (48 percent) and the federal government (56 percent). While these numbers roughly track the expectations of relative strength among various types of filers, they also reveal that such broad categories are far from coextensive with filer experience in lobbying the Supreme Court.

The previous figure treats all repeat filers as equal. But, of course, there is also significant variation in how frequently repeat filers have filed briefs in the Supreme Court. Consequently, we next turn to examine the distribution of all briefs filed. For this analysis, any brief signed by multiple filers of different types is coded according to the filer with

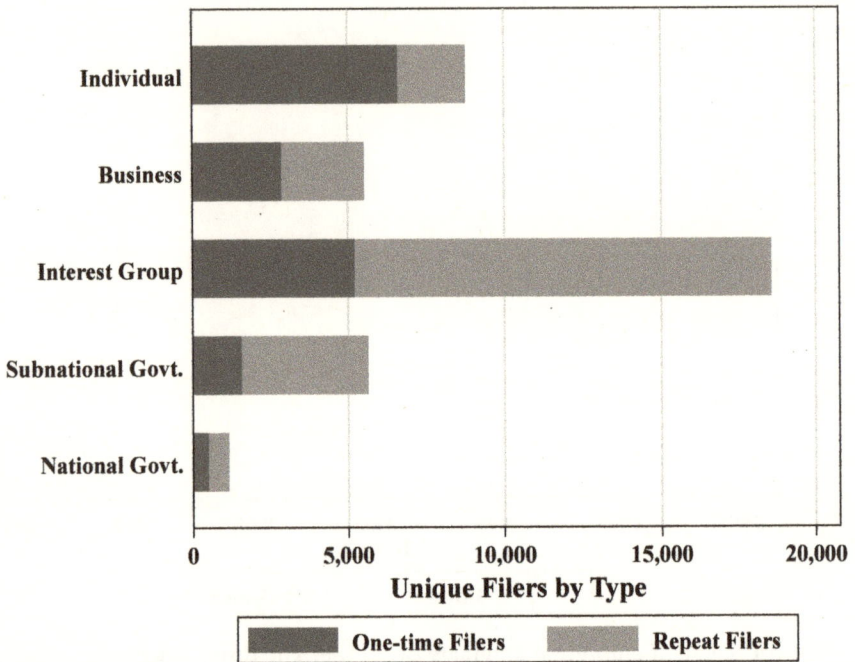

Figure 1.9. Distribution of participants in Supreme Court briefing. The distribution of uniquely identified entities that signed one or more merits brief from 1984–2015, broken down by type. The light gray portion of each bar shows the percentage of filers in each type that participated multiple times while the dark gray portion of the bar represents one-time filers. Repeat player/one-time filer status was calculated using briefs extending back to 1970.

the highest level of resources. For example, a brief signed by an individual and an interest group will be coded as an interest group brief. We also further split our analysis to examine the distribution of filer type in litigant and amicus briefs separately. Since amicus participation is entirely voluntary while litigant filers are determined based on which cases the Supreme Court chooses to hear, there may well be different patterns of participation. Figure 1.10 indicates that this is, in fact, the case. Interest group briefs are far and away the most common type of entity to file an amicus brief while individuals are the most common type of party.

Next, we look at the interest groups that have participated most frequently in Supreme Court briefing. Table 1.2 lists the top ten interest

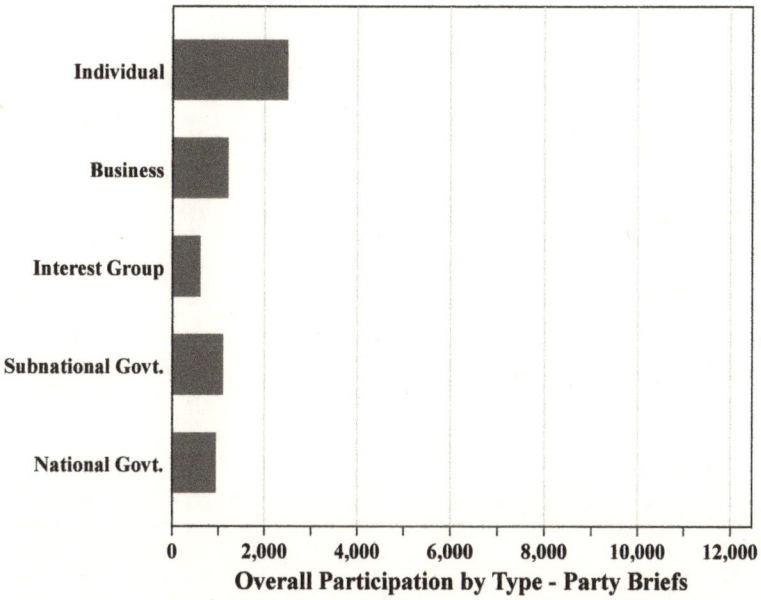

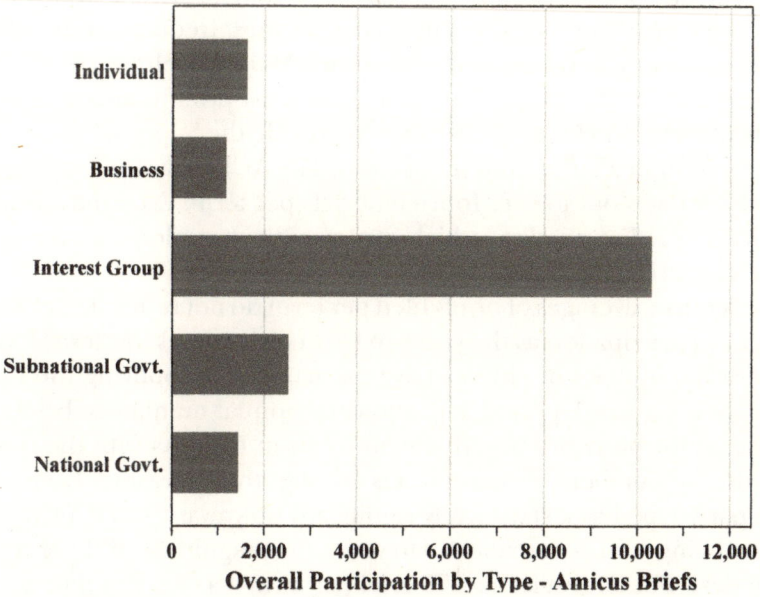

Figure 1.10. Distribution of overall briefs by type. The distribution of total briefs signed by type of filer and type of brief. The panel on the top shows the distribution of participants in main party briefs. The panel on the bottom shows the distribution of participation by filer type within amicus briefs.

Table 1.2. Top Ten Interest Groups by Frequency of Brief Signing, 1984–2015

Interest Group	No. of Briefs
American Civil Liberties Union	467
National Association of Criminal Defense Lawyers	409
Chamber of Commerce of the United States	298
National Association of Counties	285
US Conference of Mayors	271
Washington Legal Foundation	261
Council of State Governments	212
National Conference of State Legislatures	206
American Association of Retired Persons	194
Criminal Justice Legal Foundation	187

groups and the number of briefs they have signed. Since a sizable majority of our briefs are amicus briefs, it is not surprising that our results track nearly identically with lists of the most frequent amicus filers (Collins, Corley, and Hamner 2015; Lynch 2004; Hazelton, Hinkle, and Spriggs 2019). The totals show that these most prolific interest groups participate very extensively, seeking to provide the Supreme Court with information in a large number of cases. The ACLU has filed 467 briefs, which averages out to over fourteen briefs per term. Even the Criminal Justice Legal Foundation, which ranks tenth, has filed an average of nearly six briefs per term.

Of course, averages of briefs filed per term do not reflect the changes in filers' participation as the years go by. In order to take a closer look at how different types of entities have participated in lobbying the Court over time, figures 1.11 and 1.12 show the annual number of briefs per filer type for party briefs and amicus briefs in turn. As with the overall trends, the numbers for party briefs are slightly decreasing. Each separate party type has a statistically significant downward trend (with all p values being 0.001 or smaller). However, the magnitude of these trends is modest. The largest is the 1.75 brief per term decrease for individuals.

Interestingly, although the total number of amicus briefs has been growing recently, figure 1.12 does not reveal across-the-board dramatic increases for every type of filer over time. On the one hand, there is no significant time trend for three of the filer types: business, subnational government, and national government. On the other hand, interest

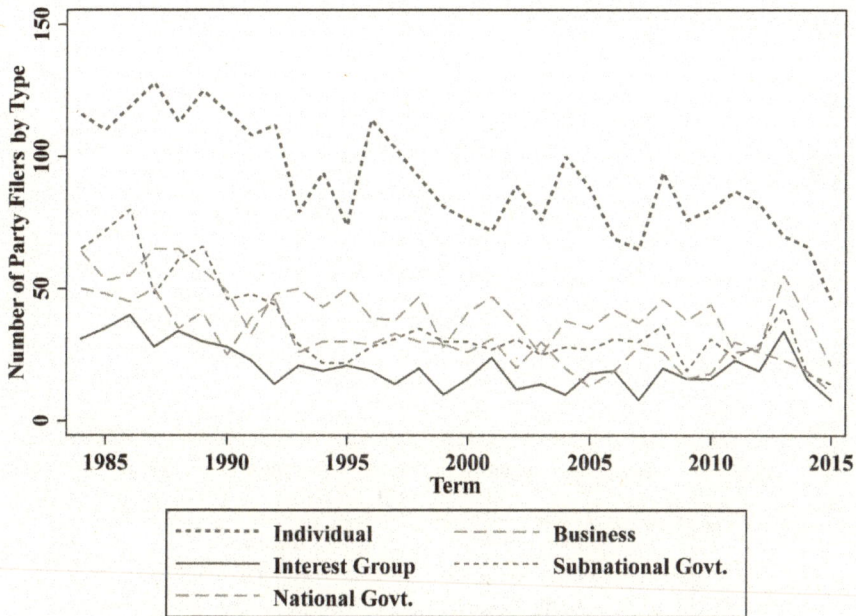

Figure 1.11. Distribution of litigant briefs signed over time. The distribution of total party briefs signed by each type of filer for each year covered by our empirical analyses, 1984–2015.

groups file an estimated 11.6 additional amicus briefs with every successive term ($p = 0.003$), and individual filers show a similarly sized 10.5 amicus briefs per term trend ($p < 0.001$).

The Attorneys

Different types of organizations may be more or less effective at presenting information to the Court depending on the lawyers who are crafting their brief. One hypothesized mechanism behind the often-observed repeat player advantage is that such "haves" typically possess greater resources, which permits them to hire more expensive attorneys. Those higher-priced attorneys presumably have greater experience and expertise, which, in turn, contributes to the higher likelihood of securing favorable outcomes in court settings (Wanner 1975; Wheeler et al. 1987; Atkins 1991; Songer and Sheehan 1992; McCormick 1993;

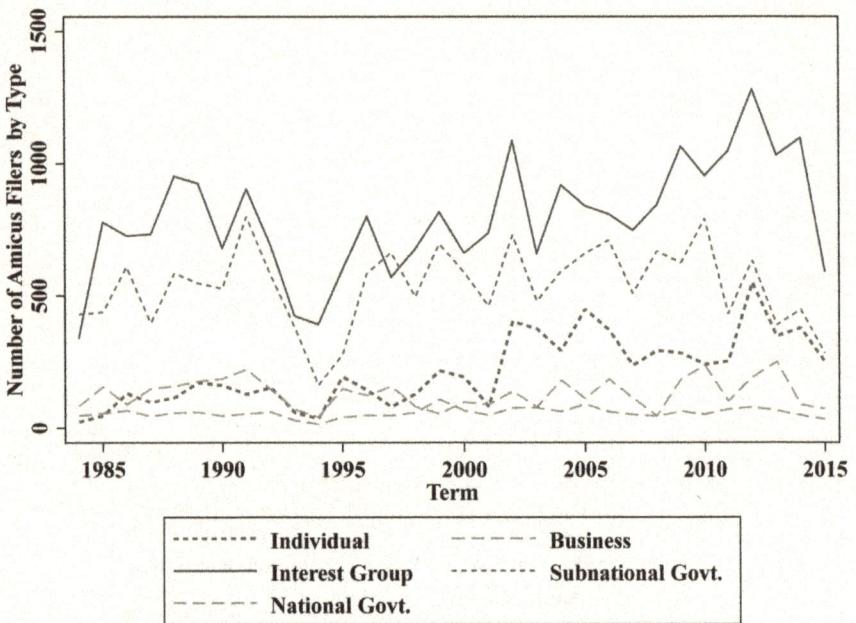

Figure 1.12. Distribution of amicus briefs signed over time. The distribution of total amicus briefs signed by each type of filer for each year covered by our empirical analyses, 1984–2015.

Albiston 1999; Farole 1999; Songer, Sheehan, and Haire 1999; Szmer, Songer, and Bowie 2016). Furthermore, it is the attorneys who determine which information is presented to the Court and how as they compose each brief. As such, we seek to obtain an overview of the attorneys who participate in the brief-writing process. We begin by simply looking at which attorneys are themselves repeat players in the Supreme Court brief-writing game.[15] Figure 1.13 shows that single appearances are more common, but that a substantial portion of attorneys are repeat players. There are nearly forty thousand individual attorneys who signed at least one brief between 1984 and 2015. Forty-three percent of those attorneys signed more than one brief (using data going back to 1970 to look for repeat player experience).

There is considerable variation among the 16,870 attorneys who have signed more than one brief. Table 1.3 shows the top ten most prolific brief writers. Unsurprisingly, this list is heavily populated by attorneys who have served as US Solicitor General. There are seventy-three attor-

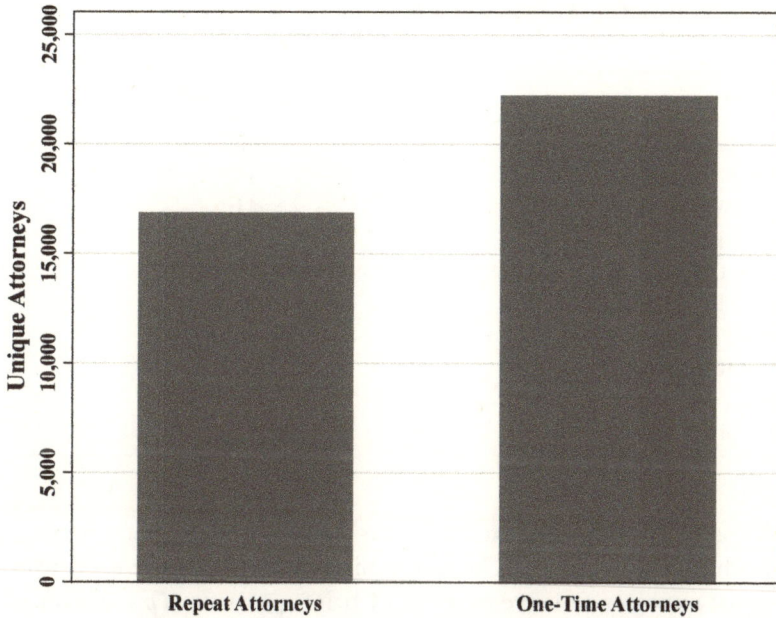

Figure 1.13. Distribution of attorneys in Supreme Court briefing. The distribution of uniquely identified attorneys that signed one or more merits briefs, broken down by whether the attorney in question signed only one brief or more than one brief.

neys in the data who have signed one hundred or more briefs. However, the modal number of briefs signed by repeat attorneys is three.

Gathering nuanced data on nearly forty thousand different attorneys who have practiced before the Supreme Court over several decades is quite a challenge. The most informative piece of information we have for the attorneys who sign briefs is available due to the structure of our own data set. We can compile the brief-writing experience for each attorney previous to a particular case. As with our measures of filer experience, we use our data going back to 1970 to compile experience measures so that everyone does not start at zero in 1984 where we begin the analysis. Attorney R noted that Supreme Court practice has changed in terms of the bar becoming more elite over time. Therefore, we look for changes in this experience measure for each passing year. Figure 1.14 shows the average number of previous briefs signed for all the attorneys who signed a brief in a given term. The experience level of

Table 1.3. Top Ten Attorneys by Frequency of Brief Signing, 1970–2015

Attorney	No. of Briefs
Edwin S. Kneedler	452
Steven R. Shapiro	442
Seth P. Waxman	416
Charles Fried	415
Paul D. Clement	389
Donald B. Verrilli Jr.	373
Michael R. Dreeben	363
Kenneth W. Starr	352
Lawrence G. Wallace	337
Theodore B. Olson	318

both party and amicus attorneys has increased with parties setting a somewhat steeper trend. Overall, amicus attorneys have seen average previous experience increase by 0.14 briefs per term ($p < 0.001$) while litigant attorneys have seen an increase of 0.31 briefs per term ($p < 0.001$). Since 1995, litigant attorneys have had a higher level of average experience than amicus attorneys.

Although consistent data on many thousands of attorneys is largely impractical to compile, we do account for two types of job experience that signal particularly adept attorneys: clerking for a Supreme Court justice and service as the United States Solicitor General.[16] Both of these qualifications are fairly rare. Of the pool of unique attorneys who appeared in our data set, 3.3 percent were former clerks and 0.03 percent were former solicitors general. However, these elite attorneys participate at a higher rate than their small numbers suggest. More than 11 percent of all attorney signatures on briefs are by former clerks while 0.37 percent of such signatures are by former solicitors general. More than 30 percent of briefs are signed by at least one former clerk and 1.7 percent are signed by a former solicitor general.

Conclusions

In this chapter, we presented a detailed overview of merits briefs filed in the Supreme Court from 1984 to 2015, including both litigant and

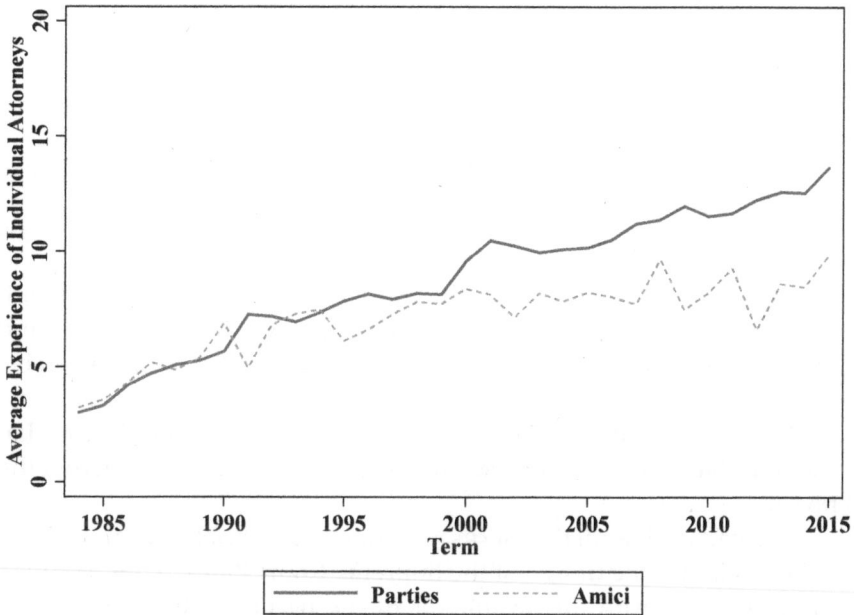

Figure 1.14. Attorney experience over time. The distribution of the average previous experience of all attorneys who signed a brief in a given year, separated by amicus and party briefs.

amicus briefs. Our nuanced data on the informational content of briefs, as well as the number and nature of both filers and attorneys, shed considerable additional light on well-known patterns in Supreme Court briefing such as the increasing number of amicus briefs over time. The patterns reveal that litigant briefs contain quite a few more citations to Supreme Court precedent than amicus briefs while amicus briefs are consistently both more textually complex and more emotional in tone. We also explored the varying participation by different types of filers by previous experience and across time. There is considerable variation in both dimensions. One interesting pattern that emerges is that while the number of amicus briefs has been increasing with each term, only two types of filers—interest groups and individuals—have a statistically significant increase in their amicus brief submissions over time. Finally, we also offered insights into temporal patterns in the number and experience of attorney participation. For example, we find that the average experience of attorneys has been increasing for both party and amicus briefs.

2 | Crafting a Brief

The previous chapter illustrates the considerable variation found in both the informational content of briefs and the people who commission and produce them. In this chapter, we begin to explore the connections between people and the briefs they submit for the Court's consideration. We begin by returning to *Florida v. Harris*. The eleven briefs filed in that case exhibit in microcosm the variation that exists in briefs across the board.

The party briefs on the merits were the longest briefs filed in the case in keeping with the design of the Supreme Court Rules.[1] They included the facts along with the arguments of the parties. Gregory G. Garre, a former law clerk to Justice Rehnquist and former solicitor general, and Brian D. Schmalzbach from Latham & Watkins LLP, in addition to the Florida Attorney General and her team, represented Florida. Their opening brief was a bit over eleven thousand words. All together, these attorneys had signed a total of 165 previous Supreme Court merits briefs dating back to 1970. The respondent's brief filed on behalf of Harris was submitted by Public Defender Nancy A. Daniels and Assistant Public Defender Glen P. Gifford, the same attorneys who had represented Harris since the original trial of his case. They submitted a brief that was only 209 words short of the fifteen-thousand word limit. Neither of these attorneys had any previous experience in the Supreme Court.

Additionally, a range of information from a variety of interested entities also flowed into the Court via amicus curiae briefs. The Court's own rules allow for such submissions, and the Court's practices encourage them (Supreme Court Rule 37). In the modern era, they are standard features in cases before the Court. Explicitly, the Court asks the briefers to bring new information to the Court. Despite this request, amicus briefs often include information similar to what is provided in other submissions (see Hazelton, Hinkle, and Spriggs 2019; Collins 2008; Corley 2008). The solicitor general wrote in support of Florida's position, as did a collection of twenty-six states and territories and the National Police

Canine Association and *Police K-9 Magazine.* On the other hand, five amicus briefs from nonprofit groups, scholars, criminal defense lawyer associations, and a branch of the ACLU bolstered Harris's position. The amicus briefs ranged in length from 4,363 to 9,606 words.

In addition to varying in terms of length, the amicus briefs also varied notably in terms of filers and attorneys. On the one end of the spectrum, Virginia and twenty-five other states and territories joined together to submit an amicus brief, and a total of thirty-three attorneys signed that single brief. Furthermore, the cumulative experience of those participants was staggering. Since states are frequent participants in submitting Supreme Court briefs, it is unsurprising that this group of filers combined for a total of more than seven thousand previous briefs dating back to 1970. Their large team of attorneys was similarly very familiar with the Court, having signed on to a total of more than twelve hundred briefs. At the other end of the spectrum, two amicus briefs in the case were signed by a lone attorney with no previous high court experience. The puzzle we seek to untangle in this chapter is the extent to which this type of variation in filers and attorneys affects the content of briefs.

Scholars have long theorized about the role party and amicus briefs play in providing influential information to the justices (Epstein and Kobylka 1992; Collins 2004, 2007; Collins, Corley, and Hamner 2013; Corley 2008; Hansford 2004; Hansford and Johnson 2014; Kearney and Merrill 2000; Spriggs and Wahlbeck 1997). Yet, virtually all of the empirical work examining legal briefs has focused on their impact (a topic we turn to in later chapters) rather than on the factors that influence their composition. Furthermore, there is scant inquiry into the connection between filer and attorney characteristics and the information they produce. The decisions of parties and amici in conjunction with their attorneys regarding what to convey to the Supreme Court sets the stage for everything that comes later. Thus, it is important to understand the factors that influence the information they provide.

Existing scholarship reveals links between both certain types of parties and higher success rates (Sheehan, Mishler, and Songer 1992; Szmer and Ginn 2014) and certain types of briefs and higher success rates (Black, Owens, et al. 2016; Feldman 2016). In this chapter, we develop and test the theoretical expectation that these two separate patterns are part of a larger process in which particular kinds of parties are capable of producing higher-quality briefs that contain especially useful information and present that information in a skillful manner. In *Florida v. Harris*, Florida's brief was drafted by a team of six attorneys compared to a pair of attorneys for Harris. There is also disparity in Supreme Court experience between the sides. Florida had participated in 361 previous cases while Harris was in the Supreme Court for the first time. Previous work has struggled to determine why the Floridas of the world are more likely to win in court than the Harrises of the world. A frequent explanation is that the repeat player advantage reflects the ability to use resources like experienced and expert attorneys to craft more persuasive legal arguments. We set about testing this mechanism. First, we discuss scholarship on the role of resources in litigation broadly. Second, we articulate a theory of how resources influence the way briefs are constructed. Third, we go about testing how well our theory predicts the determinants of the quantity, type, and presentation of information in briefs. We reveal a rich tapestry of connections between filer and attorney characteristics and how briefs are drafted, many of which we anticipated and some of which we did not. As we hypothesize, more experienced attorneys and those who have clerked in the US Supreme Court craft briefs with a larger amount of information, more strategic citations, and a higher concentration of future-oriented language. However, both former and current solicitors general tend to defy our expectations. For example, they both draft party briefs with less information than other attorneys. In the final section, we provide an overview of all of our findings and summarize our conclusions.

Resource Advantage

While not the focus of practice guides, existing scholarship indicates that entities with more resources have greater success shaping policy. This pattern emerges in a variety of contexts. Lobbyists with greater resources, and those who can hire them, are more successful in shaping legislation (Baumgartner et al. 2009; McKay 2012). Similarly, parties with better resources enjoy an advantage in court. In 1974, Marc Galanter first suggested a distinction between repeat player litigants and one-shot litigants and argued that repeat players tend to obtain more favorable judicial decisions (Galanter 1974). One reason for this is because repeat players (also referred to as "haves") typically possess greater resources than one-shotters (also referred to as "have-nots"); they can hire more expensive attorneys who presumably have additional experience and expertise, which, in turn, contributes to the higher likelihood of securing favorable litigation outcomes (Wanner 1975; Wheeler et al. 1987; Atkins 1991; Songer and Sheehan 1992; McCormick 1993; Albiston 1999; Farole 1999; Songer, Sheehan, and Haire 1999; Szmer, Songer, and Bowie 2016). While Galanter initially proposed this theory in the context of trial litigation, his general expectation that courtroom participants who enjoy greater resources and higher status in society tend to enjoy higher rates of success in courts has proved to describe empirical realities in a variety of contexts.[2] Scholars have demonstrated that status and resources carry an advantage in a wide variety of courts, including the US Supreme Court (Sheehan, Mishler, and Songer 1992; Szmer and Ginn 2014). This result applies beyond the litigants themselves as well. Amici who are repeat players are also more likely to achieve their desired outcome (Buckler 2015).

Despite the substantial number of studies that uncover the type of repeat player advantage that Galanter hypothesized, we still have a relatively poor understanding of the mechanism or mechanisms that underlie this well-established advantage (Szmer, Songer, and Bowie 2016). Galanter himself proposed multiple explanations for such an effect. Repeat players may be able to shape the law to their advantage over time due to their long time horizons, they may be better able to select which cases should be litigated (rather than settled), and they may devote more resources to litigation (Galanter 1974). While scholars have continued to restate and discuss these mechanisms, efforts to disentangle them have been largely thwarted by methodological difficulties. Primary among these difficulties is the inherent limitation posed by the prevailing method of quantifying litigant resources (Songer and Sheehan 1992; Songer, Sheehan, and Haire 1999). For decades this line of work has relied on classifying litigants (or amici) into general types that reflect overall resources or status in general, such as whether a litigant is an individual, a business, or a government entity. This was an eminently sensible strategy in view of the difficulty of obtaining more specific information. However, more recent work that engages the question of mechanism provides some insight into how research can move forward (Feldman 2016; Szmer, Songer, and Bowie 2016).

Examining the features of attorneys involved in litigation in addition to characteristics of the parties has begun to shed light on the mechanism(s) behind the repeat player advantage (Feldman 2016; Szmer, Songer, and Bowie 2016; Szmer and Ginn 2014). A key element of the resources explanation is that greater resources allow higher-status litigants to hire better lawyers (Galanter 1974). This mechanism is based on the idea that the quality of legal counsel is related to the probability of success. There is a considerable amount of empirical evidence that this is the case. For example, McGuire (1995) studies the role of experienced attorneys in merits cases before the Supreme Court and finds that attorneys who have more Supreme Court experience than opposing counsel are more likely to win. Several other studies find similar evidence that more capable attorneys achieve better litigation outcomes in the US Supreme Court (Feldman 2016; McGuire and Caldeira 1993; McGuire 1995; Wahlbeck 1997; Szmer 2005; Szmer and Ginn 2014; McAtee and McGuire 2007; Corley 2008). In these articles, the scholars find at least some relationship between higher levels of attorney expertise (either overall or in relation to opposing counsel) and an increased incidence of success.

The link between attorney expertise and litigation success suggests that having the resources to hire more expensive (and, presumably, higher-quality) attorneys explains at least part of the often-observed repeat player advantage (Feldman 2016; Szmer, Songer, and Bowie 2016; Szmer and Ginn 2014). But the reason why attorneys with better qualifications or more experience are more successful presents its own puzzle. Two major explanations for the greater success of better attorneys concern the credibility of an attorney as an information provider and the capability of attorneys with more experience and knowledge to make more persuasive arguments (Box-Steffensmeier, Christenson, and Hitt 2013; Szmer 2005). The credibility explanation is that judges are more likely to trust an attorney who appears in front of them frequently both because they have prior knowledge of that attorney's abilities and because they know such attorneys have an incentive to be faithful information providers in order to build and preserve a reputation as an advocate judges can trust (McGuire and Caldeira 1993; McGuire 1995; Wahlbeck 1997; Haire, Hartley, and Lindquist 1999; Szmer and Ginn 2014). This mechanism can work *for* filers too. The importance of filer reputation was raised by Mayer Brown (n.d.) with regard to clerks reporting that "some organizations develop positive reputations and, as a result, the court relies on their briefs more than those of other organizations."

There was a somewhat mixed picture from our interviewees regarding the extent to which the importance of experience stems from reputation. Most attorneys who mentioned reputation saw it as an important aspect of Supreme Court practice. Attorney and Former Clerk H noted that when the Court deals with attorneys that they don't know there is "less trust and reliance." Former Clerk N mentioned that experienced interest groups develop reputations regarding having something to say in amicus briefs. Relatedly, Attorney O stated that "justices and clerks pay attention to whose name is on the brief when they start reading." On the other hand, Attorney and Former Clerk M said they could "speak only for myself" but that the "brief spoke for itself" rather than the author being important. Though they did acknowledge that some attorneys have reputations. In interviews conducted by Lynch (2004), the majority of clerks she spoke with indicated that reputation mattered.

The importance of reputation was implied by our interviewees who discussed the risk of losing credibility with the Court. Attorney O noted that reputable attorneys can lose credibility. They observed that "some [attorneys] play fast and loose, especially at the cert stage." Such attorneys can include state solicitors general who do things like "exaggerate circuit splits and are trying too hard." This can happen because "many attorneys are chasing oral arguments and take risks to get in." Attorney and Former Clerk B thought too many attorneys wrote advocacy pieces, sacrificing their reputation and credibility. Attorney and Former Clerk H advised that attorneys focus on their "credibility" and take a "high degree of interest and accounting in what you are saying." This is especially true where the individual plans to be in front of the Court again. Specifically, "[you] don't need to say it is the end of the Republic." Instead, focus on producing a "well-written" and "quality" brief.

The second explanation for the success of experienced advocates is that such attorneys are more intelligent, have more extensive substantive knowledge, and are more skilled in presenting arguments to a court (Feldman 2016; Miller, Keith, and Holmes 2015; Wahlbeck 1997; Haire, Hartley, and Lindquist 1999; Szmer, Songer, and Bowie 2016; Szmer and Ginn 2014). The reason these qualities would matter is because the adversarial system sets up litigants' attorneys as the judge's primary source of information (Marvell 1978; Szmer, Johnson, and Sarver 2007). Many interviewees accentuated the importance of attorney experience as related to skill and knowledge. For example, Attorney and Former Clerk M noted that experience "matters generally in almost anything." The same is true at the Supreme Court according to them. Attorneys with experience know the "vocabulary, norms, etc." As with "any court, it matters." It is a type of "specialized knowledge." Attorney J described wanting the "right author" with "experience and gravitas," such as a "professor," attorneys from "big firms with pro bono departments," or other individuals with experience. The kind wanted can "read... the tea leaves" and predict the likely outcome of the case. They have "meticulous thinking" and provide the "larger community with a favor." There are justice accounts that also bolster the idea that more expert attorneys make better arguments. Justice Scalia recounted that during an arduous session of reading briefs, he ran across one that was very well written (Garner 2010, 52): "And I turned over the front, it made me so happy to see that it was one of the best lawyers in Washington, and it made me very happy to know that you could tell the difference."

The relationship between experience and understanding the unique nature of Supreme Court practice was also noted by multiple interviewees. Attorney O volunteered the importance of experience without being asked about it. They described "a widening gap regarding experience" at the Supreme Court, which "confirms the cliques." The practice is moving to a "small highly trained bar." It is "justified" because such attorneys "do a much better job." They "really believe in handing [cases] over to experts." The practice "has changed." Experienced attorneys "understand nuances of particular justices" and know "what kinds of arguments will be well received by the Court"—in other words, the types of arguments where the justices will be "sympathetic." "Frequent flyers" get a "much more receptive hearing." For example, former clerks have a "better chance to make their case."

Furthermore, the increasingly elite nature of the Supreme Court bar was a common topic of conversation in the interviews. Former Clerk K noted that "you don't go to the Supreme Court without lots of experience and coaching." As a practitioner, they "learned at the knee or hand of famous lawyers." It is like an "apprenticeship." For them, this is an "art, not a science." They also noted that the Supreme Court bar is a "very closed network" that "taught each other." Attorney and Former Clerk H also described the Supreme Court bar as "specialized" and populated by "repeat players." They noted that you are "unlikely to see a novice [practice in the Court] now." Attorney R noted that the Supreme Court practice now consists of "ten to twelve law firms" that are "there all of the time." They noted both an increase in the money involved and amount of policy being produced. When you see lawyers from states, they are there for subject matter expertise.

Similarly, Attorney and Former Clerk B noted that the Supreme

Court bar is a "narrow group" with "very trained" members who show "lots of care" in their craft. Furthermore, they felt that inexperienced attorneys treated Supreme Court briefs like other briefs and that was a mistake. They noted that Supreme Court justices are different because they have more resources than other judges. While they deal with more difficult questions, they have fewer demands and more resources. So, what works below does not work at the Supreme Court. Likewise, Former Clerk N noted that the Supreme Court bar is "elite" and very "good." They are the "best in the biz," "generally good," and "not shitty." Thus, they don't remember seeing obvious mistakes in the thousands of party briefs that they have read. Supreme Court practitioners write these briefs at a "very high level." It is "very different than the Courts of Appeals." The party briefs at the Supreme Court are "not missing cases or indirect precedent." (Though, they did note that the quality of party briefs at the cert stage was much more variable.) Similarly, Attorney O noted that less experienced attorneys tend to reargue cases as they did in the courts below. Thus, they include "elements not of interest" and "give short shrift regarding jurisprudence, which is more important at the Supreme Court than lower courts." They noted cases where a lawyer focused on a standing issue that was not important to the matter at hand. However, Attorney E was less impressed by experience: they felt that attorneys who focused on the Supreme Court tended to be a little too "cutesy" with elements such as turns of phrase.

Another interviewee (Attorney A) thought that experience helped with the pressures of Supreme Court practice: they noted that the "hoopla" of Supreme Court proceedings can impact how attorneys write briefs. They also observed that some attorneys write such briefs all the time whereas many more only write one or two. There is "lots of excitement" that "could be overwhelming and distracting." Where attorneys have been with a case the entire way, there may be less distraction. Though the attorney described being struck with "the grandeur of the occurrence" on the day of argument, they thought it would vary by attorney.

Finally, two interviewees offered contradictory advice for more novice attorneys faced with the possibility of litigating in the Supreme Court. Attorney J noted that one should ask, "Why are you best to argue this point?" when preparing a brief in terms of type of brief and expertise. On the other hand, another attorney who had appeared before the Court (Attorney Q) thought it was mistake to have "experts" argue another's cases at the Court. They called it "a shame" to give up the opportunity to "make the argument yourself" because it is an "honor to address in briefing and [in person]" and a "once in a lifetime shot."

The broad takeaway from this literature and the interviewee comments is that resources matter. Parties with more resources are more successful. More expert attorneys are also more successful. This means that hiring better attorneys is one specific way resources may help improve the probability of success. These overall patterns are likely to be influenced by the unique context of the Supreme Court. In that arena, the stakes are so high that the justices are typically provided with information of considerable quantity and quality on both sides of each case (Buckler 2015, 78). In fact, Galanter's party capability theory has more limited explanatory power in the Supreme Court (Sheehan, Mishler, and Songer 1992). This is unsurprising. Simply examining the relative capacity of the litigants on each side only tells a fraction of the story when a variety of entities are also filing amicus curiae briefs (Songer, Kuersten, and Kaheny 2000). Just as litigants vary in terms of resources and capability, so do amici (Box-Steffensmeier, Christenson, and Hitt 2013; Spriggs and Wahlbeck 1997). The work on party resources that explores the greater litigation success of entities with higher status in society and more experience in the legal system has focused primarily on litigants. As we move forward to theory building, we seek to extrapolate the insights of the work on resource advantage to apply to amici as well as parties.

The Role of Information in Resource-Based Success

In addition to observations about the greater success of stronger parties and lawyers, there is evidence that the content of briefs can be pivotal in determining the outcome of the case (Black, Owens, et al. 2016; Feldman 2016). This link likely flows through the amount and type of information found in the brief as well as how that information is presented. The success of certain types of parties and lawyers and the success of certain types of briefs is not likely to be a coincidence. After all, a key function of attorneys is to provide information to the Court (Marvell 1978; McGuire 1995; Wahlbeck 1997; McAtee and McGuire 2007; Szmer, Johnson, and Sarver 2007). Moreover, as discussed previously, one reason more skilled attorneys (often hired by those with more resources) may obtain better litigation outcomes is that they are better at presenting the justices with information in an effective way (Haire, Hartley, and Lindquist 1999; Hanretty 2014; Szmer, Songer, and Bowie 2016; Szmer and Ginn 2014; Wheeler et al. 1987). As Spriggs and Wahlbeck (1997) describe, "Justices are trained in legal reasoning and the composition and persuasiveness of legal arguments therefore affect them" (368). Repeat player theories frequently cite the idea that better attorneys are more skilled at presenting information to judges in a persuasive fashion (Larsen and Devins 2016).

In several interviews, former clerks and attorneys who have filed briefs with the US Supreme Court noted that more experienced attorneys are able to present a compelling story regarding the most desirable outcome in terms of policy. Attorney P said that it is a "classic mistake" to tell the Court, "Don't worry regarding the consequences" because the Court is "really concerned regarding the floodgates and future cases." There is an "instinct to try to avoid admitting possible changes" but "[you] need to wrestle with implications." They acknowledge this is "hard to do." One should appear "honest." While Attorney R described goals in drafting briefs in terms of "politics," they also noted that there is "an art" to putting forth a "client's cause." As noted previously, Attorney O also alluded to the importance of experience in making policy arguments.

Yet little work directly explores the link between attorney characteristics (or other indicators of party resources) and the text of the briefs submitted to a court. Collins, Corley, and Hamner (2015) show that from 2002 to 2004, amicus briefs with greater cognitive clarity and shorter sentences had more of their exact phrasing repeated in the US Supreme Court's majority opinions. While this study does not look directly at attorney characteristics, it is plausible that more experienced attorneys are better able to craft the type of clear and simple briefs that are effective. In the only direct examination of that link to date, Feldman (2016) finds that in the Supreme Court attorneys who have appeared in one or more previous cases produce higher-quality party briefs in terms of writing style than attorneys in their first appearance at the Court. Specifically, repeat player attorneys craft briefs that are clearer and less emotional and that avoid undue passivity and wordiness (Feldman 2016). However, Feldman (2016) offers no measure of the informational content of the briefs, only how material is presented.

Our focus in this chapter is assessing the explanation that the success of stronger parties and amici and more expert attorneys lies in the ability to make better legal arguments. In particular, we explore whether those with greater resources and expertise actually produce noticeably different, and presumably better, legal arguments than those with fewer resources and less expertise. While most research on party and attorney capability focuses on either litigants or amici, we develop a theory that is comprehensive enough to provide and test explanations for all merits briefs submitted to the Supreme Court regardless of the source. We focus on all those who file briefs, including litigants and amici of all types, from individual persons to the federal government. Moreover, rather than look only at the entities involved in litigation or their attorneys, we examine both. As Flemming and Krutz (2002) point out, "Lawyers and their clients, that is the agents and their principals, can independently affect the process of litigation" (812). This approach allows us to distinguish between different types of repeat players. Some filers may be frequently involved in litigation while others rely on hiring attorneys with considerable experience (Albiston 1999). We begin by setting forth our hypotheses with respect to the overall patterns we expect to see emerge in brief writing before proceeding to describe our approach to empirical testing.

Filer Resources

Building a theory of what kind of filers or attorneys are likely to craft quality briefs is a challenging task. We both use and expand on existing concepts. Broadly speaking, we seek to capture three dimensions that are likely to lead to higher capacity to produce better briefs: resources, experience, and expertise. First, briefs written by filers with more resources are likely to be higher quality. In general, a higher-quality product can be created by investing more resources in its production. In the context of Supreme Court briefs, filers with more resources can hire more expensive attorneys, hire a larger number of attorneys, obtain expert opinions, and obtain information that may be costly to compile or procure. Scholars have long classified litigants into broad categories to use as a proxy for litigant resources. Following previous work, we expect the federal government to have the greatest amount of resources at its disposal and individuals to have the least amount of resources with other types of entities falling between those two extremes (Black and

Boyd 2010; Szmer and Ginn 2014). We expect higher-status filers to produce better briefs.

We move beyond simple filer type to theorize regarding two more nuanced facets of filer resources. The first is primarily motivated by the inclusion of amicus briefs in our study. There is substantial variation in the number of entities that cosign each amicus brief. A single person or interest group might write a brief, or a collection of organizations or persons may band together to present their cumulative concerns to the Court in a single brief. Those submissions presented by a greater number of filers should have a greater amount of resources available than briefs composed by a lone filer or a smaller number of filers. There is evidence that briefs with more signing parties have a greater chance of success (Box-Steffensmeier, Christenson, and Hitt 2013; Buckler 2015). It is possible that dynamic is related to the better quality of briefs generated when groups come together and pool resources. One interviewee (Attorney D), on the other hand, said they were wary of group briefs because of concerns regarding the quality of the arguments that type of collaboration produces. While variation in the number of cosigners is most flexible for amicus briefs, there is variation in the number of cosigners for litigant briefs as well since litigation can involve more than one party on each side. For both types of briefs, there is a larger pool of resources available to contribute to constructing a higher-quality brief when there are a greater number of filers. So, we expect briefs with more cosigners will be higher quality.

Next, we turn to the number of attorneys who sign a brief. Although there may be some exceptions, in general it costs more money to hire more attorneys to work on a brief. Moreover, there is empirical evidence that litigants in higher-status categories do hire more counsel (as well as more experienced counsel) (Farole 1999; Haire, Hartley and Lindquist 1999; Szmer, Songer, and Bowie 2016). The addition of more attorneys working on a brief should also contribute directly to producing a higher-quality brief (Szmer, Johnson, and Sarver 2007). As Szmer, Songer, and Bowie (2016) point out, "Presumably, larger litigation teams have several advantages over smaller teams, including enhanced abilities to anticipate and respond to counterarguments." (71). There is also evidence that larger litigation teams lead to greater success (Haire and Moyer 2007; Szmer, Johnson, and Sarver 2007). Consequently, we expect briefs with more attorneys to be higher quality.

Experience

In addition to resources, scholars have also shown that experience plays a key role in the repeat player advantage. A filer with virtually unlimited resources that hires a phalanx of high-priced attorneys may still not generate the most effective brief if neither the filer nor any of the attorneys have ever participated in litigation before the US Supreme Court. Attorneys who are familiar with a given court are better able to effectively persuade that court (Haynie and Sill 2007; Flemming and Krutz 2002; Sheehan and Randazzo 2012; Szmer, Johnson, and Sarver 2007). While this is true to varying degrees in many courts, there is reason to expect experience to be particularly important in the context of Supreme Court litigation (Owens and Wohlfarth 2014). Larsen and Devins (2016) note that "Supreme Court practice is different in kind than other litigation and requires highly specialized skills" (1918). Feldman (2016) found that attorneys with more experience before the Supreme Court produced higher-quality briefs. Several other studies have found more generally that greater attorney experience leads to a greater chance of success (Dumas, Haynie, and Daboval 2015; McGuire 1995; Szmer, Johnson, and Sarver 2007). This might be due to their ability to write better briefs. As we discussed previously, multiple interviewees noted the increasingly elite nature of the Supreme Court bar and its importance in addition to the influence of attorney experience.

We expect this pattern to hold for filers as well. Although filer experience has not previously been evaluated in this precise way, scholars have noted that the same logic applied to attorneys could be applied to parties or interest groups as well (McGuire and Caldeira 1993; Szmer, Johnson, and Sarver 2007). Along similar lines, Box-Steffensmeier, Christenson, and Hitt (2013) find that more well-connected amici are more successful using a complex network metric of connectedness in which the number of previous briefs an interest group has filed is an important component. While connections are weighted differently based on the power of the groups in question, the score is fundamentally based on the number of other organizations with which a filer has cosigned a brief. Filing more briefs overall tends to be correlated with cosigning with a higher number of other filers. That is to say, although we do not account for links between filers in precisely the same way that Box-Steffensmeier, Christenson, and Hitt (2013) do, our theoretical framework rests on the same foundation: the idea that filers have varying ability to be successful in the Supreme Court. While we focus on variation in resources, experience, and expertise, it is worth noting that these are likely important elements of connectedness to other organizations and entities. In other words, powerful parties and attorneys within the core of Supreme Court litigation are generally replete with such attributes. Our hypotheses regarding experience are that we expect that when both filers and their attorneys have submitted more briefs to the Supreme Court in the past, they are able to submit better briefs.

Attorney Expertise

Experience litigating in a particular court is one way filers and attorneys can gain expertise in crafting effective briefs. But there are other routes to gain such expertise as well. We examine three attributes of attorneys that reflect particularly high levels of knowledge regarding the operations of the Supreme Court. The judicial deliberation that occurs, both individually and collectively, in order to generate a judicial opinion takes place almost entirely behind closed doors. Only the justices themselves have full access to the process. But their law clerks have considerably more access than the public at large. Clerks read case documents and briefs, research the law, write memos with legal analysis, discuss cases with their justice, and sometimes even produce initial drafts of opinions (Ward and Weiden 2006). Moreover, each year the justices hire a new batch of clerks, and their outgoing clerks enter the legal profession. Many of these former clerks participate in litigation before the Supreme Court throughout their subsequent career (O'Connor and Hermann 1994). There is evidence that they are more successful than other attorneys (especially with respect to convincing the justice for whom they clerked) (Black and Owens 2020). As described in chapter 3, one attorney with Supreme Court experience discussed how helpful former clerks can be in preparing briefs, including volunteering their time and unique expertise. We theorize that former clerks will be able to put their insider knowledge to work to craft higher-quality briefs.

While only selected work has looked directly at the impact of clerkship experience, most research on party or attorney capability accounts for the presence of the solicitor general. A wide variety of studies have documented the large advantage enjoyed by the solicitor general at virtually every stage of Supreme Court litigation (Bailey, Kamoie, and Maltzman 2005; Black and Owens 2012). The solicitor general is more likely to obtain their desired result at the cert stage as well as on the merits, and their arguments are more likely to be reflected in the Court's majority opinion. The powerful role of the solicitor general is highlighted in practice guides (Mayer Brown n.d.) and qualitative studies (Lynch 2004).

Our interviewees also noted the importance of the solicitor general and attention paid to their briefs. When it comes to amicus briefs, Former Clerk and Attorney H noted that there are two types: "those from the SG and everyone else." Attorney P believed that if the United States is not a party, that it is "worth trying to get it to submit" an amicus brief. It is "difficult to get." The "parties separately meet with the SG and try to persuade" them to submit a brief on their behalf. Moreover, solicitor general briefs are important. Former Clerk N explained, "One of the most important briefs in a case is the one filed by the Solicitor General. Even when the United States is not a party, often the SG will file a brief in support of one side (or in support of neither side). The SG's views are essentially treated as party briefs by the Court, even when the United States is an amicus."

Much of the solicitor general's success is attributed to the institutional advantage of representing the most powerful actor in the legal system, the national government. However, the position is also highly specialized since it directly focuses on practice in the Supreme Court representing the interests of one particular client that frequently engages in litigation at that level. Interviewees highlighted the importance of the solicitor general and experience. Attorney and Former Clerk M believed expertise is "why the solicitor general gets so much weight." While they acknowledged that it is true that the solicitor general represents the United States, they highlighted "more collective experience" and the presence of "repeat players" in the office. It is a "feedback loop" regarding what the Court finds "persuasive." They have information regarding "veins of arguments" that are specific to justices. As with other experienced advocates, reputation is a component as well. Attorney and Former Clerk H asserted that the most credible party briefs come from the United States when represented by the solicitor general. They also spoke of those associated with the solicitor general's office as similarly benefiting from good reputations. Justice Roberts, who worked in the solicitor general's office, has noted the importance of such experience

(Garner 2010, 18). Justice Ginsburg has touted both the expertise and credibility of that office as well (Garner 2010, 136–137).

The fact that the solicitor general develops substantial expertise in presenting arguments also means that once they leave the office to return to private practice, they take that vast experience with them. The value of this experience came up in the interviews. For example, Attorney R noted the importance of talking with former solicitors general to understand Supreme Court practice. Attorney and Former Clerk H noted that former solicitors general and assistants to solicitors general are very "credible." These attorneys (solicitors general, former solicitors general, and attorneys from the office) have a "high degree of credibility and reputation" regarding both "facts and law." Consequently, we hypothesize that both current and former solicitors general will produce higher quality briefs.[3] Likewise, it is probable that current and former members of the office of the solicitor general who do not hold the top job also have the capacity to produce higher-quality briefs. However, due to a lack of available data on precisely who worked in the office of the solicitor general and during what time frame, we restrict our focus to the solicitor general themselves. Nevertheless, it is worth noting that theory suggests any empirical findings regarding former solicitors general are likely also indicative of the performance of other former members of that office.

Data and Methods

Testing hypotheses regarding the determinants of high-quality briefs requires developing a way to quantify what makes a "better" brief that provides information to the Court in a more effective way. There are many aspects of a quality legal argument that defy large-scale, objective quantification. However, there are opportunities to test our hypotheses. Rather than select a single definition, we conceptualize quality as a multifaceted concept that incorporates the amount, type, and presentation of information. We first describe the details of our empirical approach and then proceed to discuss and test the role of filer and attorney characteristics on each of these three ways of conceptualizing the quality of a brief.

As described in chapter 1, we have amassed data on over thirty-two thousand briefs from 1970 to 2015. We use the data going back to 1970 to develop experience measures for both filers and attorneys, and we run our empirical analyses starting in 1984. As a result, for the first brief we analyze in 1984, the experience measures are not all set to zero but contain variation based on data going back to 1970.[4] Our unit of analysis is the individual brief, and we examine the determinants of information in both main party briefs and amicus briefs.[5] Since the details of each case may shape all the briefs for that case, we cluster standard errors on the case. Each model has the same set of explanatory variables. We will discuss each of our outcome variables further later as we explore the different ways of measuring information. All of our outcome variables are continuous, so we run ordinary least squares regression models throughout.

Although our theory of how resources, experience, and expertise shape information in briefs largely applies to both party and amicus briefs, there are some significant differences between the two types of briefs. For example, the number of filers is much more likely to vary for amicus briefs than it is for party briefs. Additionally, litigants and amici may take different approaches. Litigants generally care primarily about the case outcome rather than the Court developing a particular policy (Spriggs and Wahlbeck 1997). As a result, litigants may provide the Court with as many reasons as possible to decide in their favor. Amici are often in the converse situation and care more about the case's implications for a particular element of legal policy (Hansford 2004; Spriggs and Wahlbeck 1997; but see Wofford 2020). As described in further detail in chapter 3, several interviewees highlighted the differences in purpose and strategy between party and amicus briefs. In order to account for such differences, we employ separate models for party and amicus briefs throughout our analyses.

Our key explanatory variables are measures of the resources, experience, and expertise of filers and their attorneys. We begin with the same kind of general filer type classification that is often employed in analyses of party capability theory (Black and Boyd 2010). Although there are some variations throughout the literature, our classification follows the overall approach. We group each filer into one of the following five categories: individual, business, interest group, subnational government, or national government.[6] We do not utilize the more detailed ten-category approach often used in research on Supreme Court litigants (Collins 2004) because there is not sufficient detail within briefs to make the fine distinctions required by that system, such as the difference between an individual and a minority or the difference between a large business and a small business. The research that uses such coding relies on the exhaustive coding of each litigant provided in the publicly available Supreme Court Database. However, since that coding does not extend to amici, we use the five-category coding scheme described previously because the name of a filer alone is sufficient to place a filer within the appropriate category without additional information.[7] Each brief is coded according to the highest status filer among all cosigners (Wheeler et al. 1987). While the relative ranking of these categories from lowest to highest status and power is often assumed to facilitate empirical analysis (Szmer, Songer, and Bowie 2016; Szmer and Ginn 2014), we model this as a factor variable (with interest group, the modal category, as the excluded baseline) (Hanretty 2014; Sheehan, Mishler, and Songer 1992). This approach allows the data to reveal both the actual rank ordering and variation in the differences between any pairwise combination.

Next, we measure the resources of the filers of each brief by counting both the number of filers and the number of attorneys on each brief. Briefs filed by a larger number of persons or organizations should have a larger pool of resources with which to work. And after controlling for the number of filers, the briefs that are signed by a larger number of attorneys should serve as a rough proxy for the level of resources the filer (or filers) are bringing to bear on the case. We log these measures (and our experience variables described later) since there are diminishing returns as these numbers increase (Black, Owens, et al. 2016; Hansford 2004; Szmer and Ginn 2014).[8]

After accounting for resources, we turn to measuring the experience of both filers and attorneys. For each filer and each attorney, we calculate the previous number of briefs they have been listed on in our data going back to 1970. Since there are often multiple filers or attorneys on each brief, we use the maximum experience among the filers and attorneys on each brief. All the filers and attorneys work together as a group to produce a brief. As a result, we expect the most experienced participants to make sure the end product reflects their experience. Previous work has used the same approach to summarize both attorney experience (McGuire 1995; Szmer and Ginn 2014) and interest group power (Box-Steffensmeier, Christenson, and Hitt 2013).[9]

Our three measures of expertise in Supreme Court litigation are fairly straightforward. First, we count the number of attorneys signing a brief who previously clerked for the Supreme Court. We identify former

Table 2.1. Summary Statistics

Continuous	Min.	25%	50%	75%	Max.
Quantity of Information	−34.08	−6.51	−0.85	5.61	61.38
Strategic Citations	0	0	1	3	64
Technical Language	2.79	6.60	7.51	8.58	23.24
Future Tense Verbs	0.00	0.68	0.84	1.03	2.96
Emotional Language	0.67	2.34	2.88	3.50	8.88
Reading Grade Level	11.83	16.13	17.06	18.15	24.18
Log No. of Cosigners	0.69	0.69	0.69	1.10	6.95
Log No. of Attorneys	0.69	1.10	1.39	1.79	4.44
Log Max. Filer Exp.	0.00	0.00	1.61	4.08	7.72
Log Max. Attorney Exp.	0.00	1.10	2.40	4.06	6.11
No. of Former Clerks	0	0	0	1	8
No. of Former SGs	0	0	0	0	2
Ideological Alignment	−1.26	−0.58	−0.08	0.58	1.26
Log Word Count LC Opinion	0.69	8.21	8.81	9.37	12.01
Term	1984	1991	2001	2009	2015

	Filer Status				
	Interest Group	Individual	Business	Subnat. Govt.	National Govt.
	46.6%	17.3%	10.0%	15.5%	10.6%

Binary	0	1
Current SG	92.7%	7.3%
Court Invited Brief	99.7%	0.3%
Petitioner's Side	50.5%	49.5%
Amicus Activity in Lower Court	60.6%	39.4%
Observations	22,282	

clerks by using a remarkably exhaustive listing of each justice's clerks in each term available on Wikipedia.[10] The next measure is the number of attorneys on the brief who previously served as the solicitor general of the United States. This variable was coded using the listing of all US Solicitors General (and their dates of service) in Black and Owens (2012). We also include a variable for whether the brief was written by the current solicitor general.

Finally, we control for features of the case that may correlate with both our measures of resources, experience, and expertise and our various outcome variables. A small number of amicus briefs are filed at the explicit invitation of the Court rather than upon the initiative of the amicus (Shaw 2015).[11] Since the content of invited briefs might vary from other amicus briefs, we control for this factor. Research shows that interest groups invest more in cases where they are more likely to win (Hansford 2004; Perkins 2018). Other filers may behave similarly. Since the Supreme Court is more likely to reverse than affirm, all participants generally expect a higher probability of success when on the petitioner's side. Therefore, we control for whether a brief is filed on behalf of the petitioner (either directly or by amici supporting the petitioner). For similar reasons, the ideological alignment between the Court and the outcome sought by a filer may be important as well. Writing a brief to convince a conservative court to produce a liberal result (or vice versa) is likely a somewhat different endeavor than writing a brief to convince a conservative court to issue a conservative ruling.[12] We use the (logged) word count of the lower court opinion and the presence of amicus activity in the lower court as proxies for the complexity and salience of legal issues in the case. We rely on the lower court opinion for these measures to ensure that the content of the briefs themselves does not shape the measure of case complexity or salience. Finally, we control for the term in order to account for the fact that both language usage and standard practice in terms of brief writing may very well shift over time. Table 2.1 shows the summary statistics for all of these variables.

The Multiple Facets of Crafting a Quality Brief

Now that we have described our explanatory variables, we will proceed to test our hypotheses. As mentioned previously, our approach is to use a range of outcome variables to explore different dimensions along which a brief might be considered to be "better" than other briefs. Specifically, we conceptualize the quality of a written submission to the Court as incorporating the amount, type, and presentation of information. We will examine each of these in turn, discussing the theoretical foundation, describing how we quantify the concept, and testing our hypotheses.

Amount of Information

The first metric of information in a brief we examine is the simple quantity. Word counts are a typical measure of textual quantity. While more is not necessarily always better, longer briefs should generally have the capacity to provide more information to the justices. However, the length of briefs is not independent of institutional constraints. There are word limits that constrain the length of briefs, even if filers often exceed the stated limits or do not use all of their allotted space (as we describe in chapter 1).

Words are not the only pieces of information in legal writing. Legal citations are an important source of a particular type of information (Collins 2008; Hansford and Spriggs 2006). Attorneys naturally incorporate references to case law in their legal arguments (Manz 2002). There are also unique aspects of the role of precedent at the Supreme Court. Attorney and Former Clerk L stated that the mistakes they saw advocates making at the Supreme Court were "101" issues—not addressing precedent and counterarguments. One needs to "acknowledge bad policy implications and precedent upfront." Attorney E noted a "dilemma" that arose because they were aware of information that could be helpful to the opposing attorney but did not describe how they resolved said dilemma. They also said that of all levels of courts, the US Supreme Court is the easiest regarding using precedent because the focus is only on Supreme Court precedent. They did note that "there is never an authority directly on point at the Supreme Court." Relatedly, Attorney C said that the use of sources is very case and issue specific. They also stated that the "Supreme Court doesn't care regarding lower court opinions unless it is about the impact of precedent." For example, it could matter if "lower courts are struggling" to apply a precedent. Also, Attorney and Former Clerk B noted that while law schools train students to include a citation for every statement in legal writing, that is not the case with Supreme Court advocacy. Also, rather than "torture" cases, advocates should "just say it." Attorney and Former Clerk B thought that citations in amicus briefs were unlikely to be unique and, thus, unlikely to help. Because of this important and unique role of precedent, we measure the number of citations to Supreme Court precedent in each brief.[13]

Two briefs with the same raw amount of information can look very different in terms of how that information is distributed. Briefs may provide a broad array of information discussing a large number of ideas and topics or they could be narrowly focused on a single legal issue. Which approach is best may depend on the context, as is discussed in more detail in the following chapters. However, in general, briefs that address a wider array of topics allow the Court more avenues to come to a favorable decision. Just like with quantity, we measure breadth of information using both words and Supreme Court citations. Instead of measuring the total amount of information in terms of words and cites, we calculate the number of unique words and citations in each brief. Narrowly focused briefs will repeat many of the same words and cite a smaller collection of precedent while broader briefs will call on a larger vocabulary and cite a larger number of cases. For purposes of empirical analysis, we combine these four metrics into a single measure of the overall amount of information in a brief.[14] Although we analyze the four constituent measures as separate explanatory variables in other chapters, we adopt this more parsimonious approach here to avoid the unnecessary proliferation of outcome variables.

The results for the models showing the determinants of overall quantity of information for both party and amicus briefs are displayed in figure 2.1. The results for "Filer Type" meet our expectations in some ways, but not in others. Amicus briefs filed by national government entities produce a significantly greater quantity of information than all other types of briefs, which is expected.[15] But subnational government amicus briefs, which should be the next highest category, produce the lowest amount of information and significantly less than interest groups. For party briefs, the only significant result indicates that the federal government produces less information than any other type of filer. These results highlight the importance of treating "Filer Type" as a categorical variable. The traditional story of each type of filer increasing in strength from individual to national government does not necessarily play out in every instance. In fact, there is considerable variation.

There is evidence for our hypotheses about the number of attorneys, attorney experience, and clerkship experience in both models. However, the effect sizes are modest. For example, moving from two attorneys to five (which is from the twenty-fifth to seventy-fifth percentile in our data) increases the estimated quantity of information in a party brief by 2.4. This is only one-fourth of a standard deviation. Each additional clerk boosts the quantity of information in an amicus brief by 1.1. There is further support for our filer quantity and filer experience hypotheses with respect to amicus briefs. It is unsurprising that these vari-

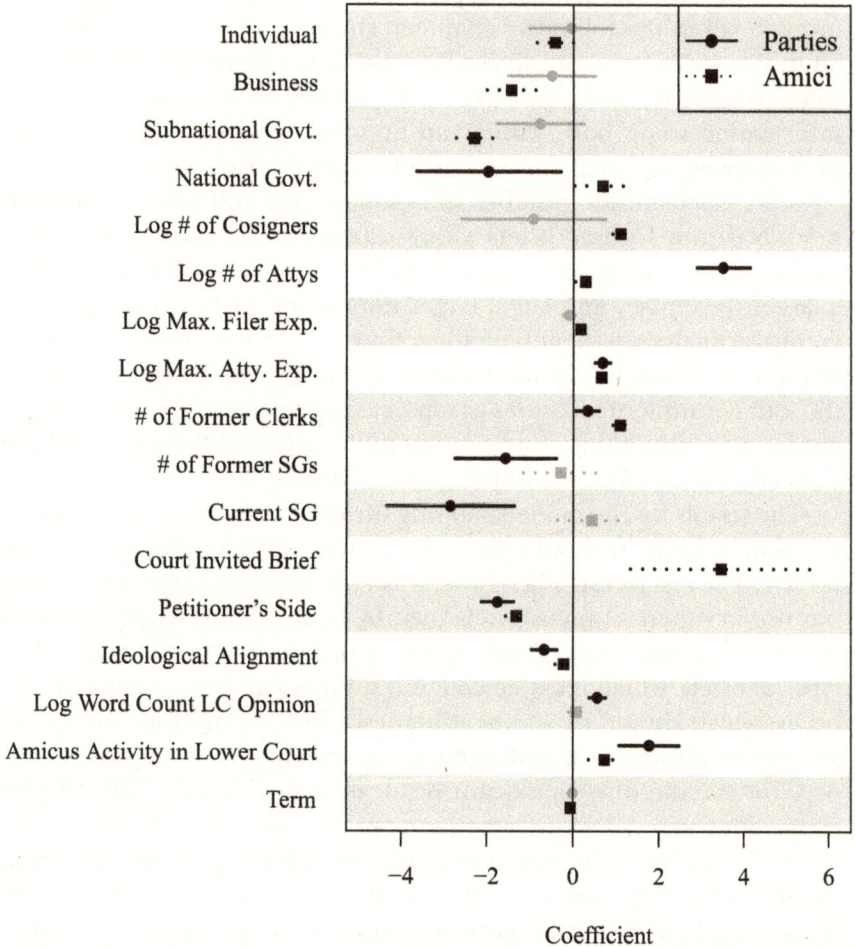

Quantity of Information

Figure 2.1. Quantity of information. OLS regression estimates of the effect of resources, experience, expertise, and a range of control variables on the quantity of information in a brief. For the party model, coefficients are marked by circles, and 95 percent confidence intervals are solid lines. For the amicus model, coefficients are marked by squares, and 95 percent confidence intervals are dotted lines. Estimates and confidence intervals in gray (instead of black) indicate that the confidence interval includes zero.

ables are only significant for amicus briefs as the identity (and therefore number and experience) of filers is fixed by the nature of the case for litigants. Amicus briefs that are specifically invited by the Court also contain significantly more information, and the effect size of 3.5 is larger than most of the other significant variables. There are two unexpected results as well. Litigant briefs filed both by former solicitors general and the current solicitor general contain a smaller amount of information.

Types of Information

Next, we turn to measure the type of information in briefs. For example, information may be strategic in nature. Including arguments crafted strategically with the current members of the Court in mind may lead to greater persuasive power. Language can be crafted strategically in a variety of ways, not all of which are subject to empirical measurement. However, one can observe the precedents cited in a brief. Given majority rule voting on the Court, observers have often commented that advocates could, should, or do disproportionately direct their arguments to persuade the justice they expect to be the pivotal voter (McGuire, Vanberg, and Yanus 2007). Expert counsel might draft briefs as "love letters" to Justices O'Connor or Kennedy (or whomever the current median is) in an effort to sway the all-important median voter.

In interviews, many attorneys who have practiced before the Court addressed their strategies regarding the audience for their briefs. While several attorneys noted that strategies vary by case and the specifics of the matter, overall, the attorneys discussed targeting strategies aimed at securing specific votes. Attorney A said that there is a debate regarding who the main audience for briefs is based on who will read them: justices or clerks. They did not resolve that debate but accentuated the importance of assuming that briefs are read and by someone with influence: "Sometimes amicus briefs are pivotal. You have to assume they might be read." Attorney Q noted that they saw both "judges and clerks" as the primary audience of briefs. Furthermore, they explained their view that the justice "guides and control[s] [their] clerks." In general, interviewees described thinking about specific justices in drafting briefs. One interviewee (Attorney J) asserted that most of the time one can "predict" the votes of most of the justices and pitch to the unknown members. They cited Justice Kennedy as an example. Such targeting is "hard to do" and focuses on "that justice's opinions": "[You] can't overdo it" or it might "backfire." Where "you can predict," one must consider who the swing or median justice is and also ask, "Is there a way to flip the unlikely [justices]?" It is "rarely possible." Mostly, one just makes the best arguments possible. Attorney R also discussed trying to "pull in the broadest coalition possible."

There was also discussion of varying strategies. Attorney J said that the specific target or audience for a brief "depends on the issue." Attorney O also said, "It depends on the case and stage" in determining the target of a brief. Likewise, Attorney P said the audience for a brief "depends." According to Attorney J, factors that matter in deciding who to target include whether the brief was "asking for radical change" or "recognizing precedent." There were "different avenues of possibility." One should think through the solutions and propose one with an eye to "what will get the support of five justices." One might target "those who are the most likely to support and those who can bring others." It is a "sophisticated issue." Also, the calculus varies between the cert and merits stages based on the numbers needed, four versus five. (The swing justice is more important at the merits stage.)

Several interviewees specifically broached targeting the swing or median justice. Attorney R noted "the Rule of Five." This was echoed by Attorney A who said the goal is generally to "appeal to five," and Attorney O discussed "counting to five" and being cognizant of the median or swing justice. Attorney D described targeting the median in a subject area. Attorney E did consider which precedent might "resonate" with the justices generally and with particular justices in building their brief. Furthermore, they described specifically targeting Justice Kennedy.

It should be noted that a few interviewees dismissed the idea of targeting briefs or indicated that it was delicate to do. Attorney and Former Clerk M said they were unsure if targeted briefs actually sway outcomes. According to J, it is a question of "how to explain [the matter] at the dinner table to relatives." One wants to avoid the "danger of being too legalistic." Rather, "pitch to mom and dad" or your "aunt and uncle who don't agree" with the presenter's opinion. Regarding targeting briefs to specific justices, Attorney A stated that they "are not that granular" when drafting a brief. Furthermore, they thought that it was "too obvious" when briefs were targeted at a specific justice. This was a sentiment that Attorney R also touched upon: "[you] don't want to appear to do that." That said, Attorney A did say they sometimes brief toward justices

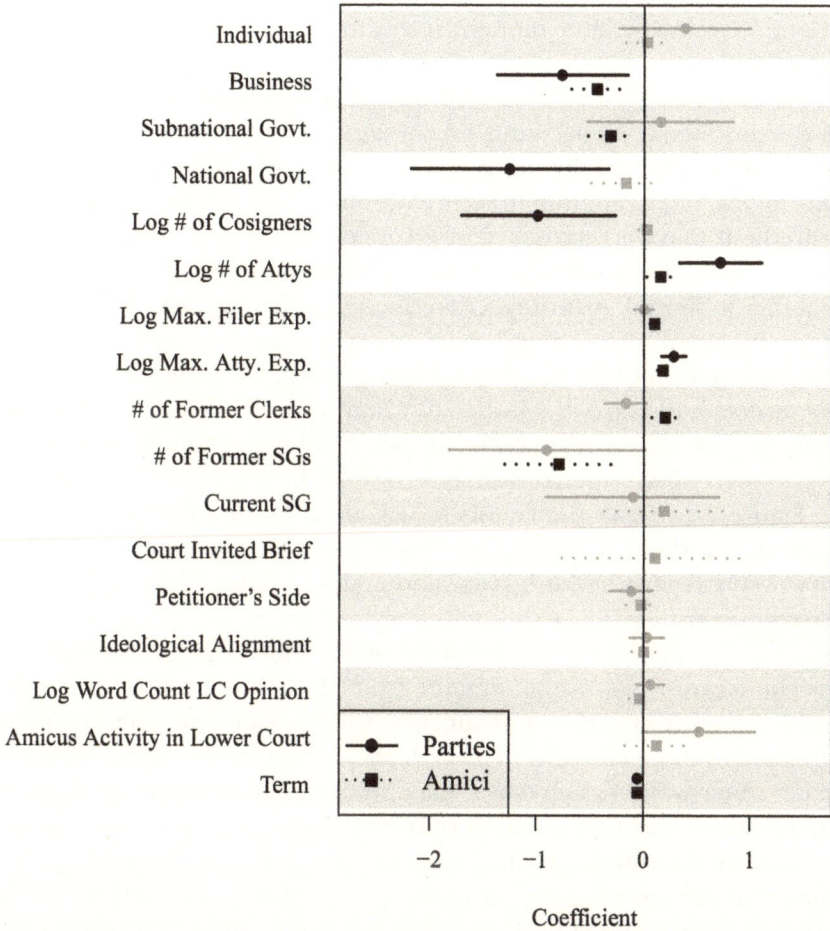

Strategic Information

Figure 2.2. Strategic information. OLS regression estimates of the effect of resources, experience, expertise, and a range of control variables on the number of citations in a brief to a precedent written by the current median justice. For the party model, coefficients are marked by circles, and 95 percent confidence intervals are solid lines. For the amicus model, coefficients are marked by squares, and 95 percent confidence intervals are dotted lines. Estimates and confidence intervals in gray (instead of black) indicate that the confidence interval includes zero.

with particular "subject matter sensitivity." The attorney said they "may include materials for some justices but am not writing for an audience of one." Generally, they thought it was too hard to be very precise in targeting briefs.

Although the interviewees did not all report strategically targeting pivotal justices, their accounts do contain sufficient discussion of such behavior to merit looking for empirical evidence of this type of strategy. One logical way to attempt to secure the all-important fifth vote is to cite precedents that were authored by the median justice.[16] In fact, Attorney P specifically discussed appealing to justices based on prior opinions that they authored. Attorney A described that their approach to getting to five included researching "what justices have said in other cases." Additionally, Former Clerk K noted that it is worth tailoring cases cited to the justices and citing the justice to whom you are trying to speak. We posit that an increased number of such citations generally indicates a higher level of strategic information in a brief.

Figure 2.2 reveals the factors associated with the inclusion of more strategic information. "Filer Type" has intermittent and mixed explanatory power regarding both party and amicus briefs. Where significant effects do exist, normal expectations are confounded. For example, national governments use the fewest strategic citations in party briefs.

The clearest results that emerge from these models are that briefs crafted by more attorneys and attorneys with greater experience contain significantly more citations to precedents penned by the current median justice. A party brief crafted by a team that includes an attorney who had signed fifty-seven previous briefs (the seventy-fifth percentile) will use an estimated 0.8 additional strategic citations compared to a team where the most experienced (or only) attorney has signed only two previous briefs (the twenty-fifth percentile). Since the average number of strategic citations included in a brief is 2.5, this is a notable effect. For amicus briefs, two of our other hypotheses are supported as well. The amount of filer experience and the number of former clerks both increase the use of strategic citations within amicus briefs, although to a fairly modest extent. Contrary to our expectations, the number of filers is significant and negative in the party model, and the number of former solicitors general decreases the use of strategic citations in the amicus model. Furthermore, since this outcome variable is new to the literature, it is interesting to note two other patterns that emerge from these models. First of all, there is no evidence of "Ideological Alignment" affecting strategic citation. This is probably unsurprising given that everyone has a reason to appeal to the Court median. Finally, the use of strategic citations appears to be decreasing over time, albeit by a small amount.

Another type of information is that which is focused more on policy implications than legal nuances. Since the advent of the famous Brandeis brief in *Muller v. Oregon*, scholars have noted that the Court may benefit from briefing not just on the law and legal theory but also social scientific or other technical information that provides the Court with the factual background they may need to assess the consequences of their decision (Margolis 2000).[17] The purpose of such a brief is "to inform courts of the context and the realities behind legal theories and arguments" (Greenhouse 2008, 1). Since the Supreme Court is faced with shaping policy for the entire country, the justices may especially require technical information from experts in the relevant field regarding how particular case outcomes may ultimately impact society (Davis 1955; Margolis 2000). Some guides specifically highlight the importance of this type of information, especially in amicus briefs (Kollross 2021; Shapiro et al. 2019; Simpson and Vasaly 2015; McGimsey 2016).

Many interviewees discussed the importance of such information for the Court; this is in keeping with previous interview studies (Lynch 2004). It was a recurring theme regarding the role of amicus briefs, with attorneys and former clerks noting that amici were particularly helpful when they provided information related to the implications of various legal policies. Multiple interviewees highlighted the unique role of the Supreme Court as a policy-making body. Attorney A observed that "highest courts are different" due in large part to the policy-making functions of those courts, which leads the judges to focus on the larger legal issues. Attorney and Former Clerk B noted that it is "unique" to the Supreme Court that "justices are always thinking beyond the participants in the case." Attorney R mentioned that the goal is to "highlight . . . the facts in the most persuasive way" because the Court is "a policy making body." Attorney P also explained that the Supreme Court was unusual in that "policy arguments can and should be made." Justice accounts provide mixed narratives regarding the role of policy. Justices Scalia and Breyer have both publicly acknowledged the importance of legal issues with broad implications over the outcomes of immediate cases (Garner 2010, 75 and 162). Justice Thomas has spoken against briefing on policy issues, though he also craves technical information (Garner 2010, 114–115 and 119).

The interviewees' discussion of the Supreme Court's consideration of policy often took the form of evaluating the larger implications of a decision. Specifically, Attorney A discussed the interest high courts have in "the question"—that is, the larger legal issues that must be resolved—as opposed to the outcome of the immediate case. The attorney noted that judges on high courts are interested in how they will form their opinions to provide guidance for lower courts. Furthermore, the structure of courts means that apex courts are dealing with important issues that are often splitting lower courts—Attorney A specifically mentioned these areas in terms of seeking cert. Attorney and Former Clerk H said they were unsure if briefing is different at the Supreme Court compared to other courts at the merits stage. (However, they said it was quite different at the certiorari stage.) But, in keeping with Attorney A, they did say that the Supreme Court "doesn't care about individual cases as much, unlike district courts." Rather, the Court is worried about "the right legal answer." Nevertheless, they were unsure if it translated into differences in briefing strategy as much as oral argument, which deals heavily with hypotheticals.

This concern with the larger legal question is one that is very much about understanding the implications of possible decisions. As Attorney and Former Clerk L explained, "[The] real world context" is important, and briefers should describe "what might happen": "How would the world look different depending on the outcome?" This is particularly true where justices have less information and experience, such as with technical issues. Similarly, Attorney and Former Clerk B was concerned about dealing with the "community context" and the potential "ripple" from the decision. Specifically, the Court needs to know "other policy options." This differs across industries. Historical information can also be useful to highlight "old problems" and "echoes." They also noted that the Court pays attention to specialized information; for example, the history of medicine. The issue is showing complexity. B said the Court is "open to receiving information" and is "hungry for [it]." They stated the importance of peer-reviewed articles (and compared them unfavorably to law review articles, which they described as "a little bit of a scandal"). Attorney R noted that we should have asked about how information gets to the Court. Specifically, they discussed the "classic story in judicial process classes" regarding the occasional importance of social science research in cases such as *Brown v. Board* and *Brown v. Entertainment Merchants Association*.[18] They also said, "Academic studies can be helpful."

Davis (1955) coined the phrase "legislative facts" to identify facts presented to a court, "which help the tribunal to determine the context of the law and policy and to exercise its judgment or discretion in determining what course of action to take" (952). This concern with policy making and information that was akin to legislative facts appeared in what attorneys we interviewed considered the best content for briefs from specific types of filers. For example, Attorney C noted that the interests of states are distinct from other types of filers. Thus, amicus briefs from states tend to focus on the interests of the state and communicating that information to the justices. These briefs tend to be in two categories: (1) a "distinct interesting take" regarding a legal issue that was "undertreated" by a party or a "particular experience or perspective," and (2) Brandeis briefs with "facts and information regarding how [the case] effects [the state] and other states." The attorney gave a specific example of a recent amicus brief in which they highlighted both a "big thing" (how a policy would affect a state) and a "small thing" (a distinct legal issue regarding standing). Litigants can provide legislative facts, such as the "big thing" described by Attorney C, by hiring experts to consult with their attorneys, and amicus briefs are often filed directly by groups or individuals with expertise in the relevant subject area. Especially for amici, providing the Court with key technical information in the form of legislative facts can potentially play an important role. Measuring the amount of technical information in a large number of lengthy documents is tremendously difficult. Rather than measure the nature of information directly, we leverage certain features of language that are more likely to be employed in the context of discussing technical concepts.

The Linguistic Inquiry and Word Count (LIWC) software provides a simple way to measure a wide variety of linguistic features (Pennebaker, Francis, and Booth 2001). We posit that three of these categories are more likely to appear in the technical discussions that are often central to legislative facts. One feature of technical information is discussing quantity. As a result, we use the LIWC category for quantitative language that includes words such as *lots* and *none*. Next, we include the use of words related to discussing causation since the purpose of describing technical information in briefs is generally to help the Court assess the effects of the Court's actions.[19] Some examples of words in the LIWC category for causation include *because*, *trigger*, and *result*. Finally, a variety of scholars note that a feature of technical information in general is an increased use of parenthetical explanations (Bennett and Slocum 1985; Nida 1992). The need to provide explanations or definitions embedded within the sentence structure signals particularly complicated or technical ideas. Consequently, we include a count of the use of parentheses. As an example of all three categories, consider the following passage from the original Brandeis brief:

> But it is shown that everything which <u>makes</u> the worker *more* strong, *more* healthy, *more* energetic, *more* intelligent, *etc.* (and these will be the <u>results</u> of *greater* leisure, and the observance of rules prescribed for hygiene, upon the subject of the hours of labor and *rest*), <u>make</u> him also *more* <u>productive</u>. <u>Therefore</u> the introduction of reforms indicates strongly that the final <u>result</u> will be a very great *increase* of <u>production</u> with a shorter time period for work. (Brandeis 1908, 68, emphases added)

This short passage of less than one hundred words contains not only a parenthetical explanation but also nine quantitative terms (shown in italics) and seven words related to causation (shown underlined). Although anecdotal, it illustrates how these three concepts play a role in language discussing policy implications.

For each of the three categories discussed previously, the LIWC software generates the percentage of words in a text that falls within each category. We sum these measures to calculate the total percentage of a brief that is more likely to be associated with a technical discussion. While this measure provides a noisy signal, we expect better-equipped filers, and especially better-equipped amicus filers, to craft briefs with a higher percentage of such information. In order to provide some face validity that our measure does, broadly, capture the type of technical information in a Brandeis brief, figure 2.3 shows the percentage of the original Brandeis brief that contains each LIWC category we are using as well as the comparable percentage from the appellant's brief in *Muller v. Oregon*. While all three categories are present in both briefs to some extent, the Brandeis brief contains a higher percentage in each category and a substantially higher percentage of quantitative language and parentheses.

Beyond containing technical information, another feature of legislative facts is that they are frequently focused on the future. This is different from traditional legal analysis since the standard application of existing law to facts focuses largely on the past. Several interviewees spoke to the future-oriented nature of Supreme Court litigation. Attor-

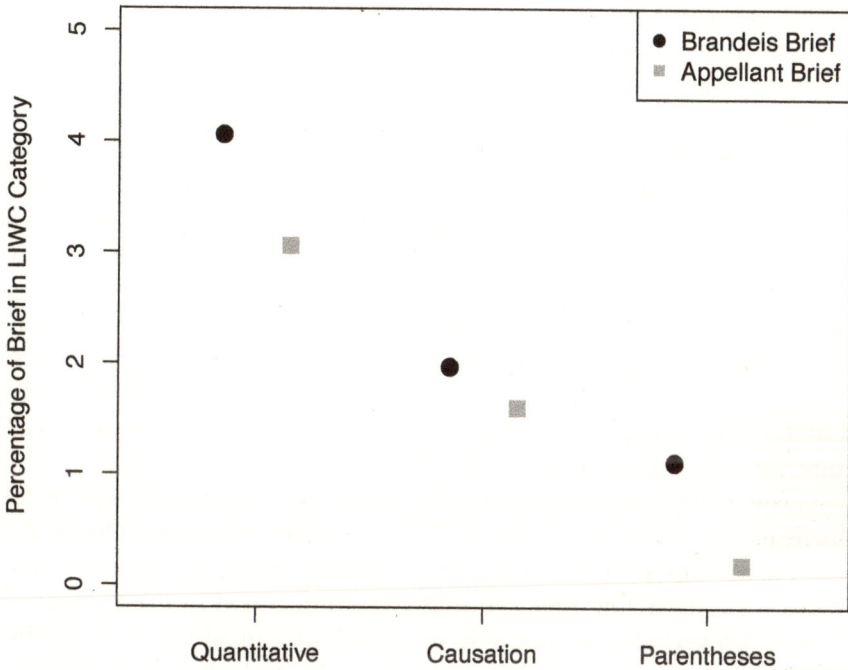

Figure 2.3. Measuring technical information. The percentage of each brief filed in *Muller v. Oregon* in each of three LIWC categories: quantitative language, causal language, and parentheses.

ney A noted that unlike many other courts, the Supreme Court is "thinking about future cases" rather than focusing on the immediate case before it. As discussed earlier, Attorney and Former Clerk B made very similar statements. Likewise, as described earlier in this chapter, Attorney P advised that it is a "classic mistake" to tell the Court, "Don't worry regarding the consequences" because the Court is "really concerned regarding the floodgates and future cases." Attorney and Former Clerk B also explained that some attorneys don't draw out consequences from potential decisions—this is a mistake because there is "no harm" in it and "some justices care [about it] a lot." Justice Scalia went so far as to say, "We don't care who wins or loses. We care about what the legal issue is and what is going to decide not just this case but hundreds of other cases" (Garner 2010, 75).

Margolis (2000) explains why discussing legislative facts often requires framing arguments in the future tense as follows:

> Policy-based reasoning involves an assessment of whether a proposed legal rule will benefit society, or advance a particular social goal. In making this determination, courts are required to identify a desirable result, and then consider whether the operation of the proposed rule will encourage that result, as well as discourage undesirable results. Because a new rule will likely be of general applicability, courts must consider how a proposed rule will work for future litigants, as well as for society as a whole. Assessing the general effect a legal rule will have is, by definition, a future-oriented enterprise. (211)

As a result, briefs that incorporate more analysis of future impact may be in a better position to persuade the Court. We test whether resources, experience, and expertise result in talking more about the future by using the LIWC category that tracks the percentage of words in each brief that are future-tense verbs.

Even though technical information is difficult to quantify, our novel measure performs well compared to our other measures. The R^2 for the parties model is 0.14, and for the amicus model it is 0.06.[20] While these seem quite low, they can better be understood in the context of how much variation we are able to explain in our other models. The models of strategic citation, future-tense verbs, and emotional language (discussed later) all have R^2 values ranging from 0.01 to 0.05. As these numbers illustrate, explaining variation in language is quite challenging. While our models of quantity of information and grade level perform better with R^2 values in the double digits, the largest is 0.23.

Figure 2.4 shows our models for both technical information and the usage of future-tense verbs. There is evidence in both the party and amicus models that briefs written by more attorneys contain more technical information. Moving from two to five attorneys writing a brief increases the amount of technical information by 0.25 for party briefs and by 0.15 for amicus briefs. The average amount of technical language in a brief is 7.76 (with a standard deviation of 1.76), so this effect size is quite small. Additionally, party briefs with more cosigners and amicus briefs with more experienced filers or more former clerks also contain a higher percentage of technical discussion. Contrary to expectation, party briefs by former solicitors general contain less technical language. The same is true for amicus briefs signed by more filers. Lastly, the results for filer type are once again a mixed bag. National government party briefs have a higher level of technical language, which tracks theoretical expectations, but subnational governments have the lowest level, which is surprising.

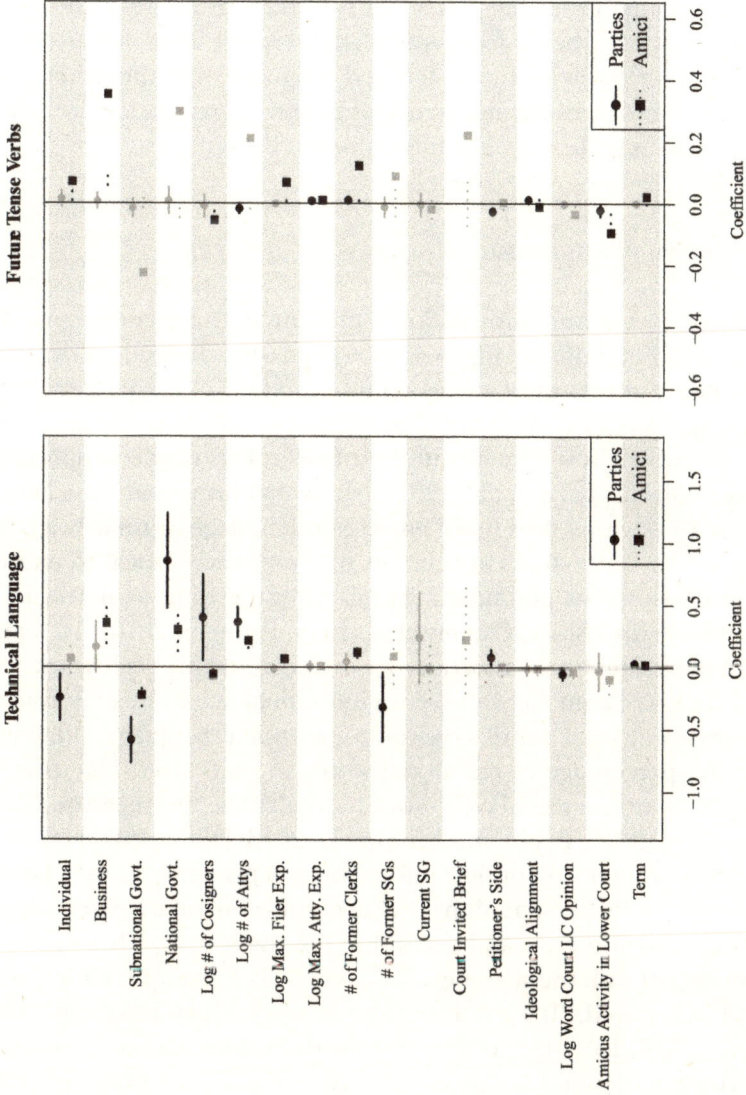

Figure 2.4. Legislative facts. OLS regression estimates of the effect of resources, experience, expertise, and a range of control variables on technical (left panel) and future-oriented (right panel) language. For the party models, coefficients are marked by circles, and 95 percent confidence intervals are solid lines. For the amicus models, coefficients are marked by squares, and 95 percent confidence intervals are dotted lines. Estimates and confidence intervals in gray (instead of black) indicate that the confidence interval includes zero.

Now we turn to explore the usage of future-oriented language. Consistent with our expectations, both party and amicus briefs are more focused on the future when they are drafted by more experienced attorneys and more attorneys with clerkship experience. As with our other models, the size of these effects is limited. Each additional clerk adds about 0.01 of future-oriented language to a brief. This is only 3 percent of a standard deviation. The effect size is quite small even considering that the average percentage of a brief devoted to future-tense verbs is only 0.87. Amicus briefs from more experienced filers also use significantly higher levels of future-focused language. On the other hand, amicus briefs signed by more cosigners and litigant briefs with more attorneys use significantly less future-focused language.

Presentation of Information

Finally, we turn to how information is presented. Guides direct practitioners to avoid emotional language (Garner 2014). Indeed, as described in chapter 1, three interviewees (with a mixture of clerking and practicing experience) mentioned that attorneys should avoid emotionality or overwrought statements in their briefs. This view is supported by research. Black, Owens, et al. (2016) show that justices are less likely to vote for a party that uses more emotional language in their brief. This is due to the contextual expectation that excessive appeal to emotion is unprofessional or potentially signals an underlying weakness in the legal arguments (Black, Owens, et al. 2016; Feldman 2016). We expect experienced filers and attorneys to understand this reality and craft their briefs with a smaller number of emotional words. Readily available dictionaries of what words constitute emotional language allow us to count the percentage of emotional words in each brief. Like previous research, we utilize the LIWC software to calculate this measure (Black, Owens, et al. 2016; Bryan and Ringsmuth 2016; Hinkle 2017).[21]

Another dimension of how information is presented is the clarity or complexity of its presentation. Practice guides regularly stress the importance of being clear and accessible (Garner 2014). These accounts are consistent with the statements of justices. For example, Chief Justice Roberts has stated, "It's got to be a good story. Every lawsuit is a story" (Garner 2010, 16). He has also discussed the importance of briefs being written to general audiences and the role of justices as generalists

(25 and 27). He further explained: "And it's just a different experience when you pick up a well-written brief: you kind of get a little bit swept along with the argument, and you can deal with it more clearly, rather than trying to hack through. . . it's almost like hacking through a jungle with a machete to try to get to the point" (11).

Several interviewees also discussed this issue in very similar terms. Regarding what is useful when consuming a brief, Attorney and Former Clerk B specifically noted a "readable prose style" with "storytelling" that one "can follow." Useful briefs include an "interesting" and "graspable structure" that is "easier to understand" as opposed to providing just the "nuts and bolts regarding legal analysis" or building "brick by brick." They noted that this is "not always possible or expected" based on the nature of the case. For example, in a technical or complex area like the tax code, a very basic approach might be appropriate. Former Clerk G noted that attorneys should "recogniz[e] the audience" as "smart generalists." It is a "skill to be able to speak in multiple registers" to both those with expertise and not. The Court "only knows what is before it." Parties are "greater experts."

In keeping with these observations of the participants in the process, a variety of research has shown that legal documents written more clearly can have a greater impact. Judicial opinions written in a clearer and simpler style are more likely to be discussed and cited positively (Nelson and Hinkle 2018). Briefs that are written more clearly are more likely to garner a judge's vote (Black, Owens, et al. 2016). Yet, writing clear prose is a challenging task (perhaps especially so for attorneys). The interviews point us in two different directions regarding clarity. First, several interviewees mentioned the importance of clarity in briefs. On the other hand, at least a few interviewees noted that attorneys should be careful not to underestimate the sophistication of their audience, noting that justices and clerks are very intelligent and educated. We theorize that one of the elements that separates the best lawyers is their ability to present information in a clear manner that avoids undue syntactic complexity. Such clarity should contribute to the persuasiveness of the arguments made (Feldman 2016).

This line of research relies on measures of the "readability" of a text originally designed to classify the approximate grade level of readers who would be able to understand a text. For example, George Orwell's *1984* is rated as appropriate for ninth- and tenth-grade readers and Jane Austen's *Persuasion* for eleventh graders. Texts with simpler sentence construction and shorter words have a lower grade level and are presumably clearer and easier to read. As there are many different formulas available to calculate this feature of a text, some scholars simply combine a wide variety of measures using factor analysis (Black, Owens, et al. 2016; Nelson and Hinkle 2018). We find that the measure selected makes very little difference to the results, so instead of using a combined measure, we employ one particular measure to provide a more intuitive scale for interpretation.[22] We use the SMOG index (McLaughlin 1969), which generates a number equivalent to the appropriate reading grade level for a text.[23] As we discussed in chapter 1, this measure provides the median estimate in our data among five commonly used measures.

Figure 2.5 shows our models of the percentage of emotional language in each brief and the reading grade level of each brief. We expect negative coefficients on our main explanatory variables for both of these outcome variables. Better briefs should be both less emotional and crafted in a clearer, less complex manner (which means registering a lower grade level).

Unlike our examination of the quantity and types of information used in briefs, the findings here provide more evidence contrary to our expectations than to support our hypotheses. Amicus briefs with more attorneys do use less emotional language as expected. Moving from two to five attorneys reduces the predicted percentage of emotional language by 0.02. The average amount of emotional language across briefs is 3 percent (with a standard deviation of 0.92). The type of filer also generally tracks use of emotional language along the lines we would expect. National government briefs employ the least emotional language, individuals employ the most emotional language (at least in party briefs), and the remaining types tend to clump in the middle. Contrary to expectations, there is more emotional language in all briefs with greater attorney experience, party briefs with more experienced filers, and amicus briefs with a larger number of cosigners. These unexpected effects are fairly modest in size too. For example, moving from one to two cosigners on an amicus brief increases the percentage of emotional language by 0.03.

The model of reading grade level presents a complex picture. We thought that more resources would lead to a lower grade level of briefs as an indication of nice, clear writing. Yet the "Filer Type" variable indicates that simpler might not always be better. Or at least that more sophisticated entities might not see it that way. Litigant briefs by the

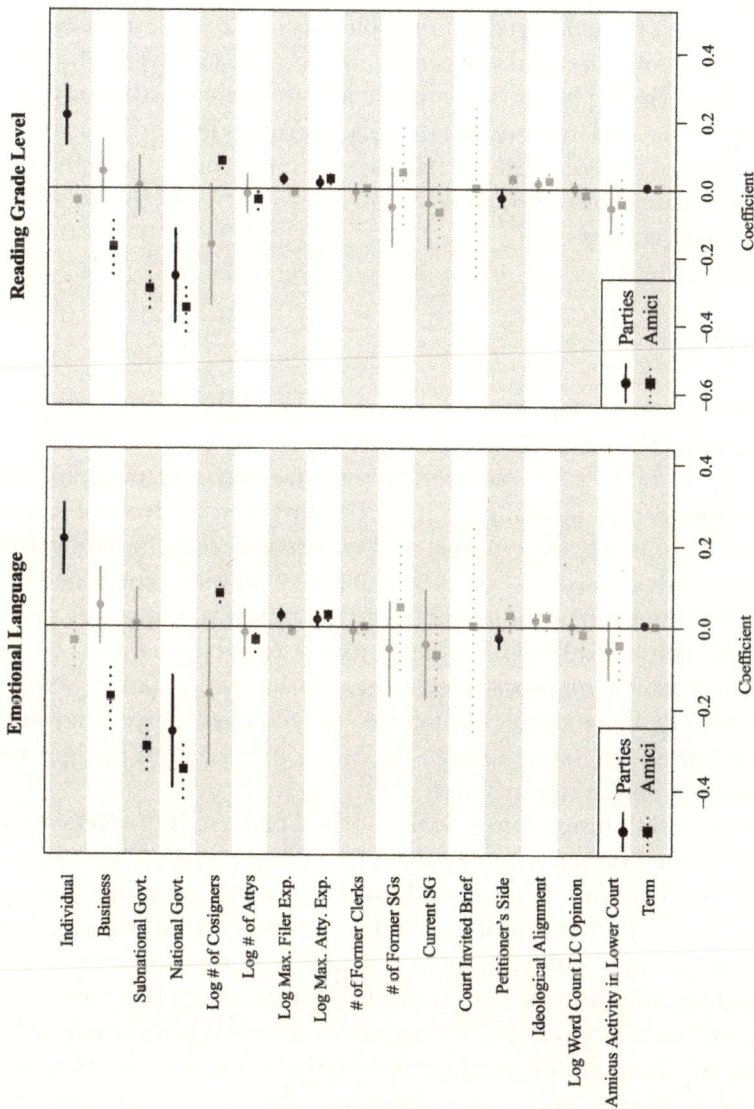

Figure 2.5. Presentation style. OLS regression estimates of the effect of resources, experience, and a range of control variables on emotional language (left panel) and reading grade level (right panel). For the party models, coefficients are marked by circles, and 95 percent confidence intervals are solid lines. For the amicus models, coefficients are marked by squares, and 95 percent confidence intervals are dotted lines. Estimates and confidence intervals in gray (instead of black) indicate that the confidence interval includes zero.

national government have the highest reading grade level (although not significantly higher than interest groups), and briefs by individuals have the lowest grade level. Along similar lines, briefs with more former clerks and amicus briefs with more attorneys are crafted with the more complex syntax of a higher reading grade level. However, consistent with our hypothesis, litigant briefs from more experienced filers and amicus briefs from more experienced attorneys and the current solicitor general are structured in a simpler way that reflects a lower reading grade level. All of these documents are quite complex. The average grade level among briefs is seventeen, and the standard deviation is only a grade and a half. So, the fact that each former clerk increases the estimated grade level of a brief by 0.06 is a marginal change, as is the similar 0.06 decrease that is associated with a move from two to five attorneys drafting an amicus brief.

Conclusions

In light of the fact that we evaluate eight hypotheses across twelve models in this chapter, we conclude by offering an overview of our findings in table 2.2 to accompany our discussion of overall trends.[24] Four overall patterns emerge from the forgoing analyses of our measures of resources, experience, and expertise across the models. First, we find fairly consistent evidence that attorneys with experience before or within the Court produce better briefs in terms of quantity and type of information. Both highly experienced attorneys and those with clerkship experience are more likely to craft briefs with a larger amount of information, more strategic citations, and a higher concentration of future-oriented language, though there is some variation in significance depending on the type of brief.

A second finding of note, rather than a pattern, is the lack of consistent expected patterns among filers of different types. The federal government sometimes performed best as expected, but individuals rarely ended up at the bottom of the ranking as the current literature would suggest. Briefs by subnational governments registered surprisingly low in some of the models in spite of the fact that such filers are typically regarded as the penultimate category in terms of litigant strength and resources. This uneven performance of the filer status variable may well be due to the fact that we are controlling for other elements of experi-

	Filer Quantity	Attorney Quantity	Filer Experience	Attorney Experience	Former Clerks	Former SGs	Current SG		Filer Quantity	Attorney Quantity	Filer Experience	Attorney Experience	Former Clerks	Former SGs	Current SG
	Party Briefs								**Amicus Briefs**						
Quantity of Information		✓		✓	✓	x	x		✓	✓	✓	✓	✓		
Strategic Citation	x	✓	✓							✓	✓	✓	✓	x	
Technical Language	✓	✓			x				x	✓	✓		✓		
Future-Tense Verbs		x		✓	✓				x			✓	✓	✓	
Emotional Language			x	x					x	✓		x			
Reading Grade Level			✓		x				x		✓	x			✓

Table 2.2. Summary of evidence supporting our hypotheses. The hypotheses are listed on the columns and the outcome variables are listed on the rows. A checkmark denotes a result that is statistically significant and in the direction we hypothesize. An x denotes a result that is significant but in the opposite of the hypothesized direction.

ence and resources, and that after accounting for these a five-category measure of filer status is not as useful. In subsequent chapters, we set aside this rough proxy and focus instead on the more direct measures of experience and resources we have developed with our expansive new data set. This makes for more parsimonious models and reduces collinearity between explanatory variables.[25]

The third finding is that solicitors general tend to defy expectations. The only evidence for either of our solicitor general hypotheses is that the current solicitor general drafts less complex amicus briefs. However, there are four instances in which the solicitor general variables have a significant effect in the opposite direction from what we expect. This may reflect the reality that their resources and experience are so qualitatively different than other attorneys and filers that different patterns emerge with respect to our measures of information. For example, the smaller amount of information presented by current and former solicitors generalin litigant briefs may be a result of a superior ability to express key points in succinct language and the confidence to only address the gist of the case without succumbing to the temptation to also address ancillary matters. Along similar lines, the fact that former solicitors general use fewer strategic citations in amicus briefs might be due to their ability to call upon a reservoir of detailed information about each justice that provides the tools to make strategic arguments in a more subtle and less ham-handed way than seeking to curry a justice's favor by citing his or her own work. The fourth, and final, general pattern we observe is that our theory appears to have more descriptive power with respect to amicus briefs than it does for litigant briefs.

3 | Coordinating and Coalescing
Investigating Information Sharing between Briefs

The extent to which US Supreme Court decisions should and do reflect aspects of public opinion and majoritarianism are hotly contested issues (Dahl 1957; Friedman 2009; Pildes 2011). Some scholars have focused on the potential capacity of amicus briefs to bring a democratic element to the unelected branch. Specifically, amicus briefing resembles legislative lobbying (Epstein and Knight 1999; Collins 2008, 2018). Accounts of such lobbying often focus on the need for information of members of Congress regarding defining the relevant issues and views of constituents (Epstein and Knight 1999). In turn, interest groups are happy to provide such information to the members in hopes of swaying the legislative outcomes and the state of policy. Our interviewees describe the art of briefing in terms that sound like lobbying. For example, Attorney and Former Clerk B stated that producing a good brief is a matter of defining the information that is useful for the justices: "What problem, dispute, or social issue are they being asked to address?" Knowing the ultimate issue is important for the attorney because it "shapes what [the justices] need to know." Once the issue is defined, they construct an "appealing answer" to the quandary that builds out the legal and moral narrative "leading them to a way of thinking" so that they "come to your conclusion."

Because those who engage in Supreme Court litigation understand the Court's function in forming policy, they focus on the importance of policy-related arguments like lobbyists do, including concerns about facts as they relate to the scope of policies created by decisions. Cases are won on "facts, not law," in Attorney P's estimation. Specifically, they believe facts account for about 75 to 80 percent: "If the law was clear, the case would not have been taken" by the Supreme Court. Therefore, one should make "floodgate" and policy arguments. Otherwise, one goes through the "motions of going through the case law." Also, Attorney and Former Clerk L voiced that advocates sometimes "assume too much knowledge regarding factual issues," as opposed to legal issues. Attorney and Former Clerk B also noted that some attorneys don't draw out consequences from potential decisions—this is a mistake because there is "no harm" in it and "some justices care [about it] a lot." But Attorney J conceptualized it quite differently: "Justices aren't deciding facts usually" but instead "pure legal issue[s]." It is best to address the legal issues in their estimation. Here, the interviewee was also focused on larger picture policy issues but with a different way of thinking about facts versus law. Although providing different perspectives, taken together these accounts paint a picture of attorneys seeking the most effective way to lobby the Court to implement their client's preferred policy.

Nevertheless, some scholars question the ability of amicus participation to act like lobbying. Specifically, Larsen and Devins (2016) attack the view of amicus briefing as a form of lobbying that may have democratic elements on the basis that parties and amici often coordinate their briefs. This criticism ignores an increasing awareness of the role that coordination plays in lobbying generally (Hula 1999; Hojnacki et al. 2012; Mahoney and Baumgartner 2015; Junk 2019). Coordination, in fact, strengthens the view of amicus activity as a form of lobbying (Hula 1999). Furthermore, this connection has largely been ignored and cries out for further exploration.

We examine coordination among briefers by looking at the content of briefs and exploring variation in similarity between amicus and party briefs. As illustration, consider our running example case of *Florida v. Harris*. In its main brief, Florida asserted that the evidence presented regarding Aldo and his training was sufficient to support a finding that there was probable cause for the search. Specifically, the state argued that probable cause was a "flexible, common-sense standard that depends on fair probabilities" and that "an alert by a well-trained drug-detection dog creates at least a fair probability that contraband exists." It further asserted that a long history of reliance by humans on dogs' superior sense of smell and the Court's repeated acknowledgment of the essential role of drug-detection dogs in law enforcement supported its position. Florida also touted the reliability of well-trained dogs and asserted that "a canine Barney Fife that regularly fails to detect contraband—or routinely alerts when contraband is absent—will be quickly identified during any genuine training regime and ferreted out." It took specific issue with the requirement that it must produce evidence of field performance, as it is less reliable than evidence from a controlled setting. Additionally, the state objected to the decision to require consideration regarding residual odors, partly because the presence of such odors is related to probable cause regarding the existence of contraband. Finally, the state asserted that the standard set forth by the Florida Supreme Court would impose "substantial and unjustifiable costs" on it.

Now we turn to the amicus briefs supporting Florida to examine the extent to which each amicus reiterated or emphasized the various arguments made by Florida. Briefs from the solicitor general, a collection of twenty-six states and territories, the National Police Canine Association, and *Police K-9 Magazine* presented a relatively consistent message: probable cause determinations regarding drug-detecting dogs should be made based on a dog's training, as opposed to field performance and the other forms of evidence required by the Florida Supreme Court. The United States, a powerful ally for the state, focused on arguing that evidence of a dog's performance detecting drugs in a controlled setting was sufficient to establish probable cause and established reliability. It also discussed why the Court should not "constitutionalize" training and certification standards and the need for clear guidelines. This brief had the greatest overall similarity to Florida's brief. Similarly, the lawyers for the states and territories argued that the Florida Supreme Court's decision conflicted with the "first principles of probable cause" and that the lower court standard would frustrate law enforcement activities. Relatedly, a brief from the National Police Canine Association and *Police K-9 Magazine* focused on an argument that a "well trained narcotics dog is entitled to a presumption of probable cause" and the ability of the state to make a prima facie showing of probable cause based on evidence regarding a dog's training or certification.

Now we turn to the other side of the case. Harris's brief argued that the Florida Supreme Court's decision should stand based on specific concerns regarding whether a drug-detecting dog "reliably alerts only to contraband" in establishing probable cause. The arguments focused on potential deficiencies in dog alerts: "The dog may be man's best friend, but as sources of probable cause, canine alerts are subject to error and misrepresentation." Such error can stem from a large array of sources, from the smell of other dogs and perfume to a desire to please a handler. The defendant argued that there are also issues regarding lingering odors from drugs that raise serious questions about probable cause regarding current possession. The law should treat searches by dogs like tips from confidential sources and require evidence regarding the reliability of the source according to the defendant, especially given the fact that dogs, like such informants, cannot be cross-examined in court. Specifically, Harris asserted that information regarding a dog's field performance is highly relevant under a totality of the circumstances standard. Moreover, his counsel argued that the state's position would erase the totality of the circumstances test in that training and certification alone would be enough to establish probable cause. Furthermore, Harris argued that the lack of current certification with the specific handler increased the need for information from the field. Finally, Harris explained that creating and maintaining records regarding field performance would be straightforward and, in many instances, was already happening.

Five amicus briefs from nonprofit groups, scholars, criminal defense lawyer associations, and a branch of the ACLU were filed to bolster Harris's position. There was more variety in the extent to which they focused on the same issues. Some of the submissions did discuss issues brought up in Harris's brief. For example, the brief filed on behalf of the Rutherford Institute was the most similar. It focused on issues of reliability in establishing probable cause, concerns with detector dogs' reliability, and the relative ease of establishing such reliability by law enforcement. The National Association of Criminal Defense Lawyers, the Florida Association of Criminal Defense Lawyers, the ACLU, and the ACLU of Florida also focused on these factors in their briefs. A group of Fourth Amendment scholars addressed issues regarding establishing probable cause under a totality of the circumstances test in detail. They also argued on behalf of the standard set forth by the Florida Supreme Court due to concerns regarding accuracy related to the warrant exception for canine sniffs. The scholars provided a more focused discussion of these issues than seen in the other briefs, including more nuanced arguments. Conversely, the Electronic Privacy Information Center focused more broadly on issues of reliability, including issues well beyond dog sniffs, such as the over-collection in digital intercepts. Additionally, the Institute for Justice filed a brief in which it opposed the assertion that evidence of training established probable cause and brought in arguments regarding civil forfeiture. These final two briefs primarily focused their discussion on arguments and issues that were not raised in Harris's brief.

The participation of a variety of interested actors as amici provided the Court with additional information and arguments, as well as some reiteration of information and arguments. How should we view such communications? To what extent are these patterns observed at large? Do such patterns indicate that the Court cares about policy implications and public support? Despite the growing knowledge that lobbying is primarily carried out by coalitions and that briefing acts as a form of lobbying, the role of coordination in the flow of information to the Court has received relatively little attention (but see Box-Steffensmeier, Christenson, and Hitt 2013; Larsen and Devins 2016). The few accounts of Supreme Court briefing that discuss the extent to which parties coordinate with amici regarding the content of amicus briefs indicate that existing theoretical and empirical approaches to considering the role of amicus briefs may miss important features of the system (Larsen and Devins 2016). Nevertheless, little quantitative research exists regarding the extent of coordination among the briefs received by the Supreme Court. In fact, researchers generally treat amicus briefs as being quite independent of litigants (Larsen and Devins 2016). This dearth of investigation is unfortunate considering coordination in briefing can help us better understand the forces that drive coordination in lobbying and information provision generally. It is an area that is ripe for further empirical investigation (Collins and McCarthy 2017; Collins 2018). Moreover, briefing allows us a particularly good vantage point to consider coordination in lobbying because the Court provides a relatively open and transparent system in which such coordination is occurring (see Hazelton, Hinkle, and Spriggs 2019).[1]

Here, we build on work regarding lobbying and briefing at the Court and investigate the extent to which there is evidence of coordination between parties and amici. Specifically, we focus on the dyadic relationship between a litigant and each of the amici who file briefs on that party's behalf (in turn). Parties and amici on the same side have similar, but not identical, goals. This fact leads to different expectations regarding the results of such relationships, including the roles of experience and repetition. These diverging expectations help explain differences across the advice in practice guides and empirical findings regarding repetition. We examine the similarity between the party brief and each supporting amicus brief. This is not to say that similarity is synonymous with coordination. On the contrary, coordination can result in either less similarity (e.g., when attorneys divvy up key topics or arguments) or more similarity (e.g., when actors agree on the importance of repeatedly emphasizing the same ideas).

Since attorneys are the actors responsible for crafting briefs, our primary focus is developing a theory of how attorney expertise shapes the extent to which party and amicus briefs resemble each other. In the previous chapter, we uncovered evidence that such expertise has an impact on the amount and types of information in individual briefs. Here, we explore how it impacts coordination regarding the content of briefs. We look at other factors as well, such as party and amicus characteristics and aspects of the litigation environment overall. The extent to which briefs correspond to each other relates to a wealth of theories of influence on the Supreme Court, including information and affected groups theory (Collins 2004). Furthermore, it pertains to the paradox of the Court asking for briefs with unique information while seemingly rewarding repetitive briefing (Collins, Corley, and Hamner 2013; Hazelton, Hinkle, and Spriggs 2019; Spriggs and Wahlbeck 1997).

We begin by discussing the existing scholarship regarding coordination in lobbying and briefing, as well as insights we gathered via interviews with Supreme Court litigators and former Supreme Court clerks. Then, we develop a model of coordination that we test on nearly twenty thousand briefing dyads between parties and supporting amici in cases from 1984 to 2015. The results are consistent with accounts of sophisticated coordination, especially concerning amici and their attorneys' experience. An amicus brief is significantly more similar to the party brief when the attorneys who signed the amicus brief have more experience or include a higher number of former Supreme Court clerks or former solicitors general. The same is true when the amici who sign on to the brief have more previous experience filing briefs in the Supreme Court. Finally, we summarize our findings.

Coalitions, Lobbying, and the Court

There is a growing movement in the legislative lobbying literature to acknowledge and contend with coordination among interest groups in lobbying activities. At the same time, legal scholars have begun to suggest and probe complex coordination among parties and amici filing briefs in the Supreme Court. Both areas quintessentially deal with providing information to policy makers. We investigate work in these veins and the accounts of interviewees to help consider the role of coordination in briefing.

Increasingly, groups attempt to influence the government through concerted action with like-minded organizations. In the realm of legislative politics, coalition building has become the norm (Heaney and Leifeld 2018; Hula 1999; Nelson and Yackee 2012; Mahoney and Baumgartner 2015; Junk 2019): "Lobbyists are not lone wolves. On the contrary, they usually work in packs" (Mahoney and Baumgartner 2015, 214) and use coalition action as one of the most prominent lobbying strategies (Baumgartner et al. 2009, 180; Hojnacki et al. 2012, 389; Nelson and Yackee 2012; Nownes 2006; Junk 2019, 1). The rise of coordination has been attributed by some to the growth in interest groups (Hula 1999, 3). The relative influence of each may diminish as the number of groups increases (Hula 1999).

Such logic also applies to the arena of Supreme Court litigation. In both situations, the amount of information has grown. Technology likely plays a role. It has increased the amount of available information and made communication between coalition members much easier (Hula 1999). Additionally, policy complexity may also encourage coordination (Hula 1999). Again, this reasoning applies to the Court as well.[2] Also, in the Supreme Court, access via briefing is limited by procedural rules that set forth word limits (US Supreme Court 2019). Filers can exceed such limits with permission (US Supreme Court 2019). Still, generally justices are seeking shorter briefs (Garner 2010), going so far as reducing word limits in recent rule changes (Mauro 2019). Thus, coalition building among briefers allows for more access to the Court via influence over a larger amount of information than one can present in one's own brief.[3]

When forming coalitions, groups must weigh the relative benefits and costs (Hojnacki and Kimball 1998; Hula 1999; Nelson and Yackee 2012). Hula (1999) asserts that "groups join coalitions to pursue strategic goals at reduced costs, to shape public debate by influencing a coalition's platform, to gather information, and to receive symbolic benefits" (7). Symbolic behavior can be beneficial as it can appease members (Hula 1999). Costs can include "organizational expenditure, resource allocation, and time lost due to coordination of the alliance" (Nelson and Yackee 2012). Additionally, coalition formation cuts against interest group competition (Holyoke 2009). Coalitions can be particularly helpful in influencing policy makers because they can signal policy convergence (Hula 1999; Nelson and Yackee 2012; Hazelton, Hinkle, and Spriggs 2019). Scholarship reveals that change is most likely to occur when groups have reached a consensus regarding policy (Hula 1999;

Nelson and Yackee 2012) and send consistent messages about it (Nelson and Yackee 2012). The Court famously allows cases to percolate, and there is evidence that they are more likely to act in ways that reflect the importance of policy agreement among interested groups (Hazelton, Hinkle, and Spriggs 2019).

Additionally, Supreme Court litigation also resembles legislative lobbying in terms of the varying roles that individuals or groups can play within coalitions based on differences in goals. In the realm of Congress, Hula (1999) notes that interest groups' incentives for joining a group generally shape the roles that they play in a coalition. Moreover, he notes that "goals, priorities and resources" influence the contours of participation (39). Core group members are focused on outcomes and include coalition brokers who help form the cooperative. They are the most invested in terms of resources. Specialists, on the other hand, care about policy goals but often in a more limited sense. Peripheral groups participate for information or "symbolic participation for their members" (46). They are the least invested in terms of resources. This research speaks to the extent to which lobbying encourages the flow of different types of information to a decision maker. Those with a direct interest in the decision are interested in a broad range of information flowing to the policy maker. In contrast, those with a less direct interest will bring more tailored policy positions.

While not a perfect mapping, Hula sets forth a typology with parallels to parties and amici, including subtypes of amici with particular attention to membership groups. Generally, parties and amici filing briefs on the same side and their attorneys all share similar goals and values, but their goals are often not identical. It should be no surprise then that many interviewees touched on broad differences regarding the role of briefs at various stages and in different cases.[4] Moreover, many interviewees described differing goals and roles for amicus and party briefs. For example, Attorney and Former Clerk L said that party briefs were "core" briefs. Amicus briefs, on the other hand, provided "stakeholder perspective," with facts and history. Amici were particularly important in complex regulation cases where the Court lacks expertise and needs factual information. Attorney and Former Clerk H noted that amici should have "slightly different approaches than parties." Similarly, Attorney E described working on "providing statistics via an amicus" with the type of "demographic information" that can't be provided in a party brief. Luckily, the group was very well-positioned to provide this information.

Attorney and Former Clerk H noted that amici can provide "some perspective not otherwise provided." In this vein, Attorney P asserted that amici can "be a little more honest" and "don't have to toe the line." Rather, they can be "nuanced" and spend "more time talking about consequences than facts compared to party briefs." According to them, there is a lot more policy in amicus briefs. Relatedly, Attorney J believed it is a mistake to discuss the specific facts of the case in an amicus brief. Furthermore, Attorney D noted that his goal in interest group briefs was to show "why the case matters," including vignettes about the type of people who are members of the group. Attorney F relatedly noted that briefs from states can include "some parochial information regarding how [the case could] influence a specific state."

The fact that so-called amicus facts (Larsen 2014) are often introduced in amici was noted by several interviewees: "Amicus have a way around rules of evidence" (Attorney A). They specifically noted this type of information coming from academics, and that appellate courts "often accept" it. Attorney R also noted that "issues outside of the record" can "be brought in" and "can be important." They think this is a "significant component regarding amicus briefs." Attorney A noted it is "sometimes unfair," as there is a difference with "published works versus private information." Attorney and Former Clerk H noted that it is surprising how the Court uses briefs with regards to occasionally pulling facts from briefs that aren't from the record, such as in a Louisiana death penalty case. These facts come from amicus briefs and are more often in dissents than majority opinions, according to H. They mentioned work by Larsen about reliance on factual assertions from amicus briefs (Larsen 2014). H also noted that they think judicial plagiarism is an important issue. The attorney and former clerk doesn't think that direct quotes are the major form of such use of materials without citation, but specifically mentioned the use of research from blogs. They also mentioned that there is "variation across justices" regarding this practice. Former Clerk N observed that parties are "constrained by the record." While amici can add "helpful. . .new facts," one has "to be careful."

The proper strategy for amici, particularly interest groups, was a matter of some controversy in the interview responses. Two interviewees noted that briefs by membership organizations often look quite different from other amicus briefs (Attorneys A and C): such groups appear to target their briefs at their members instead of justices and clerks. Attorney A believed that "too many amici just file to get their name in there." However, a different perspective was offered by an attorney with experience in interest group amicus briefs (Attorney D). Attorney D described being "very picky" about cases where they would file a brief for a specific interest group. They looked for cases "that are related to the group's mission." The group's "brand" was "very important" to this attorney. They wanted to make sure the group was presenting "well-crafted" briefs with a "consistent" message. Furthermore, Attorney D was also "very careful not to do harm" and cared about the specific facts of the underlying case and how it arrived at the Court. The ultimate question is, "Who do you serve?" For this attorney, it is the members. They also described wanting to "bring [in the] voices" of members while providing support for the party.

These accounts tie directly to existing theory regarding such actors and their goals and strategies: parties (and, thus, their attorneys) are primarily concerned with winning the case at hand, as it will directly impact them; amici, on the other hand, generally are more focused on the legal rule that will be announced by the Court because that is what is most likely to influence their interests (Marvell 1978; Collins 2008). Though, it should be noted that goals may vary across types (Wofford 2020). Additionally, membership organizations acting as amici are likely also eager to show their members that they are actively pursuing their interests (Hansford 2004). Thus, the strategies of parties and amici are likely to diverge at points. Parties behave as core group members whereas amici generally act as specialists and peripherals. Membership groups are particularly prone to behave as peripherals as their goals are often related to performing for their members.

These varying roles and goals should lead to attorney expertise manifesting in different patterns depending on the context. First, because parties are particularly interested in the disposition of the case, they are more likely to be interested in providing the Court with multiple paths to arrive at the desired outcome. Such routes can include multiple lines of legal reasoning, policy arguments, and types of technical information. Thus, parties should be more concerned with organizing amici to provide divergent information, especially where experienced attorneys who understand these nuances represent them. Amici, on the other hand, should be more interested in bolstering specific legal rules (Marvell 1978; Collins 2008). This may result in more convergence if the allied party has proposed the desired rule. As with other forms of lobbying, we anticipate that the differing goals of the key players in potential coalitions before the Supreme Court will lead them to differing patterns of behavior. But the extent to which parties and amici can carry out their goals via coordination should not be equal. Instead, resources are very likely to influence the results of coordination (Hula 1999). Next, we consider how resources in the form of experienced attorneys likely influence coordination.

The Impact of Attorney Expertise on Coordination

As discussed in chapter 2, there is a wealth of research indicating that parties with more resources obtain better outcomes in litigation (Galanter 1974). Additionally, scholars have noted that better-resourced groups have more experienced attorneys (Szmer, Songer, and Bowie 2016). In this vein, research indicates that attorney expertise is related to more positive outcomes for clients (Wanner 1975; Wheeler et al. 1987; Atkins 1991; Songer and Sheehan 1992; McCormick 1993; Albiston 1999; Farole 1999; Songer, Sheehan, and Haire 1999; Szmer, Songer, and Bowie 2016). This evidence extends to Supreme Court litigation (Feldman 2016; McGuire and Caldeira 1993; McGuire 1995; Wahlbeck 1997; Szmer 2005; Szmer and Ginn 2014; McAtee and McGuire 2007; Corley 2008). The attorney expertise literature offers a range of possible explanations for why attorney expertise may matter, including credibility with judges, skill, and case selection (Box-Steffensmeier, Christenson, and Hitt 2013; Szmer 2005). With regards to issues of coordination, these factors may be at play: the reputational cache of experienced attorneys may help them recruit others, attorney expertise may help attorneys coordinate more effectively due to increased knowledge of potential groups (Hula 1999) and how to communicate and coordinate with such groups (Larsen and Devins 2016), or experienced attorneys may choose cases in which coordination is more likely (Songer and Sheehan 1992; Songer, Sheehan, and Haire 1999; Haire, Hartley, and Lindquist 1999; Hanretty 2014; Haynie and Sill 2007). We consider these potential influences further in light of the goals and incentives to coordinate across groups.

There is evidence of coordination among briefers going back for decades. For example, McGuire (1994) notes that "it is well established that, once the Court agrees to hear a case, there is considerable activity between the litigants, their lawyers, and outside interests" (821). Work on effective amicus practice has touted the importance of "communication, cooperation, and coordination" between amici and the party (Sungaila 1998, 189). Larsen and Devins (2016, 1901) provide extensive qualitative evidence that attorneys for parties recruit and organize amici writing in support of their positions, which they call "the amicus machine."

In our interviews, respondents overwhelmingly reported that parties and amici coordinate with each other. While interviewees varied in their descriptions of how much coordination occurs between parties and amici on the same side of a case, there was a consensus that coordination is occurring. On one end, Attorney R said there is "always" coordination. Other interviewees highlighted the common nature of such efforts: Attorney and Former Clerk L and Attorney F noted there is "a lot of coordination" between parties and amici. There is a network with a "great deal" of "feedback" and "recommendations" (L). Attorney F described both soliciting amici and having offers of help from potential briefers. They also noted that potential amici sometimes can't get involved because of the interests they represent. Relatedly, Attorney E described regular calls between the parties and amici while Former Clerk H described more variation in the level of coordination: "Some reach out to everyone they can and share drafts and high-level comments." Attorney J generally has a "specific sense of what the party wants." There is a "back and forth with drafts," and they "see what the party will say." They will check in regarding specific issues where it would be helpful. "Sometimes [they] agree to write on a specific issue" while other times there is "less coordination." Attorney O said that "parties try to know who [is filing] and coordinate but some amici come out of the blue."

While there is evidence of such coordination going back for some time, the practice has grown and become the default approach in more recent years (Larsen and Devins 2016). McGuire (1994) considers how expert lawyers recruited amici at the certiorari stage. At the time McGuire was writing, such amicus solicitation appears to have been relatively rare. Things seem to have changed. Attorney C noted that parties are "more sophisticated and strategic now." Specifically, they are "good about recruiting and organizing amici" and "deliberate positioning regarding arguments." Larsen and Devins (2016) also indicate that this solicitation has increased dramatically over time, brought on in part by the increasing importance of the elite Supreme Court bar (see also Lazarus 2007). This observation is entirely in keeping with McGuire's theory regarding the critical role of attorney skill and experience in knowing the importance of amicus briefs.

In that vein, Attorney and Former Clerk B saw the level of coordination as variable and related to experience: they said coordination existed "among regular practioners and experienced attorneys." Attorney P agreed, stating there is "lots" of coordination—an "enormous amount when done properly." (Though they also recommended talking to attorneys who had more cases before the Court.) They noted that parties need greater levels of coordination, perhaps as much as possible, because it provides the "advantage of more bites at the apple." Without coordination, parties are limited in what they can communicate by their individual word limits, and "word limits are frustrating." Another interviewee tied coordination with experience: "Sophisticated advocates make lists and reach out" to others (Attorney and Former Clerk L). Attorney O also noted that "well-litigated" cases have increased coordination regarding amici. Thus, attorney experience is very likely to affect the extent to which we see evidence of coordination.

Such experience should help attorneys advance the goals of their clients. As core members, parties acting through their attorneys generally act as brokers in helping create and coordinate coalitions (Hula 1999). Because the justices seek certain types of information, such as empirical facts, from sources they can trust, the parties' attorneys are incentivized to recruit various types of amici and coordinate their briefing efforts (Larsen and Devins 2016, 1915). As McGuire (1994, 822) notes, such solicitation is helpful to interest groups who would otherwise have to monitor many petitions and potential cases to determine when they should participate. This does not mean that the goals of parties and amici will always align, but rather that coordination has potential benefits for both.

One should note that there are practical limits to the coordination that is likely to occur due to ethical concerns regarding a party dictating what an amicus will write. Since 2007, the Supreme Court has required disclosures regarding sponsorship and authorship of briefs, in part to avoid the attorneys for a party ghostwriting an amicus brief (Larsen and Devins 2016). Many of the interviewees that we spoke with touched on such ethical issues. Attorney A noted that there is some coordination among parties and amici but that it "should be and almost always is above board." They clarified that each filer through attorneys writes its own brief, though suggestions may be made by parties regarding areas to "cover" and "explore." In another instance, they noted the importance of issue coverage among the briefs. They did note that they have had experiences where attorneys for parties tried to "red line" or "ghostwrite" amicus briefs and they "won't accept" such behavior, and it is generally "not well received." Attorney D explicitly stated that they were also careful not to coordinate too much. Attorney Q noted that it is "not ethical to file if the party is dictating" the brief.

Thus, coordination generally takes a less direct form. Attorney and Former Clerk L did note that it would be "rare to see line editing or heavy direction." Generally, the coordination is at "the front end." Similarly, Former Clerk H described coordination in terms of circulating drafts and "high-level comments." Attorney and Former Clerk B also noted that there was "not complete control" by parties over the text of an amicus brief but that there was likely to be "at least a call." In such a call, the party attorney would probably express "a few ideas they would like to see explored." They would "try to shepherd [the other attorney] through" and make sure the brief would "add value." Furthermore, attorneys might read drafts of briefs and make suggestions. They were unsure to what extent inexperienced attorneys coordinate. Also, Attorney D did communicate with the relevant party. Specifically, they usually talked to the attorney for the relevant party and asked, "What do you want us to say?" After this initial discussion, they generally did not have much contact with the attorney for the party. This was echoed by Attorney Q. They did seek to play a "support position" and provide "depth, history, and legal arguments that can't be developed in the party brief" while also "representing the interests of members." With the limits on coordination also in mind, we turn to the more specific roles attorneys are playing within briefing and coordination.

Parties' Attorneys: Brokers and Whisperers

The first type of common coordination by parties' attorneys involves assembling briefs on behalf of a side. Brokers rely on expertise to form coalitions: "Institutional links can help coalition brokers estimate the interest and preferences of potential coalition members" (Hula 1999, 78). They must have information regarding such candidate members, and those with this kind of information "have an obvious advantage" (51). Those team members tasked with recruiting amici, so-called amicus wranglers or amicus queens, are keenly aware of the reputational cache of specific organizations and attorneys (Larsen and Devins 2016, 1922; Carpenter 2012; Smith 1997). Additionally, based on theoretical models and our interviews, such wranglers should be highly motivated to recruit all the major helpful players, as justices may interpret their absence as communicating information itself (Bils, Rothenberg, and Smith 2020). Attorney A noted that one of the potential functions of an amicus brief is to point out "the dog that didn't bark" from potential supporters of the opposing side. They believed that this trend is motivated by the fact that amicus participation is so high that some justices explicitly notice when certain groups are not present.

Interviewees reported that generally parties contacted potential amici. For example, Attorney Q described that they are usually contacted by a party and "ask[ed] to look at the case and decide if [they] can [contribute]" as an amicus. Attorney and Former Clerk B noted that reaching out can occur both ways, from parties to amicus and vice versa. Attorney R, on the other hand, described the coordination as occurring from parties to amici. They said coordination revolves around briefers "looking for groups that care about the issue" and getting together briefs and moot courts. They noted that sometimes parties stand alone and speculated that could happen in a case like *Snyder v. Phelps* where a party is unpopular.[5] (It should be noted that the church was supported by multiple briefs by very important players, such as senators.) Furthermore, a party may act to assign amici or block them (Attorney C). Attorney J believes parties should approach amici with "specific asks" and coordination. This is effectively "volunteer work" and the potential briefers are "too busy." So, someone asking for a brief needs "to be convincing." They are more likely to say yes to "repeat players" where "mutuality" is at play. People need "enough time . . . . Write a cogent paragraph defining what you want" and "make it easy."

Additionally, interviewees described the types of considerations that influence if such requests are successful. Attorney and Former Clerk H described getting requests to file an amicus brief and opting to file one on behalf of neither party because the requesting party has a "problematic argument." Similarly, Attorney J described being "careful regarding the party" in terms of deciding to be involved in a case. One can end up "tightrope walking" where a criminal defendant appears to be guilty. "Part of the decision to participate" is about the party and if the case is a good "vehicle" for certain legal issues: "[You] don't want to file in a loser case." They were concerned if the immediate case was the best way to present the issue. Furthermore, were the important issues "preserved?" They don't want a "procedural out for the Court." Cases that are "fact intensive" are "bad" because of the "unique facts." Instead, they "want cases with conflicts in the circuits" that have been "percolating." Know "what is in the pipeline." What "other cases are working through?" It's better to "hold on" for a better case and "save effort." Q did mention that tensions arise between parties and amici. They describe such conflict as "very interesting" when it happens. The approach the group wants to take "may not help" the party. They have "come close a couple times" and "step. . . back" when it occurs.

In addition to recruiting relevant groups, amicus wranglers will secure prestigious attorneys to author certain briefs to highlight their importance (Larsen and Devins 2016, 1923). As described in chapter 2, Attorney J discussed how much care goes into selecting skilled and credible attorneys to contribute to briefs. Attorney D echoed this description and noted the importance of former clerks. Luckily for wranglers, the opportunity to develop experience and reputation incentivizes attorneys and firms to work on amicus briefs even when they are not paid (Larsen and Devins 2016, 1932). Justice Roberts discussed the importance of dedicating oneself to superb representation in the Supreme Court, even in the absence of payment, due to reputational costs (Garner 2010, 14). Also, because amici can file with the parties' permission, attorneys for parties sometimes attempt to block briefs (Katyal 2006).[6]

More directly relevant for our purposes, the second type of coordination involves the content of the briefs. Specifically, parties want the totality of information provided to the Court to be helpful to their cause. Parties are more oriented to outcomes, and, thus, providing the justices with multiple pathways to arrive at the desired result is likely to be helpful. Additionally, justices repeatedly profess their desire for broad information. For example, Simard (2007) conducted a survey of judges at all levels of the federal hierarchy regarding amicus brief practices. Three of ten Supreme Court justices she contacted (all the sitting justices at that time and one retired justice) responded to the survey. All the justices who responded indicated that amici curiae might be helpful to "offer legal arguments that are absent from the parties' briefs" (690), inform the Court regarding the potential impact of decisions on nonparty groups (692), and provide information that is not in the record (695).[7] This is in keeping with the Supreme Court's formal rules that call upon amici to bring new information (Supreme Court Rule 37.1). Additionally, it is well documented that repetitive briefs are headaches for clerks who often filter the briefs that their justices will read (Bruhl and Feldman 2017; Lynch 2004).

Larsen and Devins (2016, 1924) provide evidence that so-called amicus whisperers work to keep the amici coordinated to reduce repetition and ensure coverage of important points. Additionally, several interviewees identified expansive roles for amicus briefs in the topologies that they offered of them. The goals and desirable features of amicus briefs are largely couched in terms of their relationship to party briefs. Their observations dovetail nicely with the roles laid out in practice guides (Simpson and Vasaly 2015; Sungaila 1998). First, Attorney and Former Clerk M described a "couple of purposes" for amicus briefs generally:

The "me too" brief, which they believe is less effective.

A brief to "bring arguments and information not adequately addressed in the party brief." They noted this is hard to do at the Supreme Court. Also, they said there is an optimal information balance that creates incentives regarding information sharing.

- Briefs that "signal . . . stakes and interests beyond the parties." This provides information on the "larger context." While M noted there is a "debate" regarding use of such information, they think it matters because it shows why the case is important and to whom beyond the parties. It can illustrate "unintended consequences."
- The briefs can act as "communication tools" to "signal" the views of the "members, constituents, or public." It is less helpful where amici are acting more as "press release[s]" to show members "your interests are being served."

Attorney and Former Clerk I described "three flavors" of helpful amicus briefs:

- Briefs that did not include the "same arguments as the party['s brief], unless [it was from a] trusted source for a justice." Instead, these briefs include "other arguments the party would make and alert clerks to" such arguments.
- Briefs that include "facts you wouldn't otherwise know." They gave the example of specific information regarding technology.
- Briefs from an academic with "methodological and substantive" information.

They gave the example of Justice Kennedy "leaning on historical evidence" and "constitutional facts." Such information can be used as "ammo" or "reinforcement." It can also help decisionmakers under-standing the extent to which certain activities fall within statutory terms.

Attorney J believed that good amicus briefs have two main elements:

- The brief should focus on a "very discreet issue" that is "narrowly defined" as opposed to the "whole case." A helpful brief will focus on an "individual legal issue." It should "fill in what the party can't include due to space [constraints] or strategy—flush it out." This can include an "issue that a party can refer to but not build out" or "can't cover in depth" or that stra-tegically it is better to have an amicus discuss. Such a brief can include a "bigger issue not as relevant to the party." Former Clerk K also described specific amicus briefs as much more helpful than general briefs. Specific briefs can "increase" understanding and are a "contribution." Further-more, they advised that "specific arguments" be made in "specific [am-icus] briefs."

- It should not focus on the facts of the case but rather the "importance of the case broadly." A good amicus brief will help show that the sought out-come is "not dependent on the specific facts." The brief should give the sense that it is "new and necessary and not repetition . . . . Who cares if you are addressing the same issue?" Rather, the brief should illustrate the "im-plications" of the case with "hypotheticals and the expertise of the specific group or filer . . . . For example, if a crime is being expanded too far," the groups should bring it up. Such briefs bring "a new perspective that is not being addressed." Specifically, the amicus can include "extrapolat[ion]" on an issue with its "expertise." Examples of such information include "statistics, anecdotal evidence, and descriptive" information that act as hy-potheticals for the Court. Ideally, "show. . . a demographic overlap with the policy" to illustrate the group's expertise and firsthand knowledge. This can include "pointing out [something is] not a big issue" or concern in "actual practice."

The need for amici to provide information resembling legislative facts generally was broached by some interviewees. Attorney and For-mer Clerk I focused on "legal policy" and the "real concern regarding the need for full information" from the perspective of the Court. This related to "waiting for percolation" and asking for the government to brief when it is not a party. Amici "jumping in give justices a wider range [of information], and justices like it." They "feel like [they] can process more [information] than they could come up with on the fly." Attorney and Former Clerk L noted positive aspects of briefs, including speaking to change, persuading on a close call, and pointing out when there is no prior law. The best briefs include "compelling legal analysis" and make arguments that "[fit] with the history of law." The "real world context" is important, and briefers should describe "what might happen": "How would the world look different depending on the outcome?" This is particularly true where justices have less information and experience, such as technical issues.

Relatedly, Former Clerk N said that "groups with track records know the purpose" of amicus briefs. They have something to say. But, when asked if they could remember a case in which an amicus brief raised a new issue that was not otherwise discussed, they could not. They said it was a "little hard to remember." They also believe amici can be helpful to show other applicable areas regarding a decision. An example would be an application to a "new technology" or the "special effect of a policy on an industry." Though they said, "You don't need a ton" of such briefs. Other areas where amici can be helpful include situations where a doctrine will have a very specific effect on a certain type of group or organization, such as corporations and free speech. Also, originalism arguments and the views of scholars are helpful. Finally, another important type of brief "that tend[s] to get attention are those filed by members of Congress or by the states. If, say, 20 states file a brief saying a particular precedent is harmful to them in some way, the Court is going to take that seriously. I can imagine such a brief being crucial in an Eighth Amendment case where the Court is looking to . . . whether particular practices have been prohibited."

On the other side of the spectrum, Attorney C listed two types of bad amicus briefs:

1. An "amicus posturing" for "an audience [that] is not the Court," such as donors or stakeholders. There the interest of the amicus is "tooting [their] own horn" and "speechifying" in an "over-the-top" manner. Furthermore, Attorney C said that many briefs went on about "first principles ad nauseam."
2. A "press-release style" brief. The attorney described these briefs as "annoying" and noted that "repetition is not effective."

In synthesizing the information from the interviews, three main areas for successful amicus briefs emerge, all of which constitute different types of relationships to the party brief.[8]

First, amicus briefs can amplify or supplement aspects of the party brief (Simpson and Vasaly 2015; Sungaila 1998). One attorney has seen situations in which parties "assigned" various parts of the party brief to amici to address. Second, the amici can provide an alternative theory or argument. Third, amici can provide specific information that they are in a better position to offer, such as information regarding the particular impact decisions would have on the interests they represent or technical information, including Brandeis briefs (Simpson and Vasaly 2015; Sungaila 1998). As described in chapter 2, several interviewees (many with clerking experience) described the need and desire for such information on the part of the Court.

It would be a mistake to think that parties would welcome all additional information that amici might provide. Interviewees indicated that parties are also motivated to coordinate to avoid trouble. Former Clerk G noted the potential for "mischief by random sentences" and that briefers should be careful regarding "cabining" while Former Clerk N noted that "occasionally" they would see "random" amicus briefs. According to Attorney E, the amici bring a different angle, as they don't care about the party: they described how the party cares about the direct outcome whereas amici have different goals aimed more at using the case as a "vehicle" to further their "agenda." They described wanting to let amici bring their perspective but "don't want them in the weeds and talking about things that don't make sense." Rather, they should focus on the main issue. As a party attorney, they tried to reduce weird interpretations and legal approaches. For example, they "tried to temper" the brief of a professor promoting what the attorney considered an extreme and "not realistic view."

Many interviewees described a divide-and-conquer approach to coordination. Attorney R noted that the "rules have changed regarding word limits," and parties "don't always have enough space." This is where amicus briefs are important. According to Attorney C, "There is some engagement with the other side, but not a lot" with regards to the arguments in amicus briefs. Sometimes there would be a pairing off with an amicus being assigned an amicus brief in support of the other side, a "deputized amicus." Additionally, they have seen a "strategy of assign[ing] amici to address specific sections of a party brief." Attorney O also thinks that amici are "value-added" when they "elaborate" and "fill . . . in lacuna and blanks." Such information is useful to "let justices go where they want to go." They had an experience of providing background information that was used by a justice. Attorney R said that amici should have a "singular issue to flesh" and say "what the party can't say." This may be jurisprudential or policy. This is "why one coordinates."

This coordination often revolves around the types of policy-relevant facts that amici can provide. Parties may reach out to amici with "specific information" that they can bring to the table (Attorney C). According to C, "parties and amici have similar information sources," but "it is easier [for amici] to expand the factual record" because "parties are bound." This is useful because the Court cites facts from outside the record in their opinions sometimes. They later noted the oral argument in *City of Hays, Kansas v. Vogt* where Justice Breyer questioned an attorney about an argument that wasn't in the record despite Justice Roberts's objections.[9] They were generally interested in the types of facts the Court would "take on." Attorney P believes that "if you are doing a competent job as [the attorney for the party], amici don't add regarding the law": "Pouring new facts into the record is good." This should come from the "expertise of the amici." Use "amicus briefs to bolster the party brief."

Two former clerks described seeing signs of coordination from their vantage point. Attorney and Former Clerk I noted that as a clerk, they sometimes thought a party would be "backing" an amicus brief. As a brief writer, they acknowledged that they coordinate briefs. It may be "close" to what others write or suggest, but they "will [always] write something else." They don't repeat but rather make a "contribution." Former Clerk K said that it was evident when there was coordination. They described "a distribution of labor" that resulted in "less redundancy." They described that "parties discuss all of the important issues" with amicus, addressing "collateral issues." Attorney and Former Clerk M was less sure about coordination due to the passage of time and also their vantage point from the Court. They also stated that one could get a "better answer from the trenches now."

Many sources regarding coordinated briefing strategy note that presenting the same information is disfavored (Lynch 2004; Mayer Brown n.d.; Simpson and Vasaly 2015; Shapiro et al. 2019). Many interviewees echoed this. Only two of the interviewees mentioned so-called me too or repetitive briefs in the typology of amicus briefs, and both thought they were less influential than other types of briefs. In fact, most interviewees discussed the importance of amicus briefs being value-added: they felt that the amici should bring something new to the table. Many attorneys expressed disdain for repetitive briefs. For Attorney C, the main question regarding amicus briefs was: "What can we add to the mix?" They noted that there are so many briefs and that they try not to submit "me too" briefs. They associated such repetitive briefs with groups that tend to file for "constituents and donors." Ultimately, they believed that such briefs are "not influential and not read." Furthermore, they stated at the US Supreme Court level, parties "do a good job regarding the merits," as opposed to intermediate appellate courts. On this topic, Attorney and Former Clerk B indicated that repetition would be more appropriate for a Court of Appeals case rather than a Supreme Court case. In Attorney C's estimation, an amicus brief should "add something else" and "something new." This something else can be "expand[ing]" on the party brief to address something that either the paper strategically did not set forth or did not have "space" to address. Attorney and Former Clerk H likewise remarked that amici can "[home] in on legal or maybe factual" issues or add some "peremptory" arguments. Attorney D, who has experience with interest group amicus briefs, described that their goal for a brief is to "add value that can't be developed in the party brief." An attorney working on amicus briefs (Q) mentioned that repetition happens "a lot." They related this to the fact that briefs "should be your own" and "not a copy."

Many interviewees framed repetition in terms of a misuse of resources. Former Clerk G described repetition in amicus briefs as "unwise" due to space constraints. For Attorney E, the goal was "not cloning." Attorney and Former Clerk L said that the issue with repetitive briefs is wanting to "make sure to cover the full range" of ideas and that repetition represented "waste." Former Clerk G described the role of amicus briefs as "buttressing points and details." They also described that it is "political who can say what." Similarly, Attorney F noted that sometimes amici are in a "better position" to make a point. Former Clerk N described repetitive amici as "distinctly not helpful." This is because even with the reduced number of cases the Court is taking, it is still "very busy," and one "can't read all" the amici in some cases. Because there are too many briefs to read, they felt that "me too" briefs did an "affirmative disservice" and "distract." Attorney P suspects that "no one reads repetitive briefs" while assuming "everyone reads merit briefs." They want amici to be as non-repetitive as possible: "Some repetition is inherent"—briefs "can't not be a little repetitive." There are "things you have to say." But, "you need to add to the conversation [something] the party can't say," such as "facts and articles not in the record" or a Brandeis brief with social science or other research. For example, in a tribal case about treaties, one would want historians weighing in. There is "a real focus" on "scholarly" works.

Logically, attorneys are basing their beliefs on how they believe the justices and clerks consume such briefs. When Attorney O was asked if repetition is ever helpful, they responded that they were the "wrong person to ask" because they weren't a justice or a clerk. But they think it is "very doubtful." They noted reports (Mauro 2005) that Justice Ginsburg has her clerks sort briefs into three piles—"ones that she 'must' read, 'should' read, and 'shouldn't' read." They speculated that the size of the piles might matter even with the "shouldn't read" briefs but were unsure. They did note that "the public interest is what the public is interested in," so it "could color assessment." But, they also thought that kind of analysis was "not applicable or appropriate at the Supreme Court."

Often, groups are encouraged to combine briefs and cosign if they are likely to be repetitive, though such behavior is relatively rare (Lynch 2004). In interviews, our participants gave differing views on this approach. Attorney and Former Clerk H believed that repetition was likely helpful at the cert stage but less so at the merits stage. While noting "the diminishing marginal return" for repetitive briefs, they believed "[you] probably can't have too many," regarding certiorari. However, when it came to the merits stage, they suggested that cosigning was "probably better." But Attorney D expressed hesitancy to combine voices in this way. Their group "very rarely join[ed] other groups on briefs" or coordinated among other groups. They said they were "squeamish" about group briefs because they are unsure of the strategy. It was a question of "numbers versus the quality of the arguments." They had made one exception in the past but were involved in all stages of discussing and editing the brief. Under the attorney's direction, the group did "partner" with others sometimes. Similarly, Attorney A did note that with amicus briefs filed by interest groups, there can be other goals because of a "greater emphasis on pleasing [members] as opposed to the justices." Furthermore, prior clerk interviews indicate that most clerks do not give additional weight to a brief on the basis that it had more cosigners (Lynch 2004).

Nevertheless, it would be a mistake to believe that some level of reinforcement or repetition does not have a place in expert briefing. For example, Ebner (2017) stresses the importance of consistency in the focus on the core questions across party and amicus briefs. Furthermore, many interviewees themselves described a need for consistency across briefs that speaks to coalescence around policy. Attorney J stated that the extent to which there is agreement on the issue within a community of interest can matter quite a bit. Parties and amici blunder when they don't "crystaliz[e] the issue or interest." Moreover, longer amicus briefs with more issues are "bad." One "learn[s] to hone over time." Former Clerk G noted that good briefs "tell a simple story." They described three types of legal thinkers: those who don't understand complexity, those who see all the complexity, and, finally, those who see all the complexity but know how to reduce it to something simple. The best attorneys can nestle the facts within a legal framework. They avoid "detritus" and keep it to what is essential.

Several interviewees described the need for themes. Attorney C discussed "common threads" in brief preparation. While Former Attorney and Clerk B was "not a fan of repetition," they did indicate that they did sometimes "[pull] a thread through" a brief. While Attorney E repeatedly described the importance of having all briefs on a side focus on an issue, they did note that they didn't want to see "regurgitate[ed] arguments." Attorney F pointed out that states seek to "harmonize the voice[s] of the state[s]" and only want to add unique information if it would be helpful. This "harmony of voice" centers on acting "collectively with others" regarding "state authority." Attorney and Former Clerk M warned against including irrelevant information. They think this is rare regarding merit briefs from parties. Rather, the problem arises with amici filing briefs that include extraneous information (e.g., "oh, look at this!"). Amici need to pay attention to not "screw up" other arguments made in the case.

Other interviewees highlighted the potential benefits or lack of detriments to repetition. Attorney and Former Clerk I described the helpfulness of repetition in highlighting "important ideas." They were aware of the existing literature regarding repetition. In fact, they said that bringing up such central ideas was "like voting," meaning it should be done "early and often." Furthermore, they noted that repetition can make ideas "seem viable." For example, if all the state attorneys general on a brief "push one theory" and "say it enough times," an idea can move from seeming "crazy" to getting "five votes." This can also happen with the number of amicus on board with an idea and the identity of the respective groups—an idea becomes "not actually embarrassing" with repetition. Furthermore, when interest groups are trying to show that they represent their members, having repetition across briefs can be a "useful signal." It is a mistake to avoid that. Attorney and Former Clerk B said that when coordinating briefs, "at the end of the day" it "doesn't hurt to have repetition," and they "don't discourage repetition." Similarly, Attorney and Former Clerk L said there are "no points off for repeating briefs on one side." In fact, they said the presence of lots of amicus briefs showed the "gravity" of a case and that the "pile has weight." Where many briefs were present, it was a signal to "pay attention."

Moreover, one should note that many empirical studies find that repetition is influential on the justices (Collins, Corley, and Hamner 2013; Hazelton, Hinkle, and Spriggs 2019; Spriggs and Wahlbeck 1997). Such influence likely stems from the informational and psychological effects of it (Hazelton, Hinkle, and Spriggs 2019). For example, to the extent that repetition represents coalescence, it could be helpful for decision makers, though the Court and former clerks may be reluctant to acknowledge that coalescence matters. Or, former clerks may legitimately resent the time they spent dealing with repetitive briefs without being aware of the impact that it had on them.

Thus, the role of repetition is likely nuanced. There are different flavors of repetition, including the sharing of facts, ideas, and arguments but not exact language.[10] Furthermore, with careful coordination, information can be repeated in more strategic and subtle ways. While the professional expectation is that experience will be related to the reduction of repetition, it is very unlikely to eliminate shared information. Additionally, while empirical studies generally find that repetition is helpful, the exact contours of that repetition likely vary based on the experience level of attorneys in different roles and with different goals. These complexities would help explain the disconnect between the advice in professional guides and the results of empirical studies.

The foregoing discussion leads us to three conclusions that form the basis for our first hypothesis. First, party attorneys, acting on behalf of their clients, tend to be focused on winning the case. Second, their efforts typically involve recruiting and coordinating amici to provide a wide array of additional information. In other words, they seek amicus briefs that add depth and breadth to their own party brief rather than simply repeating it. Third, more experienced party attorneys are likely to be better equipped to manage this task successfully. Consequently, our first hypothesis is that when party attorneys have greater expertise, the text of the party brief and amicus brief will be less similar.

Amicus Attorneys: Partners, Advocates, and Shadows

Attorneys for amici come to coordination with goals that can vary from those of the party. While parties may seek a broad array of information, amici may wish to reinforce specific information in favor of adopting a particular rule (Marvell 1978; Collins 2008). Furthermore, as described above, experts regarding the Supreme Court indicate that amicus briefs can expand upon points in a party brief (Sungaila 1998). To the extent that amici are coordinating with litigants to help with such points, we anticipate that party attorneys will choose experienced attorneys to further iterate important aspects of the brief. Such experienced amicus attorneys will also be in a better position to see when such an approach is warranted and potentially initiate it themselves.

Relatedly, attorneys for amici can make up for deficiencies in the representation provided by the litigant's attorney. Many interviewees discussed how amici could act to fill in where a party's counsel lacks the necessary experience. Furthermore, issues of experience for attorneys across the types of briefs were also discussed by multiple interviewees. Attorney A believed that the experience of the party attorney was important. They specifically pointed to experience at the Court itself as a potentially important factor. As evidence, they noted that while "rescue briefs" (another name for shadow briefs whereby an amicus curiae effectively writes like a party to make up for defects in the party briefs) are "relatively rare" at the Court of Appeals level, they are "common" at the Supreme Court. Relatedly, Attorneys and Former Clerks L and H mentioned the existence of shadow briefs as well. H described how both the solicitor general and amici can act to cover for inexperienced party attorneys, and they believed that amicus briefs from the solicitor general are particularly helpful when crafted to "fill in" for an inexperienced attorney. Former Clerk G described the uncertainty caused when a party does not address an issue. They mentioned that the existence of a "large looming issue" could leave a clerk with no way to "wrestle [with it] in time to write a bench memo." Former Clerk N said that where states are parties, they generally have solicitors general hiring experts, but it varies. There are some weak advocates in those cases. There, "amici can shore up" the arguments.

Additionally, experience is seen as important with regard to amicus influence. According to Attorney and Former Clerk L, the amicus briefs that were most likely to be influential were from "professors and repeated players or advocates." Expert attorneys write "more persuasive" and "clear" briefs. Furthermore, they have more "legitimacy" and "authority" with the Court. They have "a leg up." Justices are more likely to "pay attention to big names," though individual justices care about "different sets" of such advocates. Inexperienced attorneys, on the other hand, can be a "train wreck."

Similarly, Attorney D described being careful in selecting attorneys to help write amicus briefs for an interest group. They sought "smart [and passionate] authors" with "strong credentials" and "chops," such as clerkship experience. The attorney found it was "important to be engaged" and "hands on" to make sure the members' "views [were] represented." Sometimes, they were very "in sync" with specific outside counsel. As a matter of course, this attorney did not engage other attorneys "more than twice" and looked for "people who can write as the group." They specifically wanted attorneys who were "new and open to back and forth." D also noted that former clerks can be "very generous and helpful."

Relatedly, Attorney and Former Clerk I asserted that party and amicus briefs generally contain different types of information. Amicus briefs should include "doctrine only when parties don't" because they have "narrow interests and competencies." Such a practice is generally known, and justices have given mixed responses to amici acting as shadow parties (Krislov 1963; Lynch 2004; Simard 2007). Party briefs, on the other hand, should include "straight doctrine" in their estimation.

Whether an amicus attorney focuses on reiterating the policy arguments its clients hold near and dear or presenting the arguments the party should have made with a defter hand, the result would be the same. In each case, the goals of amici indicate that their attorneys would have reason to produce briefs that look more similar to the party brief. When amicus attorneys have more expertise, they should be able to accomplish this goal to a greater extent. Thus, our second hypothesis is that when amicus attorneys have greater expertise, the text of the party brief and amicus brief will be more similar.

The Impact of Filers on Coordination

Crafting the text of Supreme Court briefs falls on the shoulders of the attorneys who filers hire to represent them. However, those attorneys undertake that task with the goals and broad instructions of their clients in mind. As a result, the filers' features may also shape coordination between parties and amici and the extent to which such coordination impacts the similarity between briefs. The characteristics of filers are likely to be especially crucial for amici since they choose whether to participate in the individual case. Litigants' participation, on the other hand, is constrained by the details of their case and whether the Supreme Court decides to hear it. Due to the nature of amicus participation, some filers accumulate considerable experience filing briefs in the Supreme Court. This repeated participation in the same venue may very well provide them with greater contacts and overall facility in coordination with parties.

As previously explained concerning amicus attorneys, when amici themselves have more expertise, we expect coordination to manifest as greater similarity to the party brief. Just as well-respected amicus attorneys are in a position to boost the credibility of any arguments made by the party, so too can well-respected amici. Although somewhat less likely, a litigant that happened to be more experienced with Supreme Court litigation might also have a greater ability to coordinate amici effectively on their behalf. If evident, we would expect such an effect to run in the same direction expected for litigant attorneys. Consequently, we expect that when litigants have greater experience filing briefs with the Supreme Court, the text of the party brief and amicus brief will be less similar; when amici have greater experience filing briefs with the Supreme Court, the text of the party brief and amicus brief will be more similar.

Just as parties and amici on the same side of a case can have somewhat different goals, so too can different types of amici (Wofford 2020). Most amicus filers invest resources because they ultimately seek to affect the case's outcome and the policy that the Court develops. There is evidence that interest groups focus more on outcomes than other amici (Wofford 2020). Of course, results and policy are not the only possible motivation for such an investment. Certain types of groups, such as membership groups, may value participation and attach themselves to strong arguments more than expanding the pool of information presented to the justices (Hansford 2004). As described previously in this chapter, two interviewees noted that certain interest groups file briefs for the sake of pleasing members. Attorney C mentioned it as a source of repetitive submissions, and Attorney and Former Clerk M stated it could lead to less effective briefs. Attorneys from interest groups provided a different perspective.

As described in this chapter, Attorney D stated that they tend not to join other groups on briefs and are quite picky about the message they are putting out to ensure it is consistent with the group's mission. They are adamant that the interests of the group members have to come first. This sentiment is echoed by Attorney Q. Furthermore, Attorney and Former Clerk I felt that discouraging interest groups from repeating information on behalf of members was a mistake. It is not clear whether the broader variation among interest group goals is likely to lead to more or less similarity with the litigant brief. Still, we examine it to see if either pattern emerges.

Data and Methods

To analyze the extent to which we see relationships between briefs consistent with the theorized relationships, we take advantage of the data set described in previous chapters, including many of the same variables we used in chapter 2. As we will throughout this book, we examine merits briefs filed from 1984 to 2015. In this chapter, our focus is on examining coordination, so the unit of analysis is the dyad formed by each party brief and an amicus brief supporting that party within a case. Ultimately, we have 19,674 dyads from 2,407 cases. Our outcome variable is a computational linguistics measure of the relationship between the content of the two briefs: cosine similarity (Hinkle 2015b; Hazelton, Hinkle, and Spriggs 2019). This measure has the advantage of being "objective and scalable" while also capturing relationships that plagiarism software and other verbatim approaches cannot (Hazelton, Hinkle, and Spriggs 2019, 26). Cosine similarity is a "bag-of-words" measure, which means that the similarity between two documents is calculated based on the individual words used without paying attention to word order. On the contrary, plagiarism measures quantify the percentage of one text that is word for word in the same order as another document, though various plagiarism software allows for small differences to varying degrees. Matching phrasing is useful in some contexts (such as measuring the diffusion of state legislation [Hinkle 2015a]). However, in this context, we do not expect coordination among brief writers to result in more or less borrowing of exact phrasing but in more or less discussion of similar ideas and topics. As such, a bag-of-words measure like cosine similarity is best suited for our purpose.

This is particularly true regarding legal writing, both in terms of briefs and opinions, where it is not only legal phrases that are important but also identification and characterization of the facts of the case and the constellation of topics that will define the scope of the applicability of the doctrine in future cases (Aldisert 1989; Braman and Nelson 2007; Schauer 1987; Sunstein 1993). Many of our interviewees discussed strategizing about when and how to include information regarding the facts of the case and legislative facts in this chapter, as well as in the previous chapter. They also discussed the unique role of precedent in the Supreme Court as described in detail in chapter 2. The unusual role of precedent in a highest court stems from the fact that only prior decisions of that court are considered binding, a type of authority that operates differently and less directly than authority from higher courts (Schauer 2008; Flanders 2009). Additionally, prior quantitative work in this area has been criticized on the basis that briefs are often influential in ways that are not captured by searching for exact language or citations to the brief (Lynch 2004, 2). Thus, we compare the text of the full briefs and move beyond specific phrases or citations.

Cosine similarity scores are the normalized sum of the term-frequency, inverse-document frequency (tf-idf), scores for each word within both documents. The tf-idf score utilizes the number of occurrences in the document (term frequency) weighted by the number of documents in the corpus in which the word appears (inverse document frequency) (Manning, Raghavan, and Schütze 2008).[11] Thus, just like letter tiles in Scrabble, less common words (i.e., those that appear in fewer documents) are worth more. That is, unusual words shared across briefs contribute more to the cosine similarity score for that dyad than common words. Cosine similarity scores exist between zero and one, where higher values indicate more similar documents. In our data set of party-amicus brief dyads, the mean cosine similarity score is 0.51, and the standard deviation is 0.16. This suggests that while two briefs arguing for the same outcome in the same case tend to be similar in general, there is still considerable variation.

As a matter of comparison, in *Florida v. Harris* the brief by the solicitor general was very similar to Florida's main brief, with a cosine similarity score of 0.77, the highest score for any amicus brief relative to the party brief of the side it was supporting in that case. To provide a substantive example, we begin with text from Florida's petitioner's brief:

> Some have speculated that, because a large percentage of U.S. currency reportedly has come into contact with cocaine at one time or another, residual odors emanating from currency may trigger false alerts. That theory, however, has been debunked "by studies showing that the particular chemical from cocaine that dogs detect does not remain in currency for an extended time under normal circumstances." *Foster*, 252 P.3d at 300 n.8 (citing, e.g., *United States v. Funds in the Amount of $30,670*, 403 F.3d 448, 461 (7th Cir. 2005) (explaining that "rigorous empirical testing" supports the conclusion that "it is likely that trained cocaine detection dogs will alert to currency only if it has been exposed to large amounts of illicit cocaine within the very recent past") (citing studies); see also Kenneth G. Furton et al, Identification of Odor Signature Chemicals in Cocaine Using Solid-Phase Microextraction-Gas Chromatography and Detector-Dog Response to Isolated Compounds Spiked on U.S. Paper Currency, 40 J. Chromatographic Sci. 147, 155 (2002)[.] ("[I]t is not plausible that innocently contaminated U.S. currency contains sufficient enough quantities of cocaine and associated volatile chemicals to signal an alert from a properly trained drug detector dog.")[12]

When we compare it to text from the brief filed by the solicitor general on behalf of the United States, the similarity is apparent:

> The concern that drug-detection dogs might alert to trace amounts of cocaine residue reported to linger on much of the U.S. currency in circulation, see, e.g., *Illinois v. Caballes*, 543 U.S. 405, 411–412 (2005) (Souter, J., dissenting), has been debunked. *See United States v. Funds in the Amount of $30,670*, 403 F.3d 448, 459 (7th Cir. 2005) (crediting study demonstrating that "circulated currency, innocently contaminated with [microgram] quantities of cocaine would not cause a properly trained detection canine to signal an alert even if very large numbers of bills are present") (brackets in original) (quoting Kenneth G. Furton et al., *Field and Laboratory Comparison of the Sensitivity and Reliability of Cocaine Detection on Currency Using Chemical Sensors, Humans, K-9s and SPME/GC/MS/MS Analysis, in Investigation and Forensic Science Technologies*, 3576 Proc. SPIE 41, 46 [Kathleen Higgins ed., 1999]); Richard A. Medema, Drug Enforcement Admin., U.S. Dep't of Justice, *Guide to Canine Interdiction* App. E (2000 ed.)[.] ("[A] positive alert to U.S. currency by a trained narcotics detection canine indicates that the currency had recently, or just before packaging, been in close or actual proximity to a significant amount of narcot-

ics, and is not the result of any alleged innocent environmental contamination of circulated U.S. currency by microscopic traces of cocaine.").[13]

The cosine similarity score for these two paragraphs on their own is 0.44.[14] When we compare these paragraphs using the plagiarism software WCopyfind.4.1.5 and the same settings as Collins, Corley, and Hamner (2013), we find no matching phrasing whatsoever.

The states' amicus brief had a cosine similarity score of 0.69 with Florida's main brief, indicating a fair amount of overlap. The relationship between the National Police Canine Association brief and the petitioner's brief came in at 0.6. Thus, the amicus briefs supporting Florida were similar to the party brief, with an average cosine similarity of 0.69. For the other side, the Rutherford Institute brief had the highest level of overlap with Harris's response with a cosine similarity score of 0.7. The brief filed jointly by the National Association of Criminal Defense Lawyers, the Florida Association of Criminal Defense Lawyers, the ACLU, and the ACLU of Florida also had a score of 0.7. The brief filed by Fourth Amendment scholars had a cosine similarity score of 0.51. Meanwhile, the two amicus briefs that brought in other topics were the least similar—the Electronic Privacy Information Center's brief had a score of 0.34 and the Institute for Justice brief had a score of 0.25. Overall, the amicus briefs supporting Harris were less similar, with an average score of 0.5.[15]

To provide an example of dissimilar text, we compare two paragraphs from the least similar party and amicus briefs on one side in *Florida v. Harris* (0.25). First from Harris's brief, we have:

> To justify using such a variable tool with little scrutiny, the State puts forth an ideal: the well-trained dog, one that alerts only in the presence of contraband. How can we know a dog is well trained? Because someone trained the dog, then that person, or someone else, declared the training a success. *See United States v. Howard*, 621 F.3d 433, 454 (6th Cir. 2010) (describing canine certification as "simply a statement by an institution that an individual has satisfactorily completed a particular course of study"). Once this occurs, the State says, the Court should defer to the "canine professional" i.e., typically one who profits from training and certifying dogs, and accept on faith that the dog's alert always justifies a search. State Br. at 24. This bright-line rule erases case- and dog-specific reasonableness determinations, regardless of whether the dog, though arguably "well trained" performs poorly in sniffing out drugs on patrol. By seeking a rule that shields judges from how infrequently a dog has

successfully led its handler to drugs in comparable settings, the State avoids the Fourth Amendment "totality of the circumstances" test.[16]

This excerpt is clearly on a different topic than the following paragraph from the Institute for Justice's amicus brief:

Second, in contrast to most of American history in which the proceeds from civil forfeitures went to a general fund to benefit the public at large, modern civil-forfeiture laws allow law-enforcement officials to keep most of the forfeiture proceeds. In 1984, Congress amended parts of the Comprehensive Drug Abuse and Prevention Act of 1970 to allow federal law-enforcement agencies to keep a portion of the forfeiture proceeds in a newly created Assets Forfeiture Fund. Initially, any forfeiture proceeds exceeding $5 million that remained in the Assets Forfeiture Fund at the end of the fiscal year were to be deposited in the Treasury's general fund. Moreover, the government's use of proceeds in the Assets Forfeiture Fund was restricted to a relatively limited number of purposes, such as paying for forfeiture expenses like storing the property or giving awards for information that led to forfeitures. However, subsequent amendments eliminated both the $5-million cap and dramatically broadened the scope of expenses the government could pay for with the Assets Forfeiture Fund, including purchasing vehicles and paying overtime salaries. In short, after the 1984 amendments, federal agencies were able to retain and spend forfeiture proceeds—subject only to very loose restrictions—giving them a direct financial stake in generating forfeiture funds. Many states followed the federal government's example by amending their civil-forfeiture laws to give law-enforcement agencies a direct share of forfeited proceeds. Law-enforcement agencies in 42 states receive some or all of the civil-forfeiture proceeds they seize.[17]

The cosine similarity score for these two excerpts at the level of the paragraph is 0.007. Unsurprisingly, we detect no matching phrasing using WCopyfind.4.1.5. It is worth noting that this is the same plagiarism score as the more similar paragraphs provided above.

Our first set of explanatory variables captures the expertise of the attorneys representing parties and amici in the dyads. Based on our theory of differing goals, increased expertise of party attorneys should lead to a broader provision of information by amici, and, thus, we expect coordination to manifest primarily as a reduced similarity between the briefs. Conversely, more elite amicus attorneys are likely to act in ways that lead to greater similarity with the party brief. To capture attorney expertise, we utilize three variables looking at their prior experiences. First, we include variables capturing the number of previous briefs[18] signed by the attorney with the most experience among those signing a brief.[19] Then, because the impact of experience is likely to decay as the measure increases, we take the natural log of the relevant attorney's experience.[20] The next set of variables regarding attorney experiences are how many attorneys signing the respective briefs were former Supreme Court clerks, "Former Clerks, Party" and "Former Clerks, Amicus." Finally, we include "Former Solicitors General, Party" and "Former Solicitors General, Amicus," capturing the number of attorneys who signed each brief who served as US Solicitor General prior to the case in question. Commentators often laud solicitors general as particularly elite Supreme Court advocates, and many former solicitors general take cases at the Supreme Court, going so far as providing pro bono services (Larsen and Devins 2016, 1929).

In addition to accounting for the attorney expertise in a party-amicus pairing, we also examine previous collaboration. For each pairwise combination of attorneys on the party and amicus briefs in a dyad, we count the number of previous briefs in our data set that both attorneys signed. This type of collaboration is not terribly common. It is present in less than 1 percent of our cases. There is, however, considerable variation in the extent of this collaboration where it exists, ranging from one to 289. Like our experience variables, we log this to create a variable named "Log Prev. Atty. Collaboration."[21]

Our final set of main explanatory variables focuses on the filers directly rather than their attorneys. We include measures indicating the number of previous briefs filed by the most experienced filer who signed a brief. Like our measures for attorney experience, we use data going back to 1970 to calculate filer experience. Again, we log the raw number of previous briefs to account for nonlinear effects. Next, we use a binary variable that equals one if one or more of the filers on an amicus brief is an interest group and zero otherwise.

We also include essential control variables, whose omission could confound our results. We begin with variables that capture participation by the current solicitor general acting on behalf of the United States. One attorney and former clerk stressed the importance of conceptualizing the solicitor general as quite distinct from other filers. The solicitor general is a remarkably successful litigant.[22] As with other aspects of Supreme Court litigation, the solicitor general occupies a unique role in terms of coalition building. Certainly, there is qualitative evidence that the solicitor general behaves differently. Usually, the solicitor general does not solicit or coordinate briefs when acting as a party (Larsen and Devins 2016). Attorney O also noted that the solicitor general's office is the exception to coordination—"they don't coordinate much at all." Additionally, the solicitor general is a very desirable amicus to recruit (Millett 2009).[23] Thus, parties are especially incentivized to recruit the solicitor general and have little negotiating power over the relationship. Additionally, an attorney and former clerk noted that the solicitor general would sometimes be brought in by the Supreme Court to make up for a lack of experience by the attorney for a party. Thus, we include "Solicitor General, Party" and "Solicitor General, Amicus," which equal one if the current solicitor general signed the brief in question and zero otherwise, as this status carries particular weight and allows for unique and potentially countervailing strategies. The role of the solicitor general, or any filer, may also be greater in cases where the Court specifically invited an amicus brief. Many of these invitations are extended to the solicitor general, but they can be extended to other filers as well (Shaw 2015). Thus, we include a variable to capture if the brief was a "Court Invited Amicus Brief."

Coordination among groups signing on to the same brief might influence the content, so we include the "Log No. of Amicus Cosigners" to capture such effects. Additionally, we include "No. of Ally Briefs" to account for the number of briefs on one side in a case across which actors can spread information. The Supreme Court generally grants certiorari in situations where they are more likely to reverse than affirm (McGuire et al. 2009); to account for this fact, we include "Petitioner's Side," a binary variable capturing whether the brief dyad consisted of briefs in support of the petitioner. We also measure the extent to which the dyad is advocating a position ideologically aligned with the Supreme Court's median. When the litigant and amicus in a dyad are seeking a conservative outcome, the variable "Ideological Alignment" is the Martin-Quinn score for the median of the Court. Where the two briefs advocate for a liberal result, "Ideological Alignment" is the Court's median Martin-Quinn score multiplied by −1. It is also possible that features of the case itself, such as the complexity of legal issues and the salience of the case, may influence coordination (Hula 1999). Prior work indicates that this is particularly true when the Court has solicited the solicitor general's opinion (Larsen and Devins 2016). This is in keeping with research on

Table 3.1. Summary Statistics for Brief-to-Brief Dyads

Continuous	Min.	25%	50%	75%	Max.
Cosine Similarity	0.03	0.40	0.52	0.64	1.00
Log Max. Attorney Exp., Party	0.00	1.39	3.30	4.62	6.11
Log Max. Attorney Exp., Amicus	0.00	1.10	2.30	3.85	6.11
No. of Former Clerks, Party	0	0	0	2	7
No. of Former Clerks, Amicus	0	0	0	1	8
No. of Former SGs, Party	0	0	0	0	2
No. of Former SGs, Amicus	0	0	0	0	1
Log Prev. Attorney Collaboration	0.00	0.00	0.00	0.00	5.67
Log Max. Filer Exp., Party	0.00	0.00	0.00	1.10	7.71
Log Max. Filer Exp., Amicus	0.00	0.00	2.20	4.32	7.72
Log No. of Amicus Cosigners	0.69	0.69	0.69	1.39	6.95
No. of Ally Briefs	2	7	12	22	156
Ideological Alignment	−1.26	−0.55	−0.08	0.52	1.26
Log Word Count LC Opinion	0.69	8.29	8.92	9.56	12.01
Term	1984	1994	2004	2011	2015

Binary	0	1
Interest Group Amicus	35.1%	64.9%
Current SG, Party	92.7%	7.3%
Current SG, Amicus	95.6%	4.4%
Court Invited Amicus Brief	99.7%	0.3%
Petitioner's Side	52.6%	47.4%
Amicus Activity in Lower Court	50.1%	49.9%

Observations	19,674

the importance of recruiting government officials to lobbying efforts (Mahoney and Baumgartner 2015). Measuring such features of a case with data available from before the briefs in question are drafted presents a challenge. We use the log of the length of the lower court opinion to reflect the complexity of the case and the presence of one or more amicus briefs in the lower courts to measure case salience.

Finally, there is evidence that coordination has increased over time (Larsen and Devins 2016), as has the number of amicus briefs (Collins 2008) and the sophistication of the Supreme Court bar (Lazarus 2007).

To capture such trends, we include a variable for term. Summary statistics are in table 3.1.

Because our outcome variable, "Cosine Similarity," is bounded between zero and one, we use fractional logistic regression to assess the relationships between the outcome variable and the explanatory and control variables. Additionally, due to the relationship across briefs within the same case, we also include robust standard errors clustered on the case.

Results

We provide the regression results in figure 3.1. The analysis yields several interesting and important results. First, while overall the results are mixed, we do find evidence that attorney experience matters with regard to brief similarity. Party and amicus attorney expertise in the form of prior filings influences the similarity of an amicus brief to the party brief. "Log Max. Atty. Exp., Amicus" is positive, as we expect, and significant. "Log Max. Atty. Exp., Party" is positive, not in keeping with our hypothesis, and significant. This result is, however, consistent with the larger law and courts literature on the positive effects of repetition (Collins 2008; Hazelton, Hinkle, and Spriggs 2019). We find statistically significant evidence that when former clerks and former solicitors general represent amici, they are more similar to the party brief filed on behalf of the same side. This is in keeping with our expectations. We fail to find evidence of a relationship between other types of experience and similarity for attorneys representing parties. Moreover, in the case of "Former SGs, Party," the point estimate is positive, though the estimated effect is not statistically significant. The estimate for "Former Clerks, Party" is negative, as we anticipated, but also not statistically significant.

Our results also provide evidence in favor of our hypotheses regarding party experience. The past experiences of both litigants and amicus filers influence coordination in the ways that we expect. When entities with greater experience filing briefs in previous Supreme Court cases are involved in crafting a party brief, it is less similar to amicus briefs filed in support of the party's position. On the other hand, when more experienced filers sign an amicus brief, that brief is more like the party brief. The final hypothesis was that amicus briefs signed by one or more interest groups would exhibit different patterns concerning coordina-

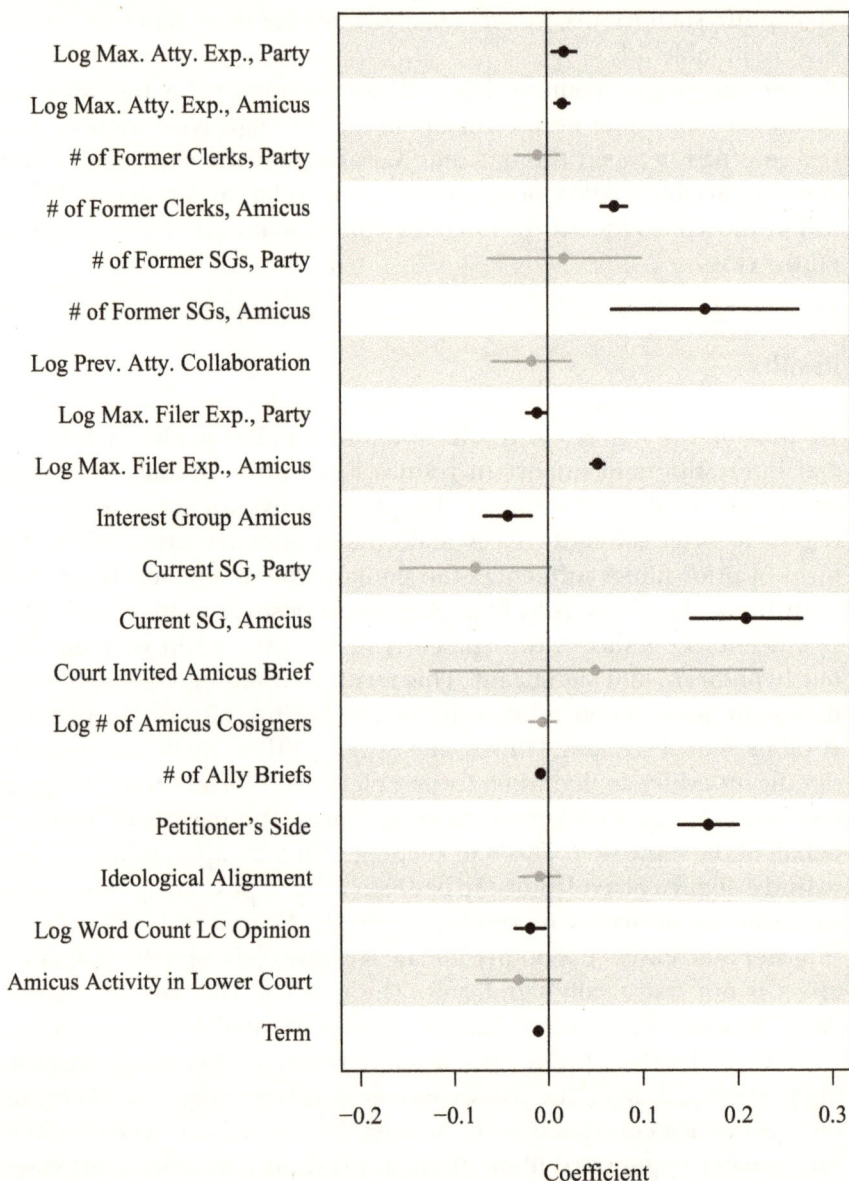

Figure 3.1. Cosine similarity. Fractional logit estimates (and their 95 percent confidence intervals) of the effect of party and amicus characteristics, and a range of control variables on the cosine similarity between the text of each litigant brief and each amicus brief filed on that litigant's behalf. Estimates and confidence intervals in gray (instead of black) indicate that the confidence interval includes zero.

tion. Our results provide evidence that is the case. Amicus briefs with an interest group are significantly less similar to the party brief than amicus briefs filed by other types of entities.

Other factors also appear to affect coordination. For example, amicus briefs are more similar to the party brief when the solicitor general files the amicus brief. The proliferation of participation reduces similarity. The amicus and party brief pairs are significantly less similar when there are a greater number of overall submissions in the case filed advocating the same outcome. Briefs submitted on the petitioner's side are more similar than those presented on the respondent's side. Longer lower court opinions appear to reduce similarity. Finally, we find evidence that the brief dyads are becoming less similar over time, consistent with qualitative evidence that an increasingly sophisticated Supreme Court bar is carefully coordinating briefs. We do not find significant effects regarding previous attorney collaboration, the appearance of the current solicitor general for a party, court-invited amicus briefs, when more people or groups sign a particular amicus brief, ideological alignment, or amicus participation in the lower court.

While these results are interesting in their own right, we explore the substantive size of each variable's effect. Understanding which variables are statistically significant is an essential first step, but understanding the relative size of such effects adds important nuance to our findings. In figure 3.2, we present the change in predicted similarity that results from moving each variable from its twenty-fifth to seventy-fifth percentile value or from zero to one.[24] We present the estimated changes with their 95 percent confidence intervals.

Many of the significant effects our model uncovers are fairly modest in size. Recall that our outcome variable of cosine similarity ranges from zero to one. The standard deviation for that measure is 0.16. This means that even the largest effect size presented in figure 3.2 represents a change that is roughly a third a standard deviation. In addition to presenting a realistic picture of the size of our effects, figure 3.2 also reveals the relative size of effects. An interesting picture emerges. There are two variables related to parties that are statistically significant and both have small effect sizes. First, attorney experience for the party results in a change of 0.015 when moving its values from the twenty-fifth to seventy-fifth percentile. In more intuitive terms, this is the difference generated by having the most experienced party attorney have three previous briefs under their belt and having a party attorney who has

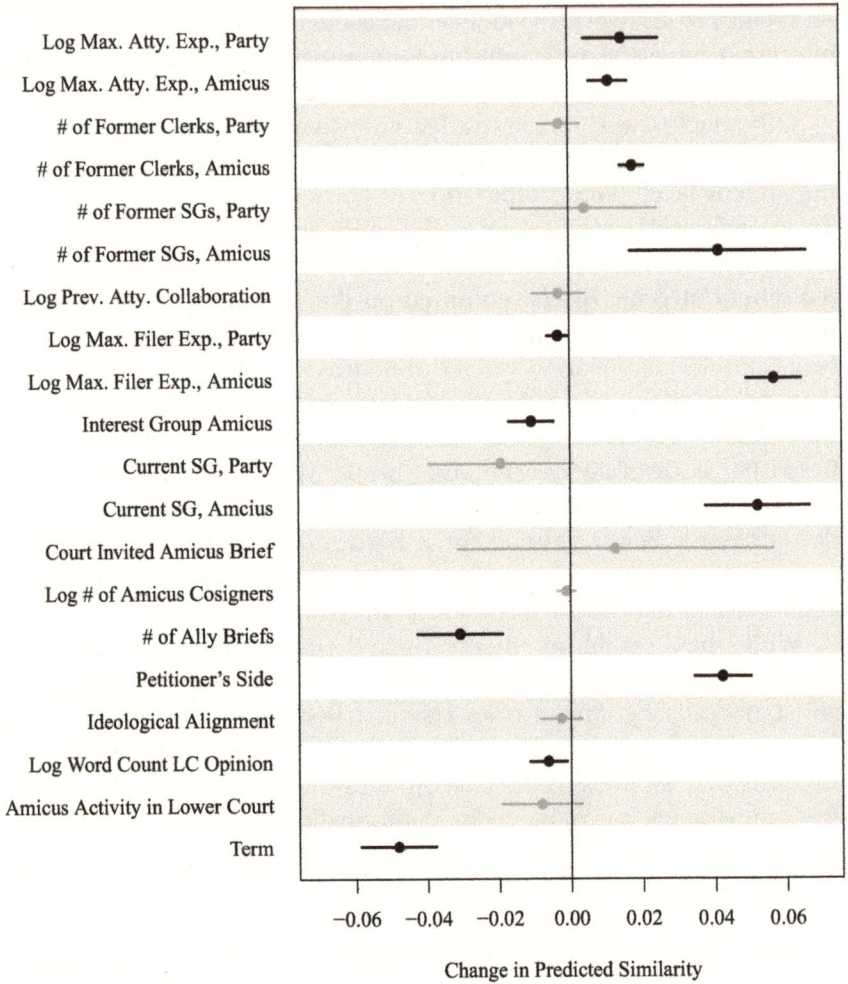

Figure 3.2. Changes in predicted cosine similarity. Estimates with 95 percent confidence intervals of the change in the predicted cosine similarity generated by moving each variable from a low to high value while holding all other variables at their medians. All binary variables, previous attorney collaboration, former clerks, former solicitors general, and invited briefs are moved from zero to one. All other variables are moved from their twenty-fifth to seventy-fifth percentile values. Estimates and confidence intervals in gray (instead of black) indicate that the confidence interval includes zero.

filed 101 previous briefs in the Supreme Court. Filer experience for parties has even a slighter influence, with a change of −0.003.

Conversely, the variables that tend to have larger effects (though still rather modest in substantive size) are related to the characteristics of amici and their attorneys. Changing "Log Max Attorney Experience, Amicus" from its twenty-fifth to seventh-fifth percentile value (from two to forty-six previous briefs) increases the predicted similarity between the party and amicus briefs by 0.011, which is in keeping with the effect for party attorneys' experience.

For amicus, the difference between one former clerk (as opposed to none) being on a brief is 0.018. The remaining effects are larger in size, but again only around a third of a standard deviation in similarity. An amicus brief signed by one former solicitor general has a predicted similarity to the party brief that is 0.04 higher than an amicus brief with no former solicitors general. At the same time, an amicus brief filed by the current solicitor general is 0.05 higher than an amicus brief filed by another attorney. And, increasing amici's previous experience from zero to seventy-four increases the similarity to the party brief by 0.06. Finally, briefs advocating reversal are a little over 0.04 more similar than briefs in favor of affirmance.

Conclusions

Our analysis yields some evidence in favor of our hypotheses, albeit with small substantive effect sizes. It provides an interesting perspective on when party briefs and the amicus briefs written to support them are more or less likely to be similar. We find that such brief dyads are more likely to be similar when the attorneys for either the party or amicus have more experience in cases before the Supreme Court. This finding indicates that attorneys may be well aware of the benefits of at least some repetition despite statements in practice guides and interviews opposing repetition. Furthermore, the experience of individuals and groups filing amicus briefs has a similar effect. Attorneys for amici who have the inside experience of working at the Supreme Court and current and former solicitors general produce briefs that are more like the party brief, indicating that they may be focusing on specific aspects of the arguments that they find beneficial or are acting to bolster the arguments of the party. These results are consistent with our expectations that parties will seek out skilled attorneys to help make their case. Finally, dyads for the petitioner's side tend to be more similar.

A range of other variables lead to greater divergence between two briefs. When a more experienced litigant files a party brief, the dyad formed with a supporting amicus is less similar. This may stem from more skilled filers encouraging their attorneys to cast a wide net through amici, though it is the opposite effect to what experience yields regarding their attorneys. This may indicate complex issues around varying goals and tactics. Additionally, interest group amici file briefs that are less similar to party briefs compared to other amici. This likely stems from their broader range of goals. Large coalitions (where many entities sign a single amicus brief) also craft less similar briefs, indicating that greater participation may increase a brief's scope. Greater textual divergence between briefs also occurs where lower court decisions are longer and in more recent cases.

These findings help us to begin to tease apart coordination using rigorous quantitative methods. They provide novel information regarding the relationships among groups in information-providing coalitions. Furthermore, learning about coordination among briefers helps us understand the nature of the interests recognized by the Supreme Court. Rather than threatening a conception of briefing as a form of lobbying with representative ramifications (Larsen and Devins 2016), coordination accentuates this approach. Finally, these results open up new avenues for further inquiry.

4 | The Win/Loss Column
Influencing Case Outcomes

On February 19, 2013, the US Supreme Court released a unanimous opinion in *Florida v. Harris* declaring Florida the winner and Harris the loser. Our in-depth exploration of factors that shape the creation and coordination of briefs in the previous two chapters sets the stage for examining how those documents influence such ultimate determinations of winners and losers. The political importance of the Supreme Court reaches far beyond simply determining who wins each case. We will take up the question of more nuanced policy content in future chapters. Here we look at the simple, yet powerfully informative, determination of whose arm is metaphorically raised in victory at the conclusion of a case. Many explanations of Supreme Court decision-making focus on the justices themselves—particularly their ideological predispositions (Epstein and Posner 2016; Segal and Spaeth 2002). Still, much of the variation in justice voting and case outcomes remains to be explained. For example, in *Florida v. Harris*, all nine justices voted in favor of the state. Although the majority of the Court was certainly conservative, making the outcome in favor of law enforcement unsurprising, what motivated all nine justices to vote for the outcome in this case? We posit that a wide range of features of the briefs and the resources used to produce them have the potential to shape justices' votes and case outcomes.

There are indications that justices care about outcomes. Former Clerk K relayed a story in which they were working over the weekend. They ran into their justice, and the clerk joked with the justice that they were the boss and didn't need to come in on the weekends. In response, the justice earnestly noted the importance of the cases to the litigants as a reason to take them seriously and put in additional work. Specifically, the justice "pointed out that the thirty minutes of oral argument is often the most important thirty minutes of the parties' lives." Justice Thomas has also discussed the importance of the votes in terms of the questions presented (Garner 2010, 117).

Furthermore, while litigants and amici have varying goals, as we discussed at length in chapter 3, the case outcome is important to both. Although amici do not have a direct stake in the facts of a case (Collins 2018; Wofford 2020), success in pursuing their broader policy goals often requires the victory of a particular litigant. Winning the case is frequently a necessary (although not sufficient) condition for amici to achieve their goals. Since case outcomes are both fundamentally important and straightforward to quantify, much of the existing work on the influence of briefs tackles the questions of when and how briefs can impact case outcomes. Yet, most of this work focuses on the existence of briefs rather than an examination of their content. Specifically, many previous studies focus on the relationship between the number of briefs on a side and the likelihood of that side winning a case (Collins 2004, 2007; Kearney and Merrill 2000) or securing justices' votes (Collins 2008; Pacelle et al. 2018; Szmer and Ginn 2014). These studies generally find a modest relationship between the likelihood of success and the side with the most briefs (Collins 2018).

Without suggesting that the volume of briefs is irrelevant, we also investigate the role the content of those briefs plays in the process. For example, when comparing the briefing submitted for each side in *Florida v. Harris*, the collective briefing on behalf of Florida contained a larger number and wider range of Supreme Court citations, was more focused on the future, and was written in a simpler and clearer style. These characteristics may well have helped Florida win the day in this case, but how do they (and other) elements of the content of briefs shape Supreme Court decision-making?

Another line of work closely related to the direct impact of briefs investigates the impact of resources and experience. A variety of evidence demonstrates that more experienced attorneys and litigants with deeper pockets are more likely to achieve their desired case outcome (Black, Owens, et al. 2016; McGuire 1995; Szmer and Ginn 2014). Yet there has been little development over time in how these important concepts are quantified. Nor have the measures been extended to apply to amici as well as litigants. By conceptualizing the impact of resources in tandem with the impact of information and developing more nuanced measures of each, our work sheds light on the underlying mechanisms in play. The forgoing chapters have demonstrated that resources, experience, and coordination shape the amount and type of information presented to the Court. Here, we examine the impact of litigant and attorney characteristics alongside the impact of brief contents.

In this chapter, we begin by describing both how and why we explore what it takes to convince justices and win cases. Next, we proceed to a detailed theoretical exposition of how the quantity of information presented to the Court, the type of that information, and the resources of the relevant players can play a role in securing votes and winning cases. Third, we describe our data and methods before discussing empirical results and explaining our overall conclusions. The results reveal that information, characteristics of the participants, and features of the litigation environment all shape votes and case outcomes. The side that was more long-winded in their briefs, represented by more experienced attorneys, backed by the solicitor general, more closely aligned with the Court median, or asked fewer questions at oral argument will find itself more likely to both secure individual justice votes and win cases. Furthermore, the side that files more briefs and includes more citations to the current median justice in those briefs is more likely to win cases.

Winning Votes and Cases

Justice votes and the related case outcomes are often a zero-sum game. In the vast majority of cases, each justice decides whether to vote for the petitioner or the respondent.[1] This simple and clear binary determination lends itself well to both theoretical development and empirical examination. However, its very bluntness does somewhat limit our ability to bring the full nuance of our data to bear. Our focus in the previous two chapters was on individual briefs. Here we shift to a broader focus that compares all briefs filed on behalf of the petitioner to all briefs filed on behalf of the respondent. This is necessary because an outcome favorable to the petitioner does not provide enough information to distinguish which of many briefs filed for the petitioner might be responsible for that outcome. In contrast, when the Court rules in favor of the petitioner over the respondent, we can conclude that something about all the information and resources brought to bear on behalf of the petitioner was collectively more successful than all the information and resources brought to bear on behalf of the respondent. Because votes are cast for only one side or the other, we conceptualize the impact of information and resources marshaled for each side in relative terms: the decision to cast a vote for one side or the other is driven by which side is more persuasive than the other.

Our approach of conceptualizing all briefs for a side as a unified whole has three additional advantages. First, using both party and amicus briefs provides a broad and inclusive perspective. Existing work on the impact of briefs focuses largely on either amicus briefs (Collins 2008, 2007; Manzi and Hall 2017) or party briefs (Black, Owens, et al. 2016; Feldman 2016) but not both. Work on Galanter's repeat player hypothesis focuses on the resources of parties (McGuire 1995; Sheehan, Mishler, and Songer 1992), but not amici. Second, as described in more detail in chapter 6, evidence indicates that readers generally, and justices and clerks specifically, approach briefs as interconnected documents that they consume in relation to each other and as a whole. Third, combining all of the briefs on each side also has the advantage of accounting for the reality of coordination among brief writers. The evidence of such coordination that we describe in the previous chapter indicates that the people involved in writing briefs understand that the Court views the set of briefs submitted for a side as a body of work.

Since a majority of the justices' votes are required for a side to obtain a favorable outcome, votes and outcomes are obviously closely related. Almost all of our theory and hypotheses anticipate the same type of effect on both votes and outcomes. Nevertheless, there may be subtle differences, so instead of assuming they are the same, we look at both. One interviewee expressed doubt that briefs influence outcomes, as opposed to decisions. Attorney and Former Clerk I believed that briefs "have influence in the words to justify a decision rather than votes." However, Attorney R noted that briefs represent "the chance to win the case" and "persuade" the Court. In this vein, Justices Roberts and Alito both noted that briefs can lose cases (Garner 2010).

Why bother looking at votes when it is who wins and loses that really has an impact? Case outcomes are certainly most relevant for immediate results. It is unlikely that those who present briefs to the Court will be happy with the content of the majority opinion if their side did not win the case. However, votes are far from inconsequential. A cause that prevails in a five-four decision today may be overturned in just a few short years (Hinkle and Nelson 2017). There is evidence that closer rulings are not always enforced as consistently (Black, Owens, et al. 2016) or accepted as well by the public (Zink, Spriggs, and Scott 2009), at least under some circumstances (Salamone 2014, 2018). As a result, the effort that goes into making briefs persuasive is not just about making them persuasive enough to get a majority of the available votes. Every additional vote garnered can benefit the winning side. Collins (2018) goes so far as to recommend that future studies of the impact of amicus briefs look at votes rather than outcomes. This suggestion is based on the idea that amici care more about policy outputs than who wins. Since our focus encompasses parties as well as amici, case outcomes are important too.

Scholars have done considerable work examining judicial decision-making in the US Supreme Court. There is compelling and consistent evidence that policy preferences play a substantial role in this process (Segal and Spaeth 2002). While fully acknowledging the important role of ideology, we focus here on providing explanations that both explore how attorneys may seek to tap into justices' policy preferences in particularly effective ways and examine the impact of factors extending beyond ideology. As *Florida v. Harris* makes clear, we know that liberal justices don't vote in liberal ways 100 percent of the time. Nor is the reverse true for conservative justices. Other forces are at work. Unlike a justice's ideology, many potential factors can be manipulated by the filers and attorneys who engage the Court via brief writing. As a result, our work investigating such factors will not only provide a more nuanced view of how the Court is persuaded (individually and collectively) but it also has the potential to inform the ways in which filers and attorneys go about seeking to influence the Court in the future.

Many Routes to Persuasion

The art of persuasion is a many splendored thing. Scholars have demonstrated that a variety of factors impact Supreme Court decision-making (Johnson, Wahlbeck, and Spriggs 2006; Johnson 2004; Maltzman, Spriggs, and Wahlbeck 2000; Collins 2008). The existence of such factors strongly suggests that the Court is open to various kinds of persuasion. Moreover, many theories have specific implications for possible ways to approach persuading the justices. Informational theory highlights the opportunity to sway justices by showing them how voting for your side will advance their policy preferences (Collins 2004; Epstein and Knight 1999; Hazelton, Hinkle, and Spriggs 2019). Affected groups theory indicates that demonstrating to the justices the extent to which important stakeholders in society support your side may help win the day (Buckler 2015; Collins 2004). This is particularly likely regarding individuals and groups who are invested enough to endure the cost of filing a brief (Caldeira and Wright 1990a; Hazelton, Hinkle, and Spriggs 2019). One strand of repeat player theory posits that sending familiar faces to make your arguments to the Court is beneficial since the justices know such repeat players have greater motivation to be faithful and accurate information providers (McGuire 1995; Szmer and Ginn 2014). In short, there are many possible roads to swaying the Court. We examine three broad classes of persuasion. The first is influence by sheer volume of information provided to the Court. Second, we look at the impact of what types of information are brought and how they are presented. Finally, we explore the role of the characteristics of the filers and attorneys involved in crafting the briefs.

Size Matters: How Quantity of Information Can Persuade

When determining who should win a case, the justices face potential uncertainty about how the binary determination of a case outcome will map their preferences onto policy. Informational theories of briefs focus on the fact that briefs are valuable because they contain facts and arguments that help the justices reduce such uncertainty (Epstein and Knight 1999; Collins 2004; Johnson 2001; Johnson, Wahlbeck, and Spriggs 2006; Szmer and Ginn 2014) or discover "legally relevant information" (Kearney and Merrill 2000). Under such theories, additional information in favor of a side is likely to increase support for that side because of the associated reduction in uncertainty (Epstein and Knight 1999; Collins 2004; Johnson 2001; Johnson, Wahlbeck, and Spriggs 2006; Samaha, Heise, and Sisk 2020; Szmer and Ginn 2014). In short, the side presenting the greater total amount of information should be more likely to win. Reducing a justice's uncertainty about what will happen if you win might not always be a good thing in a particular case. This is especially true with respect to influencing votes, where there is little room for nuance. Using information to reduce uncertainty may shape the details of the policy the Court sets forth in their majority opinion to a greater extent since there are virtually infinite possibilities for how precisely policy is crafted compared to only two choices for how a justice votes. However, although information may not be as well positioned to influence votes as policy content, we still expect that in the aggregate (especially after controlling for the justices' ideology) a benefit should emerge for the side that presents the most information. One way to visualize this expectation is to think of all the briefs for each side of a case stacked into two separate piles. If all else is equal, the side with the taller stack (containing more total information) should be more likely to win.

Since informational theory focuses on reducing uncertainty, it also predicts a more nuanced pattern. In addition to looking at raw totals, the amount of information presented to the Court can also be examined in terms of the breadth or coverage of that information (Hazelton, Hinkle, and Spriggs 2017). If one side's stack of briefs towers over the other, but every brief in the stack discusses the same one or two narrow issues, that repetition may leave relatively little in the way of distinct, usable information for the justices. As such, it is not just the total quantity of information but also the breadth of information provided that should lead to an advantage. Consequently, informational theory also predicts that the side which provides a wider range of information will be more likely to win.

Contrary to the expectations of information theory, some scholars theorize briefs are more persuasive when they contain repetitive information (Collins 2004; Collins, Corley, and Hamner 2013; Kearney and Merrill 2000; Szmer and Ginn 2014; Wofford 2015). The idea underlying this persuasion theory is that the number of voices repeating an argument is more important than the total amount of information presented by a side (Collins, Corley, and Hamner 2013; Szmer and Ginn 2014; Wofford 2015). As a result, repetition is persuasive both as a signal of society's preferences and as a basic psychological mechanism (Collins, Corley, and Hamner 2013; Hazelton, Hinkle, and Spriggs 2019). If a brief that contains more repetition of other briefs has a greater impact, it stands to reason that when all the briefs for a collected side repeatedly emphasize the same themes, that side should be more successful. This would suggest that greater breadth of information might have a negative impact on getting votes and winning cases. The conflicting theoretical expectations for the breadth of issues covered by a collection of briefs and the repeated emphasis of similar arguments highlight the importance of accounting for this concept in our empirical analysis.

There is also a third way of conceptualizing the quantity of information or signals brought to the Court, and that is to simply consider the number of briefs presented for each side (Collins 2004). To use our earlier example of the two stacks of briefs filed, the idea here is to simply count the number of briefs in each pile and theorize that the stack with a greater number of briefs is more likely to be persuasive. Due to the difficulties of measuring the content of briefs and (relative) ease of counting them, this approach has long been a mainstay of research on the impact of briefs in the Supreme Court (Collins 2008; Songer and Sheehan 1993; Szmer and Ginn 2014). Many scholars have found that a greater number of amicus briefs is related to a greater probability of winning or securing justices' votes (Collins 2008). However, these results leave some ambiguity about the underlying mechanism. A greater number of briefs may have an impact because the number of briefs is a good proxy for the quantity of information presented to the Court (Buckler 2015; Collins 2004).

Since we have gathered the actual content of the briefs, we need not rely on such a proxy. Rather, as in our previous work, we can develop and explore a more targeted theory that considers the signal sent by a brief independent of its content (Hazelton, Hinkle, and Spriggs 2017, 2019). Affected groups theory suggests that it is the number of outside people or groups weighing in on each side of a case that carries the type of information the Court is looking for (Behuniak-Long 1990). Under this account, the content of the briefs does not matter at all. The theory suggests that the justices simply use the number of briefs filed for each side as an estimate of which side has more allies (Caldeira and Wright 1990a; Hazelton, Hinkle, and Spriggs 2017). We build on this theory by arguing that beyond the simple number of participants, the number of briefs signals the strength as well as the quantity of support coalescing around a particular policy choice because it captures the amount of resources invested in lobbying the Court. Briefs are not cheap talk. They are a rather expensive mechanism to participate in the conversation (Behuniak-Long 1990; Hazelton, Hinkle, and Spriggs 2019).[2] As a result, the number of briefs on each side provides the Court with a signal regarding the relative importance of each side to affected groups in society. This theory suggests that the side with more briefs in their stack is more likely to win (regardless of the relative height of the stacks).

What You Say and How You Say It: Influencing
with Content and Style

There is considerable variation in the text of briefs presented to the Court that extends beyond the raw amount of information or the number of those briefs. While the sheer complexity of the textual content is daunting, there are basic elements and characteristics of briefs that lend themselves to theorizing about relative persuasive impact. We begin by looking at strategic appeals to the median justice. Since case outcomes are determined by majority rule, strategic brief writers might craft their arguments to focus on persuading the justice most likely to be casting the critical deciding vote (McGuire, Vanberg, and Yanus 2007). There are anecdotal accounts of such behavior (Barnes 2007). In one example, Behuniak-Long (1990) discusses how amici crafted their briefs to persuade Justice O'Connor in *Webster v. Reproductive Health Services*.[3] Additionally, some of our interviewees suggested this approach, as described in chapter 2.

While there are surely highly nuanced ways to engage in such strategy, we argue that one basic method is to rely to a greater extent on citing Court precedents written by the current median justice. Such an approach both strokes the median justice's ego and appeals to precedent they are likely to find quite persuasive. Citation studies consistently indicate that judges cite their own opinions more frequently than any other judges' (Hinkle 2016). This may be partially due to greater familiarity, but it is also likely a product of judges finding their own work more persuasive and compelling (Hinkle 2016). If brief writers engage in such strategy and it is successful in persuading median justices, then the side that cites more precedents written by the median should be more likely to win the case. While the median justice is not always the pivotal voter, they are the most common pivotal voter (Enns and Koch 2013). This is the one area where we do not expect the same impact for votes. There is no particular reason to expect a concerted focus on targeting the median justice to noticeably impact all the justices' votes. We only expect an impact on the median justice's vote, which should, in the aggregate, manifest in case outcomes.

Next, we consider the importance of advising the Court regarding the future policy implications of ruling for one side or the other. The potential utility of providing such insight has been recognized since the famous Brandeis brief in *Muller v. Oregon*. A variety of social scientific and technical information can give the Court valuable information about how their ruling may play out in the long term (Margolis 2000). The object of providing this type of information is "to inform courts of the context and the realities behind legal theories and arguments" (Greenhouse 2008, 1). While Supreme Court justices are highly intelligent, they are not omniscient. Faced with shaping policy for the entire country, they often need technical information from experts in the relevant field in order to thoroughly evaluate how particular case outcomes may ultimately impact society (Davis 1955; Margolis 2000). Davis (1955) coined the phrase "legislative facts" to identify facts presented to a court, "which help the tribunal to determine the context of the law and policy and to exercise its judgment or discretion in determining what course of action to take" (952). While we expect much of the briefs to be focused on traditional legal arguments, the side that brings a greater amount of key "legislative facts" to the Court's attention may well be in a better position to persuade. Two features of such information are their highly technical nature and a focus on the future (Davis 1955; Margolis 2000). Consequently, we expect the side that presents a greater relative concentration of technical and future-oriented language to have an advantage.

There is an old adage that says, "It's not just what you say, it's how you say it." This statement is as true in Supreme Court briefing as in any other area. Style matters. Presentation can persuade. Legal writing experts recommend that lawyers present their arguments in the clearest language possible and unadorned by emotional fripperies (Black, Owens, et al. 2016; Feldman 2016; Scalia and Garner 2008).[4] With respect to emotion, this advice is backed up by empirical evidence that justices are less likely to vote for a party that uses more emotional language in their brief (Black, Owens, et al. 2016). The reason emotion is counterproductive in the context of legal argumentation is because excessive appeal to it is viewed as unprofessional and potentially signals an underlying weakness in the legal arguments (Black, Owens, et al. 2016; Feldman 2016). We expect that the side that infuses their briefs with a larger percentage of emotional language will be at a disadvantage when it comes to votes and case outcomes.

Experts also encourage lawyers to write as clearly as possible (Scalia and Garner 2008). There is some empirical evidence to back up this advice as well. Briefs that are written more clearly can be more likely to garner a justice's vote (Black, Owens, et al. 2016; Long and Christensen 2011). This kind of impact may very well be due to arguments that are stated more clearly having greater persuasive value (Feldman 2016). However, as described in chapter 1, our interviews with former clerks and attorneys who practice before the Supreme Court suggest that the value of clarity is not necessarily a simple matter in this unique context. There, several interviewees brought up the importance of clarity (e.g., interviewees M, G, E, and R). Furthermore, Attorney and Former Clerk L described clear writing as a bare minimum standard for good briefs. On the other hand, at least a few interviewees noted that attorneys should be careful not to underestimate the skill level of their audience. Attorney R said one of the biggest mistakes is failing to understand the "sophisticated" nature of the practice. Former Clerk K warned against "stating the obvious." This is something that Attorney and Former Clerk B also touched on, saying, "Don't forget the intelligence of the tribunal" as well as its "carefulness." On balance, we hypothesize that the side with briefs that are written in a clearer style that avoids undue syntactic complexity are more likely to win votes and cases.

Money Talks but How Loudly? The Role of Resources in Winning

As we demonstrated in the previous two chapters, the resources brought to bear in writing briefs affects both informational content and coordination. It is also possible that even after controlling for the amount and types of information presented to the Court, as discussed prior, resources may continue to impact case outcomes. Scholars have demonstrated that status and resources carry an advantage in a wide variety of courts including the US Supreme Court (Buckler 2015; Galanter 1974; Szmer and Ginn 2014). Although the pattern is widely recognized, it is less clear what underlying mechanism or mechanisms are responsible (Szmer, Songer, and Bowie 2016). Some explanations focus on the ability of resources to secure high-quality legal representation that can, in turn, produce high-quality legal arguments (Wanner 1975; Wheeler et al. 1987; Atkins 1991; Songer and Sheehan 1992; McCormick 1993; Albiston 1999; Farole 1999; Songer, Sheehan, and Haire 1999; Szmer, Songer, and Bowie 2016). We discussed this dynamic at length in chapter 2. There are other possible reasons that resources influence Court decisions as well. In this section, we explore these as we consider how the side with more resources might do a better job of securing votes and winning cases. We think about resources in a cumulative sense, including the total number of filers and attorneys on each side, the overall experience of filers and attorneys, and the expertise of the attorneys. While previous work on the impact of amicus briefs frequently controlled for the type of parties involved (individual, interest group, government, etc.) (Black, Owens, et al. 2016; Collins 2008; Szmer and Ginn 2014), there is very little work that comprehensively integrates an examination of the resources of amici into the exploration of how resources have an impact on votes and outcomes in the Supreme Court.

We estimate cumulative resources by counting the number of filers and attorneys who sign the briefs for each side. This departure from the more typical approach of classifying litigants according to type provides a simple and informative measure when looking at cumulative resources. Comparing the resources of one petitioner and one respondent is a substantially different task than the type of cumulative comparison we are doing here, which is why the classic variable of litigant type is not very useful in this context. Even comparing the highest status type of all filers, party or amici, on each side is not very informative. Such a measure would only capture a rough proxy of one entity on each side. Instead, we opt to measure the cumulative level of participation in briefing.[5] Many different types of people or groups can sign each brief, and many briefs are filed on each side. Regardless of the nature of all those participants, the more people or groups that sign on to briefs, the larger the overall resources available. And the number of attorneys they hire to write those briefs is an indicator of the resources actually expended on producing the briefs. Consequently, we predict that having a greater number of filers or attorneys on one side of the case should lead to an advantage.

However, before we move on to discuss other measures of resource and experiential advantage, it is worth noting that the number of entities who sign the brief may reflect more than resources. That is to say, any advantage associated with a greater number of cosigners may instead be explained by affected groups theory. Affected groups or interest group theory indicates that the number of groups filing briefs on a side may be important, regardless of the amount of overall information provided, because it indicates general support for the position (Collins 2004; Scott 2013; Simard 2007) or specific support from powerful groups (Kearney and Merrill 2000). Both Collins (2004) and Buckler (2015) compare the impact of the number of briefs to the number of cosigners in order to disentangle information theory and affected groups theory. Our approach builds on their work by providing further measures of information and drawing the link between the number of cosigners and resources.

Next, we turn to the impact of experience. Often repeat players have substantial resources. But resources and repeat player status are not necessarily coextensive. We use the total filers and attorneys as an indicator of resources on each side of a case, but the previous experience of both is important too. Scholars have documented that attorneys with more past experience in the Supreme Court have a better success rate (Black, Owens, et al. 2016; Feldman 2016; Kearney and Merrill 2000; McGuire 1995). Work also suggests that amici who are repeat players are more likely to achieve their desired outcome (Box-Steffensmeier, Christenson, and Hitt 2013; Buckler 2015). Although counting previous Supreme Court experience of litigants is not common, many studies have shown that parties that are presumed to be repeat players, such as government actors and certain key interest groups, are more likely to succeed (Buckler 2015; Black, Owens, et al. 2016; Collins 2007).

In several interviews described in chapter 2, former clerks and attorneys who have filed briefs with the Supreme Court noted that more experienced attorneys are able to present a compelling story regarding the most desirable outcome in terms of policy. There is also a reputational component to repeat player status in the Supreme Court, as is mentioned by some interviewees (H, N, and O) in chapter 2. An attorney who is familiar to the Court may have increased credibility both because they are perceived to have more expertise and greater trustworthiness (Black, Owens, et al. 2016). Research on persuasion has long shown that communications from more credible and trustworthy sources are more likely to change someone's mind (Black, Owens, et al. 2016; Miller and Levine 2019; O'Keefe 2015). Such source effects emerge even when the content of a message is exactly the same and only the credibility or trustworthiness of the source of the message is manipulated (Berlo, Lemert, and Mertz 1969; Hovland and Weiss 1951).

Judicial politics scholars have provided evidence that judges are more likely to trust an attorney who appears in front of them frequently because they know such attorneys have an incentive to be faithful information providers in order to build and preserve a reputation as an advocate judges can trust (Black, Owens, et al. 2016; McGuire 1995; Szmer and Ginn 2014). There is experimental evidence that trustworthy sources are more persuasive (Hovland and Weiss 1951). While research focused on the trustworthiness and credibility of attorneys has not typically been extended to filers, the same logic applies to them as well. Organizations such as the ACLU that frequently file amicus briefs likely understand that if they are caught providing inaccurate information, they will sacrifice their credibility in future cases (Buckler 2015). The result is a dynamic in which the justices can view repeat filers as more trustworthy information providers because such repeat filers have more to lose if they are caught providing low-quality, inaccurate, or deceptive information. Box-Steffensmeier, Christenson, and Hitt (2013) note that, in general, groups that participate in politics more frequently are more likely to affect governmental policies, and they suggest that this general observation may apply to brief writers as well. As a result, there are multiple reasons to expect that the side that has more experienced filers and attorneys will be more likely to secure votes and win the case.

The impact of resources is certainly more nuanced than just the number and experience of filers and attorneys. In order to delve even deeper, we consider two types of credentials that are likely to indicate particularly high-quality attorneys. Expertise specific to the institution is especially valuable in the Supreme Court (McGuire 1995; Owens and Wohlfarth 2014). Therefore, we focus on two types of credentials that provide an attorney with knowledge of the Supreme Court far beyond that enjoyed by the typical attorney. The first focuses on the insider knowledge gained by the experience of clerking for a Supreme Court justice. The vast majority of the Court's work is done behind closed doors, and a clerkship grants a year of access to much (if not all) of that private world (Ward and Weiden 2006). There is evidence that this access can give a former clerk special insight into how to best persuade justices (especially the justice for whom they clerked) (Black and Owens 2020). The second type of credential that we examine is previous service as the solicitor general. While the solicitor general does not have the same kind of insider access that clerks do, they do have the benefit of close institutional links to the Court and full-time immersion in the task of persuading the justices (Black and Owens 2012). In short, both positions give an attorney a considerable amount of access to the Court and the opportunity to accumulate substantial insight into what arguments and approaches are most likely to be effective.[6] In addition, the obtaining of such positions is highly competitive, and the individuals who secure them are likely to possess extraordinary legal minds (Black and Owens 2012; Ward and Weiden 2006). Therefore, we expect that the side of a case that employs more attorneys who were former clerks and solicitors general will be more successful.

One final, but critically important, resource that may be available to one side in a case is the support of the current solicitor general. The solicitor general is remarkably successful as both a party and an amicus (Black and Owens 2012; Collins 2008; Kearney and Merrill 2000). As noted in chapter 2, Attorney and Former Clerk H felt that the credibility of the solicitor general was a key feature in the unusual position they held with the Court (see also Larsen and Devins 2016). The fact that the solicitor general is a valuable ally is not lost on filers and attorneys. They are a very desirable amicus to recruit (Millett 2009). One interviewee (Attorney P) also noted that parties work especially hard to persuade the solicitor general to file a brief on their behalf due to the power of such a brief. Some scholars attribute the success of solicitors general to institutional factors since the solicitor general represents a key player in the political system: the United States government (Epstein and Knight 1998). Still others attribute it to the expertise of the attorneys in that office (Spriggs and Wahlbeck 1997). Both of these explanations suggest that the solicitor general filing a brief for a particular side will give that side a higher probability of both securing votes and winning the case. To the extent that the latter explanation, focused on the personal expertise of the attorneys who hold the position of solicitor general, is driving this relationship, we should observe a similar effect for past solicitors general as we hypothesize previously. Any difference we observe between the success of the current solicitor general and past occupants of that office will indicate the institutional effects of representing the federal government.

Data and Methods

Next, we explore the cumulative effect of all the briefs filed by both litigants and amici on each side of a case. Our first unit of analysis is the case vote, and the outcome variable equals one if a justice voted in favor of the petitioner (and zero otherwise). The second model is at the case level, with the outcome variable equaling one if the petitioner won the case and zero if the Court ruled in favor of the respondent. Information on both justice votes and case outcomes was obtained from the Supreme Court database. Since both outcome variables can only take on two possible values (zero or one), we utilize probit models. The first model, of justice votes, also includes standard errors clustered on the case.

Language, Citations, and Briefs

Our first set of explanatory variables are a series of measures of the relative content presented to the Court. For each of these measures, the difference is calculated by subtracting the relevant quantity for briefs filed on the respondent's side from the relevant quantity for the briefs filed on the petitioner's side.[7] For example, the variable "Difference in No. of Briefs" is the number of briefs filed urging reversal minus the number of briefs filed urging affirmance. Each side includes all relevant briefs filed by both parties and amici. Since the outcome variable is whether a justice voted for the petitioner, positive coefficients on our difference measures indicate that more is better (the pattern generally anticipated by our hypotheses).

We go beyond simply counting the number of briefs on each side to measure both relative aggregate information and the relative breadth of the information presented on each side. For our first measure of total information, we begin with the standard approach of using a simple word count as a rough approximation of the information in a document (Huber and Shipan 2002; Huber, Shipan, and Pfahler 2001). However, the impact of additional information will tend to decrease as the total word count grows. The difference between one thousand and two thousand words should be much more substantial than the difference between eleven thousand words and twelve thousand words. Consequently, we take the standard precaution of using the natural log of the word count of the briefs on each side before calculating the difference.

Our second measure of the total amount of information on each side is the number of citations (in hundreds) to Supreme Court precedent. Legal citations are an important source of a particular type of information (Collins 2008; Hansford and Spriggs 2006). Attorneys naturally incorporate references to case law in their legal arguments to the Supreme Court. Citations to precedent from the Supreme Court are the most theoretically relevant sources because they are most likely to influence the Court. While research shows that precedent-level characteristics such as vitality and age lead to varying persuasive force (Hansford and Spriggs 2006), here we simply look at the number of citations. The average brief contains about one hundred and fifty citations, and we would have to aggregate any precedent-level characteristics to both the brief level and then further accumulate across all briefs filed for each side in a case. Since our unit of analyses are focused on votes and case outcomes rather than at the precedent level, the benefits of parsimony and the ease of interpreting the number of citations outweigh any nuance we would gain in our measures by incorporating precedential characteristics.

We also use words and citations to calculate the relative breadth of information presented by briefs. To do so, we count the number of different individual words used and cases cited in the set of briefs on each side.[8] Each new legal issue that is raised will bring additional words and precedents into the discussion. Consequently, holding the aggregate amount of information constant, briefs that incorporate a wider vocabulary or discuss more precedents are likely to be addressing a broader set of issues.[9] Conversely, a decrease in these measures indicates a higher degree of repetition. Our final measure of the amount of information is the number of briefs.

Types of Information

Next, we explore a variety of features of the type of information presented for each side in the collected briefs and how they stack up against each other. We begin by looking at the difference in the number of strategic citations to opinions written by the current median justice. Then, we look at features common to Brandeis briefs that focus on policy implications. Specifically, we examine the difference in the technical and future-oriented language on each side. Lastly, we look at how the information is presented with measures that capture the difference in the reading grade level and percentage of emotional language in the briefing for each side. We provide more detailed discussion of how we calculate these (and other) variables in chapter 2.

Attorney and Litigant Characteristics

Our final group of primary explanatory variables captures attorney and litigant characteristics that reflect the resources brought to bear to produce the information presented in the briefs. We start with the raw numbers of both filers and attorneys on each side. Next, we turn to experience. Since cumulative experience would closely correlate with the raw numbers, which are already accounted for, we summarize the experience of the filers and attorneys on each side by using the median number of previous briefs filed or signed going back to 1970.[10] As with word counts, we expect the impact of both number and experience to diminish as the quantities grow, so we take the natural log of the number and experience variables for each side before calculating our difference variables.

We account for attorney expertise on each side using three types of expertise: a prior clerkship for a Supreme Court justice, former experience as the solicitor general, and current status as the solicitor general. For each type of expertise, we calculate a difference measure that is the number of attorneys on the petitioner's side with the relevant characteristic minus the number from the respondent's side with the same characteristic. For example, "Difference in Current SG" equals one if the solicitor general appears for the petitioner and negative one if the solicitor general appears for the respondent. Lastly, we account for how many briefs were invited by the Court. As with the other difference measures, we subtract the number of briefs on the respondent's side that were invited from the same number for the petitioner's side.

Litigation Environment

Finally, we incorporate other aspects of the litigation environment that may affect the justices' votes. Perhaps most importantly, we account for the ideology of the Supreme Court justices. In order to quantify the ideological alignment between a justice and the petitioner in the votes model, we use a standard measure of Supreme Court ideology, Martin-Quinn scores (Martin and Quinn 2002). When the petitioner is seeking a conservative outcome, the variable "Ideological Alignment" is the Martin-Quinn score of the justice, because higher Martin-Quinn scores denote greater conservatism. Conversely, when the petitioner is advocating a liberal outcome, "Ideological Alignment" is the Martin-Quinn score of the justice multiplied by negative one. In the case outcome model, we measure the alignment between the petitioner and the Court median, also using Martin-Quinn scores. Next, we account for two aspects of the lower court proceedings that may reflect the complexity and salience of the underlying case. They are the (logged) word count of the lower court opinion and a dichotomous measure for whether one or more amici participated in the case being appealed. Furthermore, the Supreme Court can show its hand at the oral argument stage by asking

Table 4.1. Case-Level Summary Statistics

	Min.	25%	50%	75%	Max.
Language, Citations, and Briefs					
Difference in Log Word Count	−1.94	−0.27	0.19	0.59	2.89
Difference in Document Vocabulary (1000s)	−11.58	−0.57	0.22	0.92	7.42
Difference in Total Cites (100s)	−11.72	−0.29	0.17	0.69	8.44
Difference in Precedent Vocabulary (100s)	−10.11	−0.22	0.14	0.54	7.41
Difference in No. of Briefs	−56	0	1	2	32
Types of Information					
Difference in Citations to Current Median	−139	−2	0	4	139
Difference in Technical Language	−6.84	−0.62	0.13	0.89	6.31
Difference in Future Language	−1.51	−0.12	−0.01	0.12	0.7
Difference in Grade Level	−3.6	−0.59	0.04	0.63	4.42
Difference in Emotional Language	−2.47	−0.3	−0.02	0.27	1.99
Attorney and Litigant Characteristics					
Difference in Log No. of Cosigners	−3.86	−0.45	0.54	1.1	4.38
Difference in Log No. of Attorneys	−3.14	−0.27	0.44	1.1	3.95
Difference in Log Median Filer Exp.	−8.95	−3.02	0	1.39	7.96
Difference in Log Median Attorney Exp.	−7.47	−1.79	0.31	2.3	6.36
Difference in No. of Former Clerks	−28	−1	0	3	20
Difference in No. of Former SGs	−2	0	0	0	4
Difference in Current SG	−1	0	0	1	1
Difference in Briefs Invited by Court	−1	0	0	0	1

(continued on the next page)

Table 4.1. *Continued*

	Min.	25%	50%	75%	Max.
Litigation Environment					
Ideological Alignment with Petitioner	−1.26	−0.8	0.12	0.8	1.26
Log Word Count LC Opinion	0	7.98	8.57	9.11	11.1
Amicus Activity in Lower Court	0	0	0	0	1
Difference in Oral Argument Questions	−94	−14	1	15	102
Term	1984	1988	1994	2002	2015
Observations		**2,439**			

questions in a lopsided fashion (Epstein, Landes, and Posner 2010).[11] Typically, facing more questions bodes ill (Epstein, Landes, and Posner 2010), so we control for the difference between the number of questions posed to each side.[12] Finally, we control for term. The summary statistics for all of our variables at the case level are provided in table 4.1.

Results

Figure 4.1 presents the results of both models.[13] As we expect, there are similarities in the results for individual justice votes and case outcomes. Nearly half of the variables that are statistically significant are so in both models. Broadly consistent with previous research, we find that the side that presents a greater quantity of information has more success. However, our results offer more nuanced insight into why that advantage is obtained. The side with more words is significantly more likely to win votes and the case. Quantity and breadth of citations are both significant in the votes model (although not the outcomes model). While the breadth of precedents cited does improve the probability of securing a justice's vote, a greater overall number of citations actually decreases that probability. Furthermore, there is no evidence of the number of briefs affecting votes, but there is such evidence for outcomes. Even after controlling for the relative scope and breadth of written argumentation

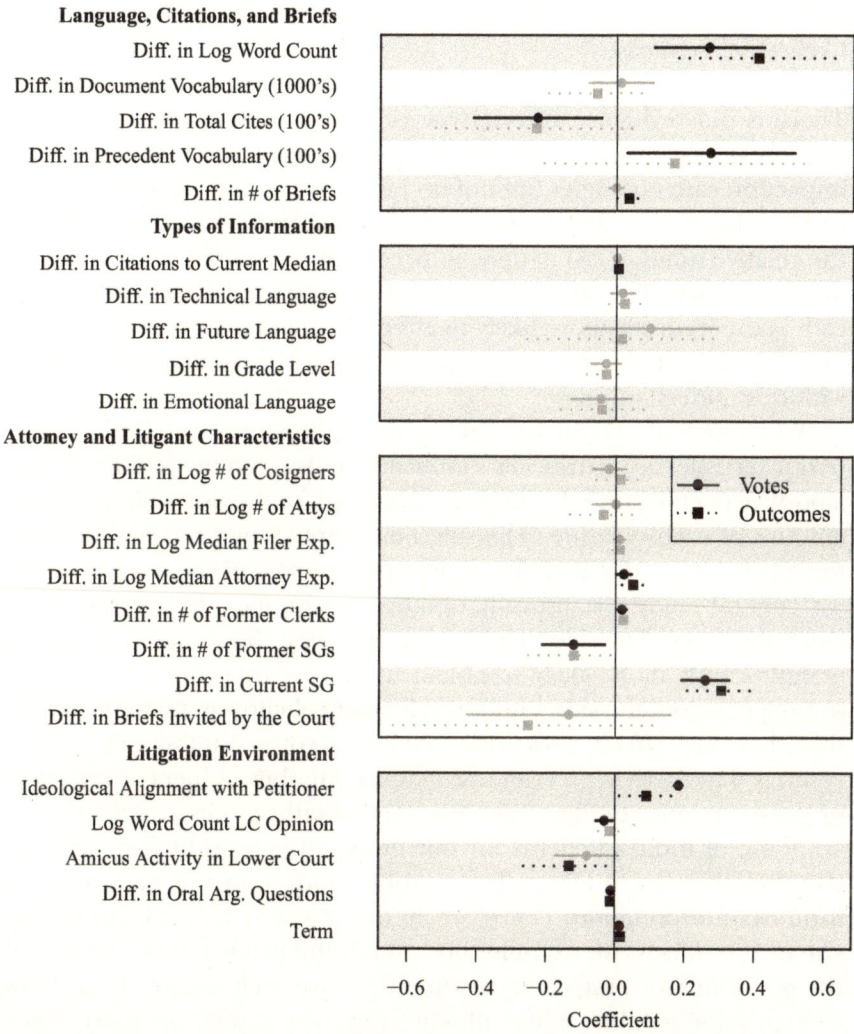

Language, Citations, and Briefs
Diff. in Log Word Count
Diff. in Document Vocabulary (1000's)
Diff. in Total Cites (100's)
Diff. in Precedent Vocabulary (100's)
Diff. in # of Briefs
Types of Information
Diff. in Citations to Current Median
Diff. in Technical Language
Diff. in Future Language
Diff. in Grade Level
Diff. in Emotional Language
Attorney and Litigant Characteristics
Diff. in Log # of Cosigners
Diff. in Log # of Attys
Diff. in Log Median Filer Exp.
Diff. in Log Median Attorney Exp.
Diff. in # of Former Clerks
Diff. in # of Former SGs
Diff. in Current SG
Diff. in Briefs Invited by the Court
Litigation Environment
Ideological Alignment with Petitioner
Log Word Count LC Opinion
Amicus Activity in Lower Court
Diff. in Oral Arg. Questions
Term

● Votes
■ Outcomes

-0.6   -0.4   -0.2   0.0   0.2   0.4   0.6
Coefficient

Figure 4.1. Modeling votes and case outcomes. Probit regression estimates of the effect of amount and type of information, attorney and litigant characteristics, and a range of control variables on the probability of the petitioner securing justice votes and case outcomes. For the votes model, coefficients are marked by circles, and 95 percent confidence intervals are solid lines. For the outcomes model, coefficients are marked by squares and 95 percent confidence intervals are dotted lines. Estimates and confidence intervals in gray (instead of black) indicate that the confidence interval includes zero.

provided, the side with a greater number of briefs is significantly more likely to win the case.[14]

Next, we turn to look at the impact of different types of information. There is only evidence of one type of information shaping who wins and loses. Strategic information has a positive and statistically significant impact on case outcomes but not on justice votes. This is not surprising considering that we are measuring strategic argumentation by counting the relative number of citations to precedents authored by the current median justice. The strategy of appealing to the median voter specifically is theoretically more likely to affect the median justice, and consequently case outcomes, than all justices' votes. The results are consistent with this understanding.

When we look at attorney and litigant characteristics, we find that two of our variables are statistically significant across both models. Both have a positive coefficient, reflecting an advantage for the side with the larger amount of each measure. The side that employs more experienced attorneys as well as the side that enjoys the support of the current solicitor general enjoy a statistically significant advantage in terms of both cases and votes. The side that hires more former Supreme Court clerks is significantly more likely to obtain individual votes. But, contrary to our expectation, the side with more former solicitors general relative to the other side actually fares worse in terms of votes. Another unexpected result is that there is no evidence that the number of filers or attorneys or the experience of filers have an effect on either votes or outcomes.

Some of the coefficients for our model appear to be very small in size, but the size of effects from probit models do not have a direct intuitive interpretation. Therefore, in order to consider the substantive size of the effects, we examine how much the predicted probability of the petitioner winning changes when we move each variable from a low to high value (while holding all other variables at their median). Since the results are fairly similar in our two models, we focus our discussion of substantive significance on the case outcomes model. After all, the change in the probability of winning the case is what many people care about. Figure 4.2 shows the impact of moving most variables from their twenty-fifth to seventy-fifth percentile value. However, for our variables that reflect the difference in the number of former clerks, former solicitors general, current solicitor general, and invited briefs, we move them from negative one to one to show the impact of moving from a one-unit advantage for the respondent to a one-unit advantage for the petitioner.

Language, Citations, and Briefs
Diff. in Log Word Count
Diff. in Document Vocabulary (1000's)
Diff. in Total Cites (100's)
Diff. in Precedent Vocabulary (100's)
Diff. in # of Briefs
Types of Information
Diff. in Citations to Current Median
Diff. in Technical Language
Diff. in Future Language
Diff. in Grade Level
Diff. in Emotional Language
Attorney and Litigant Characteristics
Diff. in Log # of Cosigners
Diff. in Log # of Attys
Diff. in Log Median Filer Exp.
Diff. in Log Median Attorney Exp.
Diff. in # of Former Clerks
Diff. in # of Former SGs
Diff. in Current SG
Diff. in Briefs Invited by the Court
Litigation Environment
Ideological Alignment with Petitioner
Log Word Count LC Opinion
Amicus Activity in Lower Court
Diff. in Oral Arg. Questions
Term

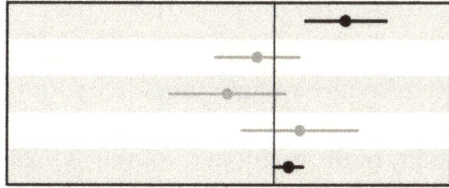

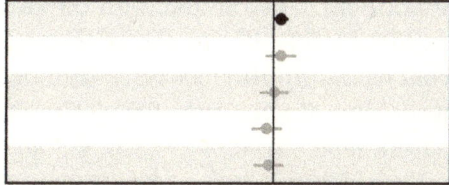

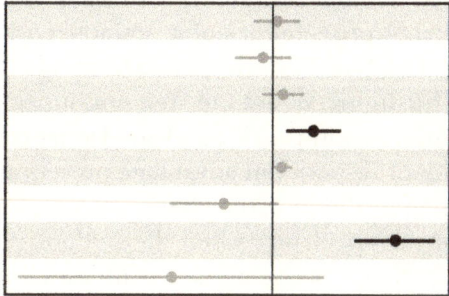

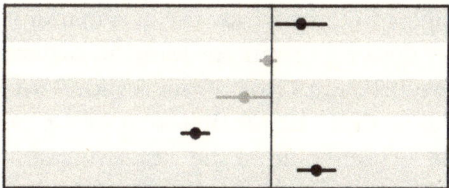

−0.4   −0.2   0.0   0.2

Change in Pred. Prob. of Pet. Win

Figure 4.2. Changes in predicted probability of petitioner winning. Estimates (and associated 95 percent confidence intervals) of the change in the predicted probability of a petitioner win generated by moving each variable from a low to high value while holding all other variables at their median. The difference variables for former clerks and solicitors general, the current solicitor general, and invited briefs are moved from negative one to one. The binary variable for amicus activity in the lower court is moved from zero to one. All other variables are moved from their twenty-fifth to seventy-fifth percentile values. Estimates and confidence intervals in gray (instead of black) indicate that the confidence interval includes zero.

Figure 4.2 reveals a number of interesting patterns. The first is that it must be nice to have the solicitor general on your side. This is the variable that generates the largest difference in case outcome. The probability of the petitioner winning is 0.23 higher when the solicitor general appears on their side compared to when the solicitor general backs the respondent. The variable with the next largest effect size is the overall length of briefs. The impact of moving "Difference in Log Word Count" from its twenty-fifth to seventy-fifth percentile increases the petitioner's probability of winning by 0.13.[15] However, for a continuous measure with considerable variation, we can get an even better picture of the impact of the relative length of briefs by examining the probability of a petitioner win across all values. We do so in figure 4.3, which shows the predicted probabilities of a petitioner win across all values of "Difference in Log Word Count" (while holding all other variables at their median). This figure shows the tremendous impact that the overall quantity of information provided to the Court can have. At the most extreme values of respondent advantage present in our data, the petitioner has less than a one in three chance of winning the case. But at the other end of the spectrum, when the petitioner's advantage is maximized, their predicted probability of winning climbs above a nine in ten chance. Furthermore, this variable alone can enable respondents to turn the tables to their advantage, a remarkable feat given the Supreme Court's tendency to grant certiorari in order to reverse cases. Yet, if the collective briefs in favor of the respondent have a logged word count that is 0.6 or more larger than that of the petitioner side briefs, then the predicted outcome of the case swings in favor of the respondent. Such an advantage in relative length of the briefs is not easy to gain. It occurs in only 11 percent of our cases. But it is possible. Two other information variables are statistically significant. Moving from an equal number of briefs for each side, a two-brief advantage for the petitioner increases the probability of a win by a modest 0.027. The substantive size of the effect of including more strategic citations to the median justice has an even smaller impact of 0.014.

What is the practical impact of the type of experience and expertise that extensive resources can procure? As noted previously, the benefit of having the current solicitor general on your side is substantial. The petitioner's probability of winning is 0.74 with the support of the solicitor general, 0.63 when the solicitor general does not participate, and 0.51 when the solicitor general supports affirming the lower court. The side with the

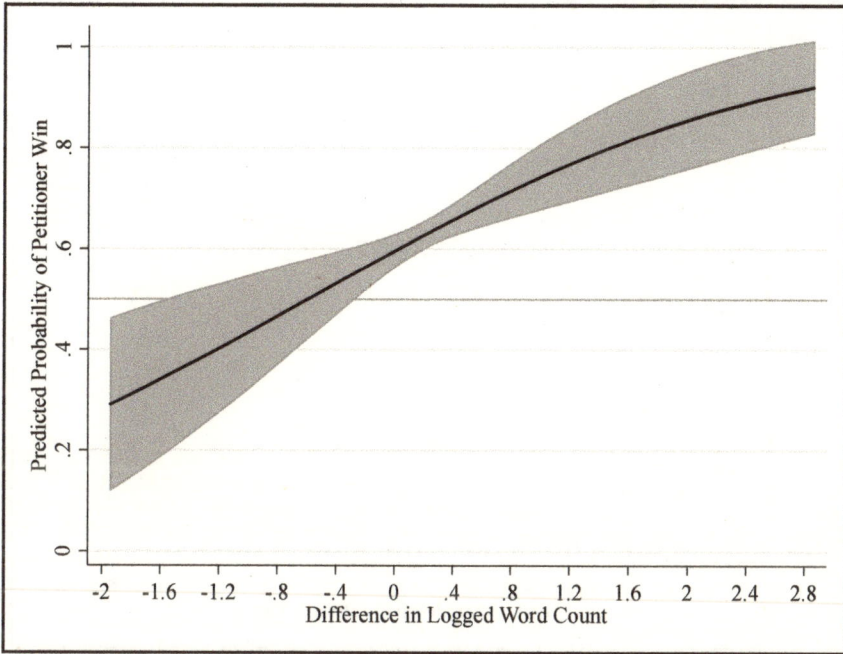

Figure 4.3. Predicted probability of petitioner win over the range of difference in log word count. All other variables are set at their median value. Any estimates above the horizontal gray reference line indicate that the petitioner is more likely to win while estimates under that line indicate that the respondent is more likely to win.

more experienced attorneys also enjoys more success, although to a lesser extent. Moving the relative experience for attorneys from its twenty-fifth to seventy-fifth percentile value increases the petitioner's chances by 0.08. Figure 4.4 illustrates the impact of this variable over its entire range. Over the range of attorney experience, the probability of the petitioner winning ranges from 0.45 up to 0.71. This effect indicates that the choices filers make regarding which attorneys they hire can impact case outcomes.

Conclusions

Our findings in this chapter build on the work of scholars (including ourselves) who have examined how briefs and resources can impact the

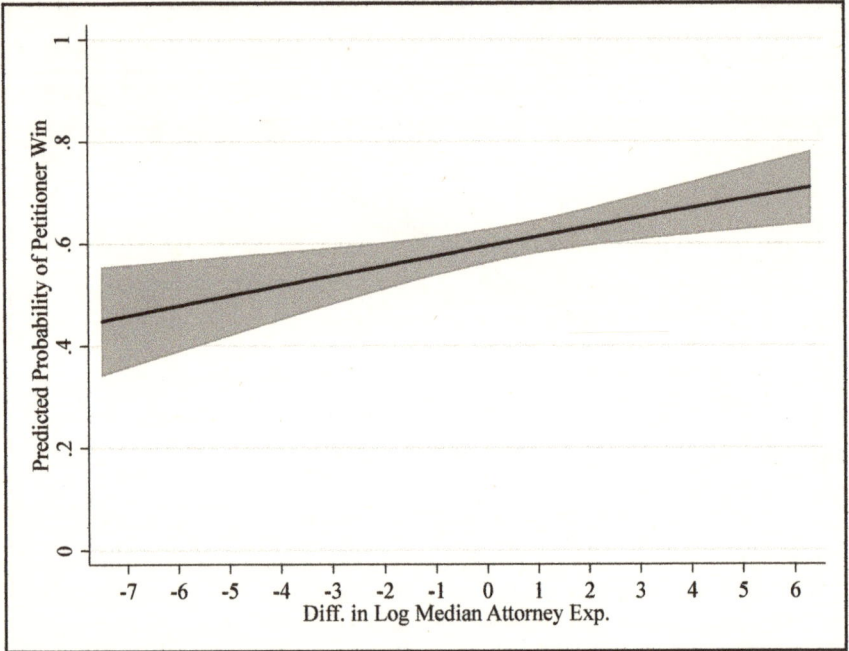

Figure 4.4. Predicted probability of petitioner win over the range of difference in log median attorney experience. All other variables are set at their median value.

way justices vote and, as a result, who wins and loses. While some of our results echo previous findings, we contribute to a more nuanced and holistic understanding of how Supreme Court justices are persuaded by considering many characteristics of litigant and amicus briefs as well as the characteristics of those who create them. This joint exploration, along with our several detailed, data-intensive measures of key concepts, provide the opportunity to better understand the mechanisms underlying patterns that have previously been observed.

A variety of scholars have provided evidence that the side with the greater number of briefs is more likely to win a case (Collins 2018). We find a similar pattern in our case outcomes model, although the effect size of the relative number of briefs is a rather small 0.03. To complement this finding, we uncover that the overall length of briefing on each side confers a larger advantage of 0.13. These findings provide an important supplement to the conventional wisdom by offering insight into why a greater number of briefs translates into greater success. The side with more briefs is often also presenting more information to the Court. This has long been theorized as one of the explanations for the impact of a greater number of briefs (Buckler 2015; Collins 2004). Our results strengthen the case for this interpretation. However, that does not appear to be the complete story. Alternative theories suggest that justices can be persuaded by the sheer number of people or groups willing to invest extensive resources in creating a brief. By evaluating the impact of the number of briefs while controlling for the extent and type of information provided, we are able to provide evidence that this mechanism is also in play, although to a lesser extent than the informational mechanism.

While previous work has focused mostly on the impact of the number of briefs rather than the number of entities who sign those briefs, we also tested the possibility that the number of filers on all briefs might be what swayed the Court. Yet that variable was statistically insignificant in both of our models. Taken together, our results indicate that the relative quantity of information marshaled for each side significantly affects votes and outcomes, and the relative willingness of participants to sink meaningful resources into creating briefs affects outcomes, but there is no evidence that the relative number of affected people or groups participating in the briefing process by cosigning a brief confers a similar advantage. However, it is important to bear in mind that the binary outcomes we examine in this chapter are not the only aspect of the Supreme Court's work product that are worth influencing. The language in majority opinions provides nuanced details of policy that have tremendous importance in their own right. There is every reason to expect that aspects of information and signals of policy coalescence that may not significantly affect who wins and loses can still shape the Court's statement of the law. We turn to this important topic in the next two chapters.

Our results in this chapter also shed additional light on the persuasive impact of resources and the experience and expertise they are able to secure. One of the reasons repeat players and the high-end lawyers they are able to afford are better able to win cases is because they can make better arguments. We have at least partially controlled for this disparity in ability. Regardless, we still find that experienced attorneys do better before the Court, suggesting that greater credibility likely plays an important role in persuading the Court even above and beyond the actual arguments they make. In a slightly different vein, the substantial impact of the current solicitor general suggests that the institutional elements of the office are important factors in persuading justices. The solicitor general is more successful because they represent the federal government and have control over which cases to appeal. This is especially true since there is no evidence of such an advantage for the side with more former solicitors general (and there is actually a disadvantage for the side with more former solicitors general when it comes to securing individual votes). The combination of these two results implies that the often-observed advantage of the solicitor general is more strongly rooted in the prestige and importance of their institutional position as representative of the United States and less linked to the individual competence and skill of the attorneys who attain that position.

The broad picture that emerges in this study is that while votes and outcomes are linked to justice ideology as we would expect, other factors can persuade the Court, often to an even larger extent. Both information and people matter. While the overall quality of legal argumentation in briefs defies large-scale empirical quantification to a considerable extent, we are able to tap into concepts that shed important light on what constitutes effective briefing. The side that presents more overall content in briefs, more briefs, and more citations to the current median justice has a significantly higher likelihood of winning a case. Even after controlling for the information in the briefs, the attorney characteristics matter too. An advantage in terms of attorney experience and the participation of the current solicitor general confer an advantage in securing both votes and cases.

5 | Standing Out or Speaking Together
How Individual Briefs Shape Opinion Content

In sports, commentators often throw around the quote, "Winning isn't everything; it's the only thing." Whether or not the sentiment is true in athletics, it is certainly not the case in Supreme Court litigation. More precisely, winning in Supreme Court litigation means something much more than the Court ruling in one's favor. While the direct outcome of a case is important to the parties and amici,[1] the legal rules announced in the majority decisions have long-reaching and remarkable impact for those involved in the case, future litigants, and society at large (Clark and Lauderdale 2010; Tiller and Cross 2006). In this chapter, we shift our focus to how the features and characteristics of the briefs and the parties and attorneys who draft and file them shape the policy spelled out in the text of the Court's opinion. Specifically, we analyze how these factors influence the similarity between each brief and the language in the decision.

Beyond the unanimous vote in favor of Florida in *Florida v. Harris*, the Supreme Court released an opinion detailing why it was reversing the Florida Supreme Court and setting forth guidance for future search and seizure cases. In short, the Supreme Court decided that "a sniff is up to snuff when it meets [the totality of the circumstances] test." It is likely unsurprising that the opinion was more like the briefs of the state of Florida and supporting amici relative to the submissions for the other side:[2] beyond ruling in favor of the state, the Court adopted the approach that Florida and the supporting amici put forth in their briefs. The Court found that Harris had failed to "undermine" the evidence of reliability provided by the state and, therefore, Officer Wheetley had probable cause to search the truck. The justices agreed that testing in a controlled setting was more reliable than in the field and should be central to inquiries into probable cause. Additionally, the Court held that a defendant could attack the rigor of the training or certification process or aspect of a specific search while rejecting the broader inquiry set forth by the Florida Supreme Court. The Court's ruling reflected the approach advocated by Florida and its supporting amici. If the opinion had been drafted differently, it would have had the potential to change arrests in all fifty states and the work of the nearly fifty thousand police dogs working in the United States (Lou 2015).

When we assess the similarity between the individual briefs and the opinion, we find that the majority opinion was most like Florida's main brief.[3] Both Harris's response and the solicitor general's briefs were similar to the majority opinion but somewhat less so than Florida's brief, which is unsurprising given the central role of party briefs generally and the importance of the solicitor general. There was a relative gulf between these briefs and the general briefs in terms of similarity to the majority opinion: the briefs of the Rutherford Institute (on behalf of Harris), National Police Canine Association and *Police K-9 Magazine* (for Florida), and Virginia and the other states (also for Florida), which had more moderate similarity. The remaining four amicus briefs were all filed in favor of Harris, with declining levels of similarity to the majority opinion in the following order: the National Association of Criminal Defense Lawyers (NACDL) et al., the Fourth Amendment scholars, EPIC, and the Institute for Justice. These patterns are in keeping with the majority opinion ultimately adopting the approach advocated by Florida and the amici supporting it.

In this chapter, we consider the influence of the textual features of briefs, the types of information found in them, the characteristics of the parties and attorneys that relate to issues of resources, and the legal and ideological environment in which the litigation occurs. While each of these categories of influence is important, our primary focus is the relationship between the relative uniqueness of information found within each brief and its similarity to the opinion. We concentrate on the impact of novel and shared information because it represents a choice vantage point from which to consider the role of information in judicial decision-making. Specifically, briefs are the primary source of information for the justices based on structure and design.[4] They encapsulate the public positions of the immediate parties and interested groups. Briefing is also an area where the Court's stated desires and empirical evidence regarding the Court's behavior seem to conflict (Corley 2008; Feldman 2017b; Hazelton, Hinkle, and Spriggs 2019; Spriggs and Wahlbeck 1997; Wofford 2015). We theorize that information shared across multiple briefs is influential because of its ability to signal policy coalescence and the psychological factors related to integrating information from numerous sources. Additionally, information only found in one brief is of dubious value based on the structures of the judicial hierarchy and Supreme Court litigation, which provide ample opportunities for briefers to be exposed to, and adopt, quality information from others.

We first engage the importance of the Court's opinions and research regarding information processing, reading comprehension, and decision-making. In doing so, we develop our theories regarding the influence of novel and shared information on judicial policy. We then set out our data and methods for capturing specific aspects of briefs and the language and information contained therein, resources enjoyed by the parties and attorneys drafting and filing the briefs, and the broader legal and ideological forces surrounding the case. As in chapter 2, we carry out our analyses on both party and amicus briefs separately, as they differ in terms of rules, goals, and tactics. The results contribute to a growing body of evidence indicating that shared information leads to more considerable influence over opinion content (Corley 2008; Feldman 2017b; Hazelton, Hinkle, and Spriggs 2019; Spriggs and Wahlbeck 1997; Wofford 2015). We also find evidence that briefs with more language regarding the future are more influential on the language in decisions, indicating that policy concerns are likely at work. Additionally, we find that many attorney and litigant characteristics and aspects of the litigation influence the similarity between briefs and opinions.

The Importance of Opinions and Their Relationships to Briefs

Here, we pivot our focus from tallying which party won or lost a case (chapter 4) to the actual content of the majority's opinion. We do so because these decisions represent the Court's announced policies (Corley 2008; Maltzman, Spriggs, and Wahlbeck 2000). These policies have an impact well beyond the immediate outcome of the case (Clark and Lauderdale 2010; Tiller and Cross 2006). It is the majority opinions, not outcomes, that lower courts and government officials interpret and implement (Canon and Johnson 1998; Hall 2010). Groups and individuals in society adapt to such changes in policy rather than the immediate outcome (Canon and Johnson 1998). Justices are aware of the importance of their writings (Garner 2010, 97). For example, according to Chief Justice Roberts, "The opinions are going to be used for lawyers, for other judges—to tell them what the law is" (Garner 2010, 8).

The entirety of the opinion has policy implications: it contains both the legal rules and tests that the Court has announced and facts and reasoning that help guide its application (Corley 2008). Because the US legal system is built on precedent and stare decisis, courts determine the applicability of legal doctrine to a future case based on analogical reasoning: if the cases are sufficiently similar along the relevant factual dimensions, then the principle should be applied (Aldisert 1989; Braman and Nelson 2007; Schauer 1987; Sunstein 1993). Thus, the text of these opinions provides the basis for legal education (Corley, Collins, and Calvin 2011). Influence over the text also appears to be the primary goal of amici (Collins 2018). Therefore, the language of the opinions themselves is key to understanding the state of the law.

Beyond announcing applicable policies, there is evidence that opinions serve other functions. They are a means by which "justices . . . engage in a dialogue with the citizenry" (Corley, Collins, and Calvin 2011, 31; see also Bennett 2001). Additionally, there is research indicating that opinion content influences legitimacy (Farganis 2012), and that justices craft their opinions with an eye towards public acceptance (Black, Owens, et al. 2016). It is essential to understand these opinions and the factors that shape them (Black, Owens, et al. 2016; Carrubba and Clark 2012; Collins 2018).

Briefs are essential documents in large part because of their role in helping justices craft opinions. In any given case, multiple avenues could support a decision in favor of either party. Briefers may present varying approaches within a matter. Based on the norm against sua sponte decision-making, the Court generally is restricted to deciding cases based on those questions and arguments brought before it in briefs (Black, Hall, et al. 2016; Epstein, Segal, and Johnson 1996; Epstein and Knight 1999; Hazelton, Hinkle, and Spriggs 2019; but see McGuire and Palmer 1996). Thus, briefs help define the contours of which policies are likely to be announced by the Court. There is also evidence that briefs do a fair bit more and shape the policy itself (Canelo 2022; Corley 2008; Collins, Corley, and Hamner 2013). As noted previously, one of the interviewees (Attorney and Former Clerk I) asserted that opinion content is where the action is concerning briefs. Therefore, the influence of information found in individual submissions on such legal policy is a worthy focus.

Additionally, the influence of briefs may vary between votes and opinions. As noted in chapter 4, Attorney and Former Clerk I believed that briefs "have influence in the words to justify a decision rather than votes." Though they said the influence varied by justice, they noted that one "lazy" approach was to simply use "recycled" language from briefs. The influence was more likely when a decision author didn't have to "fix up" the language.

Novel and Shared Information

In investigating the relationship between briefs and majority opinions, we are chiefly concerned with the role of information. There is a multitude of reasons that information may be helpful to decision-makers, but we must go beyond the broad idea of information and investigate more nuanced aspects (Hazelton, Hinkle, and Spriggs 2019). To do so, we focus on the role of novel and shared information from briefs in shaping the language found in the decisions. This allows us to explore how briefing helps shape decisions, including the role of policy coalescence among groups. Informational theories indicate that knowledge matters (Hazelton, Hinkle, and Spriggs 2019; Krehbiel 1992; Szmer and Ginn 2014; Yackee and Yackee 2006). Justices (Simard 2007), clerks (Lynch 2004), and practitioners (Forman 2016) stress the importance of new information in amicus briefs. Additionally, psychology research indicates that unique information can influence decision-makers (Collins, Corley, and Hamner 2013). Thus, some have theorized that unusual information should influence majority opinions (Spriggs and Wahlbeck 1997). However, institutional and hierarchical features make it unlikely that other briefers would not repeat valuable information (Hazelton, Hinkle, and Spriggs 2019). Moreover, repetition itself may represent information, specifically as a signal of policy coalescence among stakeholders (Hazelton, Hinkle, and Spriggs 2019). Finally, psychological research indicates that individuals are more likely to be persuaded by shared information due to issues related to social conditions and heuristic and persuasive effects (Collins 2004; Collins, Corley, and Hamner 2013; Hazelton, Hinkle, and Spriggs 2019; Wofford 2015). We also investigate other aspects of the language and information found in the briefs, resources associated with the characteristics of the parties and attorneys, and the litigation environment to provide a fuller picture of how the text of submissions translates into the content of opinions.

Novel Information

First, we consider informational, structural, and psychological theories, along with qualitative accounts, regarding the influence of information communicated by a single source among many. Our investigation includes both reasons to believe that such new information will be influential and factors cutting against such an expectation. We begin with theoretical and anecdotal accounts regarding informational and structural reasons that novel information may be influential. Informational theory indicates that sources with unique details are particularly valuable: because policy makers need knowledge regarding a host of factors when making decisions, the mere fact that individual information increases what a justice knows makes it likely to be influential (Box-Steffensmeier, Christenson, and Hitt 2013; Collins 2008; Hazelton, Hinkle, and Spriggs 2019; Stasser and Titus 1985).

The Supreme Court's own rules and norms suggest that the justices want novel information. The Court's practices regarding allowing amicus briefs are quite permissive, indicating that it wants as much information as possible (Collins 2007, 2008; Hazelton, Hinkle, and Spriggs 2019). Furthermore, the Court has explicitly stated that it is seeking novel information in amicus briefs: "An amicus curiae brief that brings to the attention of the Court relevant matter not already brought to its attention by the parties may be of considerable help to the Court. An amicus curiae brief that does not serve this purpose burdens the Court, and its filing is not favored" (US Supreme Court 2019, Rule 37.1). It is easy to imagine that reading the same material over and over could be taxing for clerks and justices in terms of both time and mental resources without the payoff of new information. Behuniak-Long (1990) suggests that repetition in briefs could be annoying (see also Hazelton, Hinkle, and Spriggs 2019). Relatedly, as described in chapter 3, nearly a dozen interviewees with Supreme Court experience indicated that amicus briefs should include information not found elsewhere. Many interviewees specifically described repetitive briefs in a negative light.

On the other hand, the structure of Supreme Court litigation and the judicial hierarchy makes it very unlikely that attorneys and filers would not repeat quality information (Hazelton, Hinkle, and Spriggs 2019). Regarding the parties, they have generally been litigating the case for years and across several courts. They have been exposed to the arguments of the other side and reasoning by judges many times. As a matter of course with iterative briefing, parties will raise and address each other's arguments, even preemptively (Hazelton, Hinkle, and Spriggs 2019; see Beazley 2010; Feldman 2017b; Fontham 1985). Furthermore, as we discuss in chapter 3, coordination is common among parties and amici who share information. In our interviews, experienced individuals addressed the need to keep amici "out of the weeds," and another warned of the "mischief of random sentences." Thus, it is improbable that only a single briefer will include relevant and accurate information. Despite this fact, the Court may still benefit from encouraging individuals to provide unique information because research indicates that it can improve debate and creative thinking (Hazelton, Hinkle, and Spriggs 2019).

Novel information may be associated with more positive outcomes due to psychological effects (Corley, Steigerwalt, and Ward 2013; Hazelton, Hinkle, and Spriggs 2019). Within psychology, theory and evidence regarding minority information indicate that it can be particularly persuasive due to its ability to command attention (Nemeth 1986; Martin, Hewstone, and Martin 2008; Baron and Bellman 2007).[5] It also influences perceptions regarding the individuals providing it (Asch and Guetzkow 1951; Crano and Prislin 2006; Packer 2011; Hazelton, Hinkle, and Spriggs 2019). Psychology research also indicates that unique information may improve a side's chances because the number of arguments in favor of a position can be influential (Hazelton, Hinkle, and Spriggs 2019; Harkins and Petty 1981a, 1981b).

Overall, however, the results of psychology experiments indicate that positions held by a single source are unlikely to be persuasive in the instant case, though they may have other benefits for the parties and attorneys providing the unique information; such advantages can include gaining valuable experience and setting the stage for future arguments and victories (Hazelton, Hinkle, and Spriggs 2019, 132). Additionally, work regarding the psychology of reading comprehension indicates that texts with unusual information will be harder for readers to process. When reading texts, humans use comprehension strategies (Afflerbach and Cho 2009; Anmarkrud, Bråten, and Strømsø 2014). Such strategies are even more useful when individuals are called upon to read and comprehend "multiple challenging, conflicting documents on a complex issue" (Anmarkrud, Bråten, and Strømsø 2014, 65; see also Myers and O'Brien 1998; O'Brien and Myers 1999), such as legal briefs in Supreme Court cases. Existing research indicates that these strategies likely vary based on the amount of semantic overlap in the documents; when such shared material is lacking, readers require more effortful strategies (Anmarkrud, Bråten, and Strømsø 2014, 65; Kurby, Britt, and Magliano 2005).

The weight of the informational, structural, and psychological theory indicates that novel information is detrimental to a filer seeking to influence the opinion the Court will produce. Prior empirical investigations regarding novel information support this proposition (Spriggs and Wahlbeck 1997; Hazelton, Hinkle, and Spriggs 2019; Wofford 2015). Thus, we hypothesize that Supreme Court opinions will be less similar to briefs with more novel information.

Shared Information

On the other hand, shared information is likely to be persuasive for several informational, structural, and psychological reasons derived from multiple literatures and qualitative evidence. While those close to the Supreme Court often tout the importance of unique information in briefs, that proposition is not without dissenters. As described in chapter 3, several interviewees articulated ways in which repetitive briefs might contribute to influencing the Court. Prior research, including a survey and interviews of clerks, indicated that clerks are more likely to pay close attention to briefs that come from reputable attorneys, especially the solicitor general (Lynch 2004). The filing organization's identity has a mixed influence (Lynch 2004). In both instances, information likely should be repeated to increase the chances that it will be seen.

Certainly, the rules and norms of the federal judiciary and Supreme Court make repetition likely (Hazelton, Hinkle, and Spriggs 2019). Usually, at least one other appellate court has heard the case before it arrives at the Supreme Court. Also, most cases come to the Court via writs of certiorari. Both stages required the parties to carefully define the issues at stake and related facts, law, and arguments (Hazelton, Hinkle, and Spriggs 2019; Krehbiel 1992; Szmer and Ginn 2014; Yackee and Yackee

2006). These public filings are also available to amici participating at the Supreme Court. Furthermore, standard briefing practices encourage the attorneys for the parties to address each of the points laid out by the other side (Hazelton, Hinkle, and Spriggs 2019). Also, qualitative accounts from our interviews (see chapter 3), prior research (McGuire 1994; Larsen and Devins 2016), and advice regarding briefing (Sungaila 1998) indicate that coordination among parties and amici is the norm. Thus, amicus briefs are likely to support the arguments presented by a party (Sungaila 1998). In fact, many interviewees noted the importance of having amici bolster aspects of the party briefs, an act that involves overlapping information. Perhaps unsurprisingly, shared information is common in briefs (Collins 2008; Collins, Corley, and Hamner 2013; Collins and Martinek 2015; Hazelton, Hinkle, and Spriggs 2019; Spriggs and Wahlbeck 1997; Wofford 2015).

While the mere fact that briefs are discussing the same underlying case accounts for some level of overlap in language, briefs that focus on the same desired policies will be even more similar (Hazelton, Hinkle, and Spriggs 2019). This is because such submissions will share language regarding the policies they are advocating, as well as the same or similar specific facts,[6] legal concepts, and precedents to build the arguments in favor of those desired policies. Such shared information among briefers likely influences justices more for multiple reasons (Hazelton, Hinkle, and Spriggs 2019): it provides them with information regarding the consistency of the preferences among invested groups about whom they are incentivized to care (Spriggs and Wahlbeck 1997) and has a psychological effect on recipients.

As is more fully described in the introduction, there are several reasons why the justices might care about public opinion and, relatedly, the views of invested groups regarding a particular issue. While the Supreme Court enjoys a fair degree of judicial independence, its decisions are not self-executing. Instead, it must rely on others to carry out its edicts (Epstein et al. 1998; Epstein and Knight 1999; Hazelton, Hinkle, and Spriggs 2019). Government officials generally implement Supreme Court policy (Canon and Johnson 1998; Hall 2010). Such officials are directly or indirectly tied to the public and its preferences. Furthermore, the public's support for the Court and its acceptance of the Court's decisions is based on perceptions of legitimacy that may be influenced by individual decisions (Hazelton, Hinkle, and Spriggs 2019; Clawson and Waltenburg 2008; Gibson and Caldeira 1992; Hoekstra 2000, 2003; Ura and Merrill 2017). Additionally, legislation can alter much of the structure and appellate jurisdiction of the federal judiciary. Therefore, the justices have reason to care if the public would support it against attacks from the other branches (Friedman 2009; Gibson and Caldeira 1992; Hall 2010, 2014; Spriggs 1996; Spriggs and Wahlbeck 1997).

Of course, the extent to which the public knows and cares about an issue and the details of any preferences may not be easily discoverable (Friedman 2009; Hazelton, Hinkle, and Spriggs 2019; Pildes 2011; Rosen 2006). Thus, the opinions of the groups interested enough to invest the resources to prepare a brief, as opposed to merely cosigning a brief, are of particular value to the Court (Hazelton, Hinkle, and Spriggs 2019). They help the Court assess the extent to which such resourced groups care, what they want, and how unified the groups are in the specific policies they seek (Hazelton, Hinkle, and Spriggs 2019; Rice 2020). Consequently, the presence of shared language across briefs filed for a side helps justices determine the extent to which policy coalescence exists among groups that are likely to be affected by a decision. A lack of a consensus among briefers for a side signals to the Court that there is increased uncertainty in the policy area, making a decision in that direction riskier (Collins 2008).

As described in chapters 2 and 3, former Supreme Court clerks and attorneys who have practiced in the Court described aspects of briefs and relationships among party and amicus briefs that indicate the importance of policy coalescence. First, many interviewees described how the Supreme Court focuses on broader issues of policy. Second, many individuals described the importance of briefers focusing on critical issues. Third, many interviewees asserted that amici could be helpful when they provided information regarding real-world implications of potential decisions, particularly regarding the potential impact for their groups.

Additionally, shared information likely exerts a psychological effect on justices for several reasons (Hazelton, Hinkle, and Spriggs 2019). Attorney and Former Clerk I noted the possible psychological effect of briefs. They also described the importance of "ideas" above outcomes. I noted that different types of briefs "help. . . move the law." In their estimation, sometimes decision-makers will want to move the law but "don't let [themselves] realize it." The judges are "not fully conscious" of the desire. So, a brief should "send a signal, not a postcard," because they "help with the psychological dance" of judicial decision-making.

Overlap in texts helps readers disambiguate difficult material using a more resonant and automatic strategy than in the absence of such shared information (Anmarkrud, Bråten, and Strømsø 2014, 65; Kurby, Britt, and Magliano 2005). Coherence is particularly crucial in complex tasks such as legal reasoning and judicial decisions (Hazelton, Hinkle, and Spriggs 2019; Holyoak and Simon 1999; Simon and Hollyoak 2002). Furthermore, research indicates that information articulated by most sources has a conversion effect on recipients that may stem from social pressures to conform (Moscovici 1980). Justices may feel related pressures to maintain popular support and legitimacy (Hazelton, Hinkle, and Spriggs 2019). Previous research also indicates that consistency in messaging across sources that share a desired outcome bolsters such majority information (Meyers, Brashers and Hanner 2000). Furthermore, the fact that multiple sources are saying the same thing can act as a heuristic for the value of a position (Spriggs and Wahlbeck 1997): it can help one assess risk (Erb et al. 2015), importance (Nemeth, Mosier, and Chiles 1992), and reasonableness (Canary, Brossmann, and Seibold 1987; Hazelton, Hinkle, and Spriggs 2019). Finally, there is evidence that repetition has an independent persuasive effect, whereby a position seems more convincing the more often it is stated (Collins and Martinek 2015). There is also evidence that such psychological effects likely operate in tandem (Toelch and Dolan 2015; Hazelton, Hinkle, and Spriggs 2019).

Prior research in this area provides evidence that shared information is influential on the policy announced in decisions. In Hazelton, Hinkle, and Spriggs (2019), we found that the more shared information a brief contained, the more similar the opinion was to the submission. Additionally, other research has shown that repeated arguments (Spriggs and Wahlbeck 1997) and rules (Wofford 2015) are more likely to be adopted by the Court and that directly overlapping language across briefs increases the chance that those phrases will appear in the opinion (Canelo 2022; Collins and Martinek 2015; Feldman 2017a).

Thus, there are a plethora of reasons to anticipate that shared information in briefs influences the content of decisions. Informational, institutional, and psychological theories all suggest that where parties and amici have a more unified focus on what they discuss, the opinion will be more likely to look like the briefs. Both qualitative and prior quantitative evidence bolster that view. Therefore, we hypothesize that Supreme Court opinions will be more similar to submissions with more shared information.

Data and Methods

Here, we explore the relationship between the content of individual party[7] and amicus briefs and the text of the Court's majority opinion. Due to differences in the types of briefs, we do so in separate models. Our unit of analysis is the brief, and the outcome variable is the similarity of the documents, as measured by the cosine similarity (see chapter 3) between the brief and opinion. As described in chapter 3, the full text of legal documents, especially briefs and opinions, are important because the articulation of facts and topics act to define the scope of the legal doctrines announced by the Court (Aldisert 1989; Braman and Nelson 2007; Schauer 1987; Sunstein 1993). Moreover, Canelo (2022) provides evidence that suggests justices can strategically disguise their reliance upon certain types of amicus briefs in order to not be perceived as overtly ideological actors. Finally, the information in briefs often influences majority opinions, even where the briefs are not quoted or cited (Lynch 2004).

For example, Simpson and Vasaly (2015) noted that Justice Kennedy adopted arguments from the amicus brief filed by Laurence Tribe and other constitutional scholars in the majority opinion in *Romer v. Evans* without citation.[8] Furthermore, a search for exact or very similar groupings of text would miss this connection: when we compare the majority opinion in *Romer* with that brief filed on behalf of the respondent using plagiarism software,[9] only 1 percent of the text of the majority opinion matches with the scholars' brief. An inspection of the overlapping text reveals that it is not related to the substantive arguments but rather are primarily references to the contested law and relevant constitutional provisions.

Thus, the influence of that important brief would be invisible using a plagiarism approach. Consequently, relying on more readily observable signals such as citation, quotation, or even unquoted use of precise phrasing from amicus briefs may well miss important aspects of how briefs influence opinions. To avoid missing these relationships, we use cosine similarity, which allows for a more nuanced understanding of the similarity between documents. The cosine similarity score for the influential amicus brief discussed above and the *Romer v. Evans* opinion is 0.57 (on a scale from zero to one). It is the highest score among the amicus briefs in that case and is second only to the respondent's brief. Thus, considering the similarity of the texts gives us a more robust means of assessing potential influence. Using cosine similarity helps broaden our understanding of the relationships between briefs and opinions. In our models, we include explanatory and control variables that capture aspects of four key areas that should influence the relationship between the brief and opinion: language, citations, and briefs; types of information; attorney and litigant characteristics; and litigation environment.

Language, Citations, and Briefs

First, we consider aspects of the language, including legal citations,[10] that appear in the briefs. We are mainly concerned with the extent to which information is unique or unusual. Thus, we investigate novel and shared information in three forms. First, we consider the overall novelty of the language found in the text generally and in the legal citations specifically (Hazelton, Hinkle, and Spriggs 2019).[11] To do so, we compare the brief at hand to others filed in the case and the lower court opinion(s). First, we consider the overall novelty of the words and citations. To do so, we take advantage of tf-idf scores (which we discuss in chapter 3 with relation to cosine similarity). Each unique word or cite within a brief is assigned a tf-idf score based on the number of times it appears within the brief inversely weighted in relation to how many other briefs and lower court opinions in the case use the same word or cite. We measure the briefs' relative novelty based on the words and cites' median score: larger scores indicate more novel content.

We also wish to measure the specific contributions of novel and shared information in terms of specific words and citations. To do so, we count the number of words (in the thousands—"Unique Words (1000s)") and citations (in the hundreds—"Unique Cites (100s)") that only that brief contains. Conversely, we also measure the number of shared words ("Shared Words (1000s)") and cites ("Shared Cites (100s)"). Additionally, if a brief reiterates more information from the lower court opinion, it may appear to have a larger impact on the Supreme Court opinion when the Supreme Court is, in fact, relying on the lower court. To account for this, we control for the cosine similarity between each brief and the lower court opinion(s) in the case. The measure, "Similarity to Lower Court Opinion," is calculated using the same procedure as the outcome variable. Finally, as we have done in previous chapters, we include a measure of the number of briefs, which here operates as a measure of the number of sources from which the Court may pull material (Hazelton, Hinkle, and Spriggs 2019).

These measures help us consider how the nature of information, whether reinforced or exclusive, is reflected in the majority opinion. As a point of illustration, we return to *Florida v. Harris*. As we noted at the outset of the chapter, the briefs filed by the parties and solicitor general were most like the majority opinion, with the cosine similarity score with Florida's main brief being the highest. The briefs of the parties and solicitor general contained less overall unique information than the remaining amicus briefs.[12] The party briefs tended to have similar levels of shared and novel information with relatively small differences. Florida's brief contained more overall novelty in terms of words, unique words, and unique citations and fewer duplicated words than Harris's response. Florida's brief, on the other hand, had lower overall novelty in terms of citations and more duplicated citations.

There was variation among the amici in terms of distribution of shared and unique information. The solicitor general's brief for the United States generally contained lower amounts of unique information overall and toward the middle for shared information for all briefs in the case. The brief filed by the states supporting Florida exhibited overall low levels of both novel and shared information. The remaining brief filed on behalf of Florida by the National Police Canine Association along with the NACDL et al. brief filed on behalf of Harris, tended to sit in the middle of measures of unique and shared information. Additionally, the brief filed by the Fourth Amendment scholars in support of Harris was generally low in unique information and high in shared information. The three remaining amici filed on behalf of Harris contained the most novel information relative to shared information. The amicus briefs from EPIC and the Institute for Justice, which were least like the majority opinion, tended to score quite highly regarding measures of unique content. Additionally, EPIC's brief had very little shared information, while the Institute for Justice's brief contained moderate amounts. The brief for the Rutherford Institute, which was moderately similar to the majority opinion, was usually in the middle of the pack for unique information but also contained among the least shared information. The patterns are mixed but overall seem to suggest that unique information is not helpful and that shared information helps carry the day. To get a clearer picture, we need to go beyond anecdote and engage our rich data set.

Types of Information

We also consider the types of information in the briefs in terms of both content and presentation. First, we include variables to capture types of informational content. To start, we consider information regarding so-called love letters to the median justice. Specifically, we measure citations to precedent authored by the median ("Citations to Current Median"). We also account for information regarding the potential impact of various policy options in the form of technical language and legislative facts (Davis 1955; Margolis 2000). Using the Linguistic Inquiry Word Count (LIWC) software, we develop a measure of technical language and legislative facts using three indicators. First, quantitative language is associated with information pertaining to the state of the world and how a decision might change that state. We also include the use of words related to discussing causation[13] and parenthetical explanations (Bennett and Slocum 1985; Nida 1992), as both indicate this type of information. LIWC generates the percentage of words in the text that falls within each category. We sum these measures to calculate the total percentage of the brief that is more likely to be associated with a technical discussion. Next, we consider the extent to which language is related to the future, as such language indicates information regarding the potential implications of a decision. Legislative facts are generally about the predicted impact of specific policies on society (Margolis 2000). Thus, the language describing such facts tends to be future oriented. Therefore, we include a LIWC variable for the percentage of future-tense verbs in the brief.

Next, our focus turns to the presentation of information. First, we incorporate a measure of the accessibility of the written information: we include a measure of the approximate grade level of education needed to understand the document. Specifically, we use the SMOG measure of reading comprehension (McLaughlin 1969). Next, we consider the extent to which the brief includes emotional language. Prior research indicates that justices are less likely to vote for a party whose brief contains such verbiage (Black, Owens, et al. 2016). This relationship may stem from the unpersuasive nature of emotional language or the fact that briefers may rely more on such expressions when they have weaker arguments (Black, Owens, et al. 2016; Feldman 2016). In keeping with prior research (Black, Owens, et al. 2016; Bryan and Ringsmuth 2016; Hinkle and Nelson 2017), we utilize LIWC to calculate the percent of emotional language in the text ("Emotional Language").[14]

Attorney and Litigant Characteristics

Our third set of variables captures the characteristics of the litigants and attorneys who filed the underlying briefs. First, we include the log of the number of cosigners on the underlying brief as a measure of the breadth of support (Collins 2004). The number of attorneys signing the underlying briefs is an indicator of the underlying resources that parties and attorneys bring to a case (Galanter 1974). Therefore, we include the "Log Number of Attorneys" in our model. Previous research indicates that the litigation experience of both the represented filers and their attorneys is correlated with success (Galanter 1974). Thus, we include variables capturing the log of the number of previous briefs signed by the most experienced filer on the submission ("Log Max. Filer Exp.") and the attorneys on the briefs ("Log Max. Attorney Exp."). We use the log of the maximum experience for both because within small working groups the most experienced party and attorney likely supervise the production of the brief and elevate its quality. Additionally, former Supreme Court clerks are elite lawyers with a unique perspective on the Supreme Court. They are highly sought-after litigators (Black and Owens 2020; Ward, Dwyer, and Gill 2014): in 2018, the "prevailing rate" for signing bonuses for former Supreme Court clerks was $400,000.[15] Because clerks may provide different types of information than other authors, we include "Number of Former Clerks," capturing their participation.

It is well understood that when the solicitor general participates in a case, the side with which they are involved tends to win. This success may stem from expertise (Spriggs and Wahlbeck 1997), the fact that the solicitor general represents the United States government (Epstein and Knight 1998), or political/partisan issues (Bailey, Kamoie, and Maltzman 2005). To capture the possibility that the attorneys' skill and expertise drive this effect, we include a variable capturing the number of former solicitors general who signed the brief. To control for the power of the United States as the government and political issues, we include a binary variable for if the current solicitor general filed the brief. Sometimes the Court itself turns to certain sources, often the solicitor general, and invites them to submit an amicus brief (Shaw 2015). This type of invitation signals a particularly high level of trust. We account for this using a control variable that equals one if an amicus brief was invited by the Court (regardless of the identity of the invitee), and zero otherwise.

Litigation Environment

We also include variables capturing aspects of the litigation environ-ment that may influence the likelihood that the decision resembles the brief. First, the Supreme Court tends to take cases to establish new law via a reversal of the lower court (McGuire et al. 2009). We must account for this reality to avoid biased results regarding the relationship between the briefs assembled for petitioners and the content of the opinions. Thus, we include "Petitioner's Side," which captures if the submission is in favor of the petitioner (1) or not (for the respondent, 0). Next, justice ideology is a well-known factor in Supreme Court decision-making (Se-gal and Spaeth 2002). To control for this important feature, we include a variable capturing the ideological alignment between the median jus-tice and the side that the brief supports. Specifically, if the brief is seek-ing a conservative case outcome, we use the Martin-Quinn score of the Court median. At the same time, we multiply that score by negative one if the side seeks a liberal outcome.[16]

The length of the lower court opinion(s) may indicate aspects of the complexity of the underlying case that could confound the relationship among other variables. Consequently, we use the log of the lower court opinion(s)' word count ("Log Word Count LC"). Case salience may also bear on the relationship between briefs and the text of decisions. To avoid concerns regarding including post hoc measures of salience, we include a measure for amicus briefs in the lower court proceedings ("LC Amicus"). The Court may also signal some level of hostility toward a particular side by posing a large number of questions during oral argu-ments (Epstein, Landes, and Posner 2010). Consequently, we control for the number of questions posed during oral argument to the side the filer of a given brief is supporting. Finally, changes in the litiga-tion environment over time, including technological advances (John-son, Spriggs, and Wahlbeck 2012) and an increasingly sophisticated bar (Larsen and Devins, 2016; Lazarus 2008), likely influence the relation-ships among texts. We include a continuous variable for the term to capture any such effects.

The summary statistic for all variables can be found in table 5.1 for party briefs and table 5.2 for amicus briefs.

Table 5.1. Party Briefs—Summary Statistics

	Min.	25%	50%	75%	Max.
Outcome					
Cosine Similarity	0	0.59	0.66	0.72	0.89
Language, Citations, and Briefs					
Overall Novelty (Words)	0.01	0.04	0.05	0.06	0.41
Overall Novelty (Cites)	0	0.01	0.01	0.02	1.04
Unique Words (1000s)	0	0.29	0.41	0.57	1.77
Unique Cites (100s)	0	0.04	0.1	0.17	1.34
Shared Words (1000s)	0.33	97.5	154.64	213.60	1,361.01
Shared Cites (100s)	0	0.21	0.39	0.6	2.14
Similarity to Lower Court Opinion	0.01	0.49	0.6	0.68	0.9
No. of Briefs	1	4	6	10	114
Types of Information					
Citations to Current Median	0	0	2	5	58
Technical Language	3.67	6.74	7.68	8.96	20.05
Future Language	0.18	0.69	0.82	0.98	2.89
Grade Level	12.78	15.6	16.34	17.15	21.86
Emotional Language	0.8	2.16	2.66	3.22	8.88
Attorney and Litigant Characteristics					
Log No. of Cosigners	0.69	0.69	0.69	0.69	2.83
Log No. of Attorneys	0.69	1.1	1.61	1.95	4.06
Log Max. Filer Exp.	0	0	0	1.39	7.72
Log Max. Attorney Exp.	0	0.69	2.4	4.44	6.11
No. of Former Clerks	0	0	0	1	7
No. of Former SGs	0	0	0	0	2
Current SG	0	0	0	0	1
Court Invited Brief	0	0	0	0	1
Litigation Environment					
Petitioner's Side	0	0	0	1	1
Ideological Alignment	−1.26	−0.8	0.07	0.8	1.26
Log Word Count LC Opinion	0.69	8.01	8.6	9.16	11.1
Amicus Activity in Lower Court	0	0	0	0	1

No. of Oral Arg.					
Questions to Side	1	43	57	71	174
Term	1984	1988	1994	2002	2015
Observations	**5,258**				

Results

Based on the fractional nature of cosine similarity (it exists between 0 and 1), we utilize fractional logistic regression to assess its relationship to shared and novel information and other important aspects of the cases. To account for interdependence between briefs within the same case, we cluster the standard errors accordingly. The results of regressions can be found in figures 5.1 and 5.2.[17] It should be noted that the results for the variables capturing aspects of language, citations, and briefs are reported in a separate figure due to issues of scale regarding the coefficients. Some of the coefficients in this grouping are much larger in scale than the other groupings. Thus, when all categories are in one figure, it is harder to discern the estimates with precision.

Our primary focus in this chapter is the relationship between novel and shared information and the Court's opinion. We begin our analysis of the results by considering how novel language and citations influence the content of the legal policy announced by the Court. For both the main party and amicus briefs, an increase in "Overall Novelty (Words)," "Overall Novelty (Cites)," and "Unique Words (100s)" are associated with a statistically significant decrease in similarity with the Court's opinion. Similarly, the estimates for "Unique Cites (100s)" are both negative, though the results are only statistically significant for amici. Thus, we find that novel information is detrimental in terms of the opinion reflecting the brief's contents. In turning to shared information, we anticipate that the opposite will be true. The results support this position: "Shared Words (1000s)" increase the similarity to the opinion for both party and amicus briefs. Additionally, "Shared Cites (100s)" increase the similarity for amicus briefs but not party briefs. We also find that both party and amicus briefs that are more similar to the lower court opinion share more with the Supreme Court opinion. For party briefs, the inverse is true with the number of submissions: where there are more briefs in the case, each individual party brief is less similar to the Court's opinion.

Table 5.2. Amicus Briefs—Summary Statistics

	Min.	25%	50%	75%	Max.
Outcome					
Cosine Similarity	0	0.38	0.49	0.59	0.87
Language, Citations, and Briefs					
Overall Novelty (Words)	0.02	0.08	0.09	0.12	0.88
Overall Novelty (Cites)	0	0.02	0.03	0.05	2.06
Unique Words (1000s)	0	0.12	0.19	0.28	1.45
Unique Cites (100s)	0	0.01	0.03	0.08	0.99
Shared Words (1000s)	0.36	27.2	48.31	73.33	565.86
Shared Cites (100s)	0	0.08	0.18	0.33	1.6
Similarity to Lower Court Opinion	0	0.31	0.43	0.54	0.89
No. of Briefs	2	8	12	21	114
Types of Information					
Citations to Current Median	0	0	0	2	64
Technical Language	2.79	6.49	7.37	8.38	23.24
Future Language	0	0.69	0.86	1.06	2.96
Grade Level	11.83	16.18	17.05	18.08	24.18
Emotional Language	0.74	2.42	2.97	3.61	8.7
Attorney and Litigant Characteristics					
Log No. of Cosigners	0.69	0.69	0.69	1.39	6.95
Log No. of Attorneys	0.69	1.1	1.39	1.79	4.44
Log Max. Filer Exp.	0	0.69	2.4	4.47	7.7
Log Max. Attorney Exp.	0	1.1	2.3	3.89	6.09
No. of Former Clerks	0	0	0	1	7
No. of Former SGs	0	0	0	0	1
Current SG	0	0	0	0	1
Court Invited Brief	0	0	0	0	1
Litigation Environment					
Petitioner's Side	0	0	1	1	1
Ideological Alignment	−1.26	−0.69	−0.12	0.58	1.26
Log Word Count LC Opinion	0.69	8.28	8.84	9.35	11.1
Amicus Activity in Lower Court	0	0	0	1	1

No. of Oral Arg.					
Questions to Side	1	47	61	75	174
Term	1984	1991	1999	2005	2015
Observations			**12,200**		

The results also shed light on several aspects of Supreme Court litigation. In terms of types of information, party and amicus briefs with more future language, which is associated with legislative facts, share more in common with the ultimate Court opinions. The opposite is true for amicus briefs with more emotional language. The results regarding party briefs and emotional language are not statistically significant. We also do not find statistically significant relationships between the opinion and citations to the current median, technical language, grade level, or emotional language for either party or amicus briefs.

Regarding attorney and litigant resources and characteristics, we find that both the log number of attorneys and cosigners on a brief are not significant for parties or amici. Experience, on the other hand, is generally useful: for filers acting as amici and attorneys for both parties and amici, the ultimate opinion looks more like the briefs of more experienced, and likely more reputable, filers and attorneys. Experience is not significant for party filers. The number of former clerks signing a brief is only significant for amici, and the number of former solicitors general is not significant in either instance. In keeping with prior research, the solicitor general is particularly influential when he or she files a party or amicus brief.

Finally, the litigation environment matters. Unsurprisingly, petitioners are more likely to prevail in shaping the content of opinions than they are in obtaining reversals. There is no evidence that ideological alignment between a brief and the median of the Court increases the similarity to the majority opinion, but this is less surprising when one considers that we are using the median of the full Court rather than just the majority coalition.[18] Both the complexity and salience of a case, as measured by the "Log Word Count LC Opinion" and "Amicus Activity in Lower Court," negatively influence the similarity between the brief and opinion. A party brief is less influential when that party faced more questions from the justices during oral argument. Finally, term is significantly negatively associated with similarity for amici but not parties.

Language, Citations, and Briefs

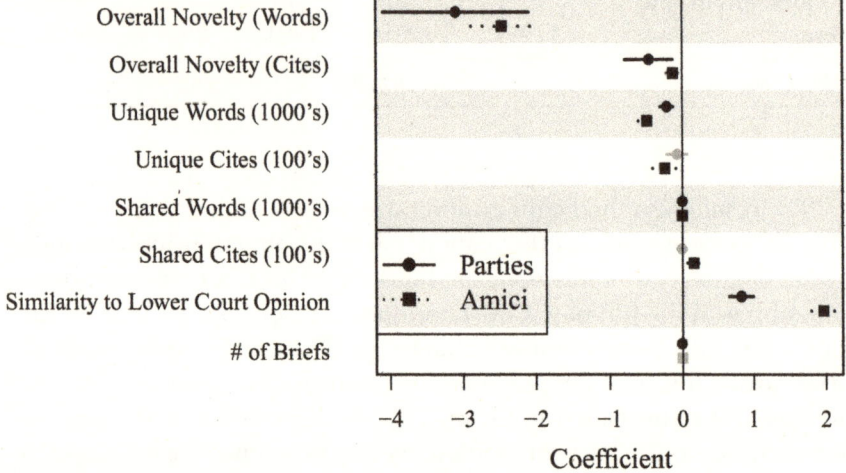

Figure 5.1. Cosine similarity. Fractional logit estimates of the effect of the characteristics of briefs, including unique and shared information, on the similarity between the text of the opinion and individual briefs for both parties and amici separately. For the party model, coefficients are marked by circles, and 95 percent confidence intervals are solid lines. For the amicus model, coefficients are marked by squares, and 95 percent confidence intervals are dotted lines. Estimates and confidence intervals in gray (instead of black) indicate that the confidence interval includes zero.

We also include the changes in predicted cosine similarity in figure 5.3 to allow for an understanding of the substantive impacts of these variables, which are relatively small. The largest effect ("Similarity to Lower Court Opinion" for amicus briefs) is 0.11, which is approximately two-thirds of the standard deviation in cosine similarity (0.16). Additionally, all of the remaining effects are within –0.05 and 0.05, and thus less than a third of the standard deviation. For example, regarding "Overall Novelty (Words)" in party briefs, moving from the twenty-fifth percentile to the seventy-fifth percentile results in a change in the predicted cosine similarity with the majority opinion of –0.014. For amicus the change results in a change in the predicted cosine similarity of –0.025. Similarly, a change from 290 to 570 unique words that appear in a party brief, but no other brief or lower court opinion in the case, corresponds to change of –0.014. For amicus, the difference between 120 to 280

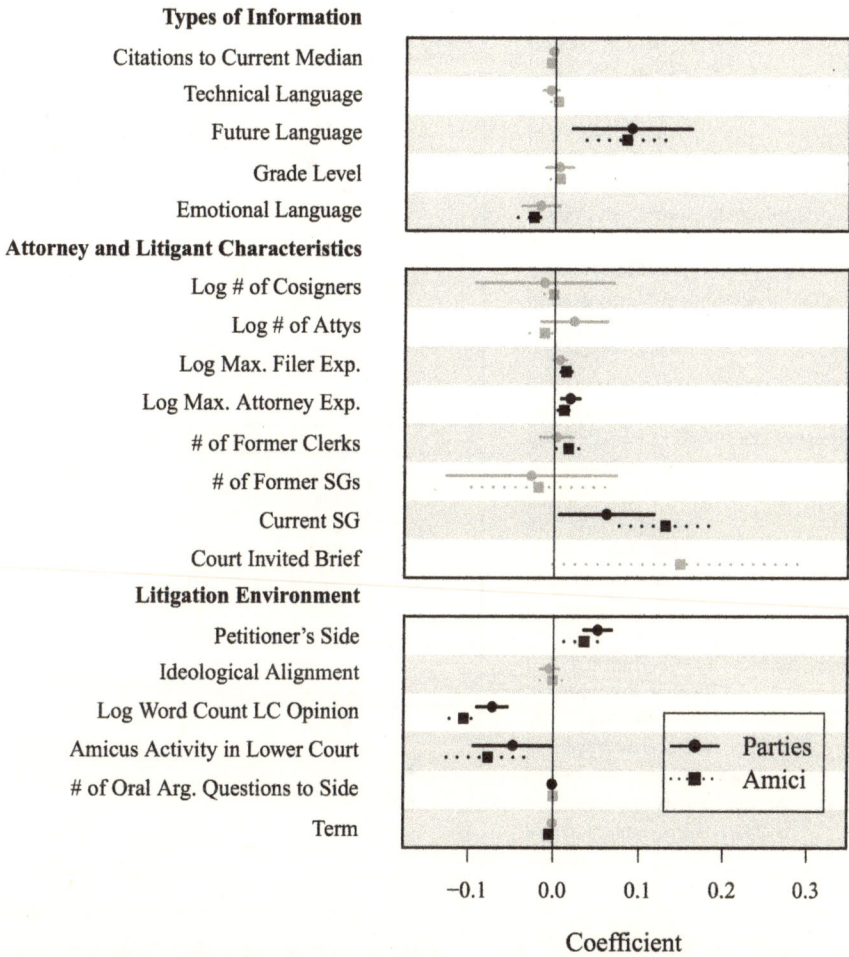

Types of Information
Citations to Current Median
Technical Language
Future Language
Grade Level
Emotional Language
Attorney and Litigant Characteristics
Log # of Cosigners
Log # of Attys
Log Max. Filer Exp.
Log Max. Attorney Exp.
# of Former Clerks
# of Former SGs
Current SG
Court Invited Brief
Litigation Environment
Petitioner's Side
Ideological Alignment
Log Word Count LC Opinion
Amicus Activity in Lower Court
# of Oral Arg. Questions to Side
Term

Parties
Amici

−0.1   0.0   0.1   0.2   0.3

Coefficient

Figure 5.2. Cosine similarity (continued). Fractional logit estimates of the effect of types of information, attorney and litigant characteristics, and a range of control variables on the similarity between the text of the opinion and individual briefs for parties and amici separately. For the party model, coefficients are marked by circles, and 95 percent confidence intervals are solid lines. For the amicus model, coefficients are marked by squares, and 95 percent confidence intervals are dotted lines. Estimates and confidence intervals in gray (instead of black) indicate that the confidence interval includes zero.

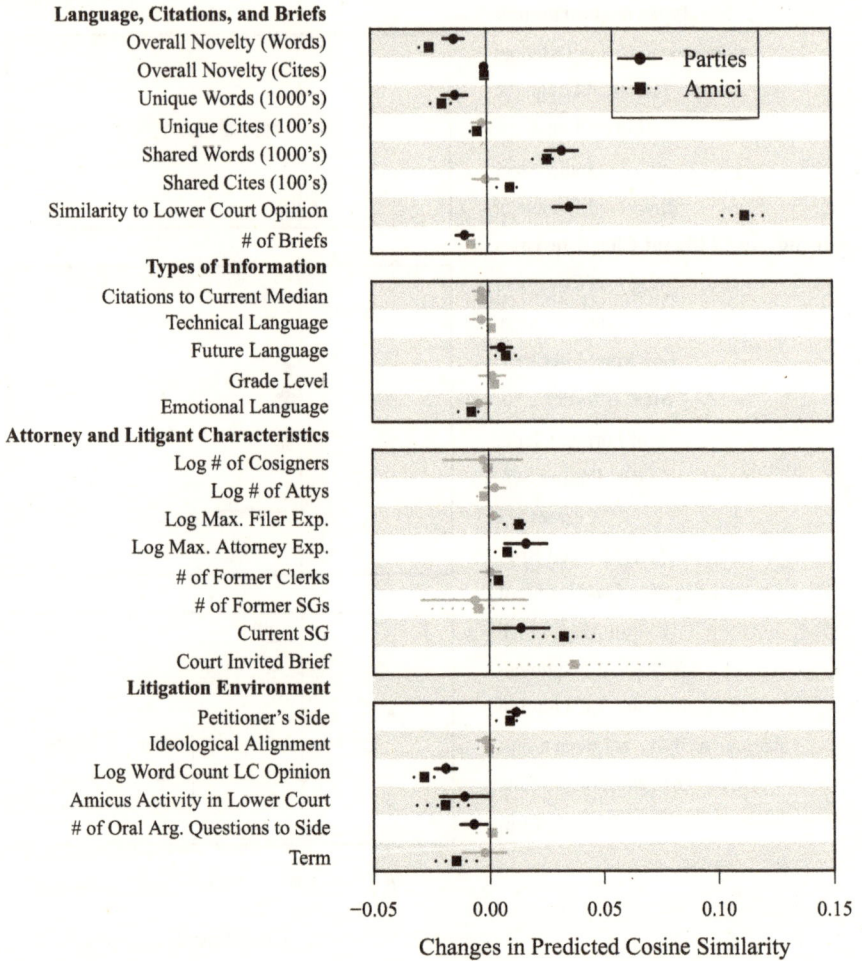

Figure 5.3. Changes in predicted cosine similarity. Estimates with 95 percent confidence intervals of the change in the predicted cosine similarity generated by moving each variable from a low to high value while holding all other variables at their medians. The difference variables for former clerks and solicitors general, the current solicitor general, and amicus activity are moved from zero to one. All other variables are moved from their twenty-fifth to seventy-fifth percentile values, except log number of cosigners for the parties model, which is held at the minimum and maximum to allow for variation. Estimates and confidence intervals in gray (instead of black) indicate that the confidence interval includes zero.

unique words results in the difference of –0.019. Thus, these effects are substantively small but statistically significant. Of course, the collective increase across many briefs may have a notable effect.

Conclusions

In this chapter, we pivoted toward considering the text of the Court's opinion. Majority opinions represent the ultimate statements of legal policy that shape not only future cases but also the behavior of individuals and officials outside of courtrooms. Specifically, we focus on the extent to which information is reflected in the Court's opinion based on whether a single filer or multiple briefers raised it. Our results provide additional support for the proposition that shared information takes the day when it comes to the Supreme Court and opinion content. Furthermore, it indicates that policy coalescence and related psychological phenomena may be at play: where parties and amici focus on common elements, they are more likely to be able to shape the opinion of the Court. The benefits of seeking novel information in amicus briefs are likely felt outside of opinion construction. When crafting majority opinions, the justices are very unlikely to reach for information that is off the beaten path and untouched by other briefs. These patterns lend credence to the idea that the Court cares about external actors and the public (or at least groups within that public). Additionally, the influence of language regarding the future indicates that the Court is keenly interested in the possible ramifications of their decisions in keeping with our interviews. Our results also suggest that experience matters for both amici as filers and attorneys generally, and that the repeat-player effect likely stems from the knowledge and skill of those involved.

Such influence may ease some concerns regarding possible countermajoritarian tendencies on the Court, but perhaps not all. While prior research indicates that amicus participation pulls from many quarters and looks pluralistic (Collins 2018), it is unclear how it shapes opinions in the absence of policy coalescence. For others, these results likely continue to raise concerns; without direct electoral accountability should justices shape policy based on input from groups in society? How can we level a playing field so heavily influenced by experience? Our research helps bring us closer to being able to address such concerns.

6 | Shaping the Law Together
Collectively Influencing
Opinion Content

Based on accounts of US Supreme Court decision-making, the justices and their clerks confronted the briefs in *Florida v. Harris* as a collection. The corpus presented to them consisted of eleven briefs. The five briefs advocating for Florida were 17,756 words in total, and the remaining six in favor of Harris included 28,687 words. From this collection of briefs, words, and information, the Court ultimately produced an opinion that reflected the consensus of the briefs asking for a reversal: Aldo's training was sufficient and the search was constitutional. If we anticipated that the raw total of information alone was likely to carry the day, this result would be surprising, as would the fact that the majority opinion was more like the collective briefs for Florida (0.78) than those assembled for Harris (0.69). But when we consider this case and, more importantly, thousands of other cases in the context of research regarding reading comprehension and judicial decision-making, a more complex picture emerges.

In our investigation of the information flowing through briefs to the Court, we present a multifaceted view providing a more comprehensive understanding. Having considered the relationship between individual briefs and the opinion in previous chapters, we turn to the influence of the collective submissions within a case. In other words, we seek to understand the forest in addition to the trees. In this chapter, we consider how the language, resources, and types of information that groups bring together on behalf of a side shape the majority opinion the Court releases. Here, we focus specifically on the combined text of briefs filed on each side of a case and their relationship to the policy announced in the decision. Building on chapters 4 and 5, other work considering the influence of the total information rallied for one side on outcomes, and the relationship between briefs and decisions, we consider the effect of bodies of text on the pronouncement of the legal rules that will define policy in the area.

Studying the texts as a collective body is warranted by theory and evidence regarding reading comprehension generally and the practices of justices and clerks specifically. While it is important to consider the relationship between individual briefs and opinions, justices and their clerks deal with groups of submissions when crafting the language that will define the judicial policies that the Court announces. Additionally, there is evidence, including our interviews and analyses in chapter 3, indicating that parties and amici tend to coordinate in the overall production of briefs with an eye toward such collective consumption. Despite evidence that coordination is common among parties and amici, researchers generally treat briefs as independent of each other. Therefore, it is also essential to probe how the text for each side as a whole influences the more refined policies announced by the Court via the text of the opinion (Collins and McCarthy 2017; Salzman et al. 2011).

We proceed by first engaging theory and research regarding reading comprehension and policy coalescence generally along with specific evidence regarding how lawyers and parties produce and justices and clerks consume such information. Next, we describe our data and methods, focusing on four types of factors that likely influence the similarity between opinions and bodies of briefs: aspects of the language, citations, and briefs; types of information; attorney and litigant characteristics; and the litigation environment. We then turn to our analyses, carried out at both the case-side and case levels, which reveal patterns consistent with our theory: the results indicate that the Court responds to policy coalescence and the psychological effects of repetition. Specifically, we find evidence that shared information within a collection of briefs influences the policy the Court announces in terms of both individual sides and relative influence. Relatedly, we find evidence, though varied, that types of information related to policy influence the text of the opinion. There is also some evidence that resources matter but the effect sizes are rather modest.

Collective Information and Decision-Making

Clerks and justices are readers who do not encounter briefs individually but rather as part of a collection of writings. As with other general types of decision-making, clerks and justices are pulling information from multiple sources (Anderson 1971; Massaro and Friedman 1990). Research indicates that the number of sources and arguments in favor of a position influences how individuals process it (Harkins and Petty 1981a, 1981b). When confronted with multiple documents, proficient readers create a mental model of the texts and a coherent global meaning (Afflerbach and Cho 2009). This "global understanding. . . is constructed by linking activities which can be explained as comparing, contrasting, relating, and differentiating information contained in each single text" (79). When reading texts, humans use comprehension strategies (Afflerbach and Cho 2009; Anmarkrud, Bråten, and Strømsø 2014). Such approaches are likely even more needed when individuals are called upon to read and comprehend "multiple challenging, conflicting documents on a complex issue" (Anmarkrud, Bråten, and Strømsø 2014, 65; see also Myers and O'Brien 1998; O'Brien and Myers 1999), such as legal briefs in Supreme Court cases. Existing research indicates that these strategies likely vary based on the amount of semantic overlap in the documents: where there is a high level of overlap, individuals integrate information more automatically whereas when such overlap is lacking, more effortful strategies are required to comprehend the materials (Anmarkrud, Bråten, and Strømsø 2014, 65; Kurby, Britt, and Magliano 2005). Thus, overlap in texts helps readers disambiguate difficult material using a more resonant and automatic strategy (Kurby, Britt, and Magliano 2005). Furthermore, there is evidence that legal documents that are easier to understand are more likely to be used by judges (Nelson and Hinkle 2018).

Within the broader model, readers create mental connections between sources regarding the extent to which they agree or disagree (Anmarkrud, Bråten, and Strømsø 2014, 65). Readers also monitor and identify aspects of the text that they do not understand as they read (Anmarkrud, Bråten, and Strømsø 2014; Afflerbach and Cho 2009). When a reader is confronted with problematic text, they will refer to other documents in the corpus to help them resolve the confusion. In processing the texts and relating them to each other, readers also form beliefs regarding the "usefulness and trustworthiness of the individual documents" (Afflerbach and Cho 2009, 79).

The construction of this global understanding across texts is directly related to assessing policy coalescence among briefs and the psychological factors related to repetition that we investigated in the previous chapter. Where briefs provide consistent, overlapping messages, justices and clerks can assess the coherent global meaning in a relatively less taxing and more cohesive manner. Again, this is consistent with prior research and our findings in chapter 5, indicating that repetition may have both heuristic and conforming effects (Hazelton, Hinkle, and Spriggs 2019). It is also compatible with existing studies that indicate that duplication in briefs is associated with more positive outcomes for briefers (Corley, Steigerwalt, and Ward 2013; Corley and Wedeking 2014; Feldman 2017a; Hazelton, Hinkle, and Spriggs 2019; Spriggs and Wahlbeck 1997; Wofford 2015). As we saw in our example of *Florida v. Harris* in the introduction, the side with the more consistent themes across briefs (Florida) ultimately took the day: the Court agreed that decisions regarding probable cause about drug-sniffing dogs should be made based on training, not other forms of evidence.

We are particularly interested in the ways justices and their clerks consume briefs. Specialized writing genres, such as legal writing, require specific knowledge, tools, and strategies to comprehend (Dewitz 1995). Prior studies indicate that novices and experts approach legal texts differently, with lawyers, skilled law students, and judges being more efficient and fluid in their approaches (Christensen 2008; Lundeberg 1987; Sinsheimer and Herring 2016). Justices and their clerks are the product of elite training (Kurtz and Simon 2007; McGuire 1993; Ward and Weiden 2006). Clerks help summarize and filter information from the briefs for the justices (Peppers and Ward 2012) as well as draft opinions (Peppers and Zorn 2008). As a result, these groups make up an expert class that can approach legal text more effectively than those who lack the relevant training and experience in the legal field.

Based on our interviews, clerks consume the information in briefs more as a whole, rather than in individual pieces. For instance, Former Clerk K described the mechanics of reading briefs. They began reading the briefs after they were all in as opposed to reading them one at a time as they were filed. The method they used was to flip the order of the briefs, reading the last of the party briefs first and working backward. "By doing that," they were able to "first pinpoint the most resonant issue in the start." In other words, by starting in "reverse," they could move from the targeted issue to the big picture. They noted that "the reply has all of it" and represents a "refined thought process." The most important "cases and authorities are usually highlighted in the final filing." They would also look at the amicus briefs as they were oriented toward the focal issue. Similarly, Former Clerk L described briefs as coming in "packages," with amicus briefs fleshing out the party briefs.

As described in chapter 3, a few former clerks reported attempting to assess the extent to which a brief presented new information in determining how closely to read the document; this implies that justices and their clerks consume briefs, in part based on their relationships with each other. Such an account is in keeping with the results of a survey of former clerks (Lynch 2004) and the statements of Justices Roberts (36) and Stevens (47) (Garner 2010). Research must reflect the reality that justices and clerks are consuming briefs in a collection (Anderson 1971; Massaro and Friedman 1990, 225).

Additionally, as we addressed in chapter 3, Supreme Court insiders (including litigators and former clerks) report that coordination is common among briefers (Larsen and Devins 2016), a characteristic that briefing has in common with lobbying generally (Hula 1999). Such coordination has become commonplace with an increasingly sophisticated Supreme Court bar (Larsen and Devins 2016; Lazarus 2008). The fact that many parties and amici are producing briefs with an eye toward how justices and clerks will read them together is another reason to consider them from a collective perspective.

Finally, the collective resources brought together in support of a side are likely to influence the opinion (Buckler 2015; Galanter 1974; Szmer and Ginn 2014). As we described in chapters 2 through 5, resources are related to many crucial aspects of briefing and decision-making. First, as discussed in more detail in chapters 2 and 4, individuals and groups with more resources can retain attorneys who have the skill and experience necessary to produce high-quality legal arguments and better informational content (see also Wanner 1975; Wheeler et al. 1987; Atkins 1991; Songer and Sheehan 1992; McCormick 1993; Albiston 1999; Farole 1999; Songer, Sheehan, and Haire 1999; Szmer, Songer, and Bowie 2016). Second, those individuals and groups with more means and capabilities enjoy advantages regarding coordination, which is explored in more detail in chapter 3 (Hula 1999; Lazarus 2007; Larsen and Devins 2016; McGuire 2004). Third, there is evidence, discussed in chapter 4, that more experienced attorneys enjoy reputational benefits. Finally, at the level of individual briefs (chapter 5), we see that resources in the form of experience result in greater similarity to the opinion. These factors indicate that the collective resources assembled on behalf of a side are likely to influence the opinion.

Thus, we undertake our investigation to consider how the collective body of information assembled in a case, both within and between sides, shapes the opinion of the Court. We anticipate that sides that coalesce regarding the information they provide to the Court will be more influential than sides with more disparate language due to the political implications of such coalescence and the psychological effects of repetition. In keeping with the previous chapter, we theorize that the more collective novel information the briefs for a side contain, the less information from that corpus will appear in the Supreme Court's opinion; alternatively, the less new information the briefs for the side contain, the more information from that corpus will appear in the Supreme Court's opinion. Relatedly, we posit that information pertinent to policy, such as language regarding the future and technical information, will be more influential. We further expect that the Court is impacted by participation when it involves a greater investment, as described in more detail in chapter 4. Finally, we hypothesize that influence will increase with resources and the collection of information related to the effects of potential decisions.

Data and Methods

We turn to our original data set to assess the influence of the collective information presented for a side via briefs on Supreme Court opinions. Here, we focus on the similarity between the text of the Court's decision and the collective text filed on behalf of a side. The similarity of these documents is important due to the broader societal impact of the legal rules announced in the opinion (Collins 2018). Additionally, considering document similarity allows us to carry out a more nuanced investigation of influence than analyzing which side won (Hazelton, Hinkle, and Spriggs 2019). As with chapters 3 and 5, we use cosine similarity, a computational linguistics measure of document similarity, to capture our outcome of interest.

We carry out two related analyses regarding the influence of the collective information brought together by a side. For the first analysis, we consider the factors that influence the relationship across the collective information for the side and the text of the decision. The dependent variable is the cosine similarity of the majority opinion and the texts assembled on behalf of the side. The unit of analysis is the side formed by the party, petitioner, or respondent and amicus briefs filed on the party's behalf. As a result, there are two observations from each case, one for the petitioner's side and one for the respondent's side. This first analysis allows us to consider overall trends between information assembled for a side and similarity to the opinion text.

For the second analysis, we consider how the differences in the relative characteristics of the two sides shape the Court's opinion. The unit of analysis is the case. The outcome of interest is the difference in the cosine similarity of each side and the opinion text. Specifically, we start with the cosine similarity across all briefs on the petitioner's side and the opinion. Then, we subtract from that the cosine score for all the respondent-side briefs' resemblance to the majority opinion. Positive values of the outcome variable indicate that the majority opinion is more similar to the petitioner-side submissions. Negative values indicate that the majority opinion is more like the respondent-side briefs. Thus, this second analysis allows us to consider how differences in the characteristics relate to differences in influence over the content of the decision. While the two investigations are closely related, testing both allows us to explore nuances between what causes similarity with the majority opinion generally and in relation to the information assembled for the other side.

As in the previous two chapters, our explanatory and control variables capture aspects of four key areas: elements of the language, citations, and briefs; types of information; attorney and litigant characteristics; and the litigation environment. However, in this chapter, the measures that we use to capture language, citations, and briefs were designed and selected to measure collective information (similar to chapter 4) as opposed to information at the individual brief level as in chapter 5. To begin, we use several measures to capture aspects of the underlying briefs filed on behalf of a side. First, we look to the underlying words in the briefs. We consider the overall length of the collective briefs per side. Specifically, we calculate the "Log Word Count"[1] of each group of briefs. We also investigate the collective vocabulary of the assembled briefs by counting the number of unique words (in thousands). By including both word count and vocabulary, we can consider the relative influence of the breadth of information instead of the coalescence around specific language (and vice versa). A larger vocabulary indicates that a set of briefs discusses a wider set of topics and ideas. Conversely, a smaller vocabulary reflects greater coalescence among briefs.

Next, we look at legal citations within the briefs, as they represent a type of specialized language within legal writing (Collins 2008; Hazelton, Hinkle, and Spriggs 2019; Hansford and Spriggs 2006). Like our treatment of words, we include the count of all citations to Supreme Court precedents in hundreds ("Total Cites")[2] within the briefs per side as well as the number of unique precedents cited in hundreds ("Precedent Vocabulary"). Finally, we controlled for the total "Number of Briefs" per side as both a measure of the breadth of support by invested parties that a side enjoyed (Caldeira and Wright 1990a) and a potential confounder regarding the number of words and citations.

Touching back with *Florida v. Harris*, we can consider how the "Language, Citations, and Briefs" variables compared across the sides in the case. As mentioned in the introduction to this chapter, the majority opinion was more similar to the total text assembled on behalf of Florida. Florida had one less brief filed on behalf of its side than Harris, had 10,931 fewer words (which we measure in terms of logged word counts), and a smaller vocabulary by 1,570 words. Regarding citations, on the other hand, Florida had twenty-one more total cites and a larger citation vocabulary by six cites. In terms of our theory regarding repetition, we would anticipate that more briefs, words, and citations and smaller vocabularies of both words and cites would be beneficial, as it would allow for the greatest levels of signaling policy coalescence. The patterns in our example case do not perfectly reflect our theory. To fully take in how these features matter in judicial decision-making, we look to the larger data.

The variables that capture aspects of the types of information, attorney and litigant characteristics, and litigation environment generally mirror those seen in chapter 5 except that they were calculated at the case-side level (please see those descriptions for further details). Regarding types of information, we capture aspects of the content of the briefs—"Citations to Current Median," "Technical Language," and "Future Language"—as well as how the information is presented—"Grade Level" and "Emotional Language." For attorney and litigant characteristics, we investigate the influence of resources by including the log number of cosigners, log number of attorneys, number of former clerks, number of former solicitors general, whether the current solicitor general was involved, and the number of invited briefs. It should be noted that by looking at the level of the case-side (and later case) level, we can tease out the relative influence of general support for a side as opposed to costly support: with both the number of briefs filed for a side and the overall number of cosigners for the submissions, we can isolate the effect of each while holding the other factor constant. This helps us explore the importance of costly involvement and information compared with the number of affected groups (Collins 2004). We anticipate that the Court is more influenced by costly participation than the number of affected parties (Hazelton, Hinkle, and Spriggs 2019). To capture filer and attorney experience, we include variables capturing the log of the median number of previous briefs signed by both all the filers of the briefs ("Log Median Filer Exp.") and the attorneys on the briefs ("Log Median Attorney Exp."). We use the median measures rather than the maximums found in chapter 5 because here we are considering the typical effect of the briefs assembled for a side.[3] Finally, we capture the litigation environment with "Petitioner's Side," "Ideological Alignment," "Log Word Count LC Opinion," "Amicus Activity in Lower Court," "No. of Oral Argument Questions to Side," and "Term."

For the second analysis at the case level, we focus on the difference in cosine similarity. Thus, we calculate all the difference variables regarding "Language, Citations, and Briefs," "Types of Information," and "Attorney and Litigant Characteristics" by subtracting the values for the respondent side from the values for the petitioner side. Regarding "Litigation Environment," we use the difference in oral argument questions and drop the variable capturing whether the briefs were filed on behalf of the petitioner, as every observation includes the differences between the two sides. All other variables regarding litigation are the same as those found on the case-side level.

Summary statistics for all the variables at the case-side level can be found in table 6.1. The summary statistics at the case level are available in chapter 4 in table 4.1.

Results

Case-Side Analysis

Because our first outcome variable, "Cosine Similarity," is bounded between zero and one, we use fractional logistic regression to assess the relationships between the outcome variable and the explanatory and control variables. Additionally, due to the relationship across briefs within the same case, we also include robust standard errors clustered

Table 6.1. Case-Side Summary Statistics

	Min.	25%	50%	75%	Max.
Outcome					
Cosine Similarity	0	0.67	0.73	0.79	0.92
Language, Citations, and Briefs					
Log Word Count	6.61	8.94	9.41	9.89	12.59
Document Vocabulary (1000s)	0.34	1.94	2.71	3.71	19.37
Total Cites (100s)	0	0.58	1.07	1.85	18.66
Precedent Vocabulary (100s)	0	0.46	0.84	1.44	14.91
No. of Briefs	1	2	3	5	71
Types of Information					
Citations to Current Median	0	1	4	12	242
Technical Language	3.77	6.85	7.67	8.74	17.24
Future Language	0.24	0.75	0.86	0.99	2.39
Grade Level	12.61	15.85	16.49	17.22	21.41
Emotional Language	0.77	2.29	2.77	3.31	8.89
Attorney and Litigant Characteristics					
Log No. of Cosigners	0	0.69	1.39	2.48	7.34
Log No. of Attorneys	0	1.79	2.4	3.14	5.92
Log Median Filer Exp.	−0.69	0	1.1	3.78	8.95
Log Median Attorney Exp.	−0.69	1.39	2.94	4.48	7.47
No. of Former Clerks	0	0	1	3	36
No. of Former SGs	0	0	0	0	5
Current SG	0	0	0	1	1
No. of Briefs Invited by the Court	0	0	0	0	2
Litigation Environment					
Petitioner's Side	0	0	1	1	1
Ideological Alignment	−1.26	−0.8	0.04	0.8	1.26
Log Word Count LC Opinion	0	7.98	8.57	9.11	11.1
Amicus Activity in Lower Court	0	0	0	0	1

(continued on the next page)

Table 6.1. *Continued*

	Min.	25%	50%	75%	Max.
	Litigation Environment				
No. of Oral Arg.					
Questions to Side	1	43	57	71	174
Term	1984	1988	1994	2002	2015
Observations		**4,912**			

on the case. The results of the fractional logistic regression analysis can be found in figure 6.1.[4]

First, we consider how aspects of the briefs themselves influence the relationship between the collective writings and the opinion. We find that the total number of words assembled on behalf of a side significantly increases the similarity between the briefs for that side and the Court's opinion. The opposite relationship holds for the side's vocabulary, which indicates the number of distinct words. In figure 6.2, we provide graphical representations of the relationships between cosine similarity and the logged word count and vocabulary, respectively. These two results together reinforce prior findings, which suggest that repetition across briefs is associated with better outcomes (Collins, Corley, and Hamner 2013; Hazelton, Hinkle, and Spriggs 2019; Spriggs and Wahlbeck 1997): holding the log of the word count constant, more unique words in the briefs results in an opinion that is less like the briefs for that side; while a larger number of words overall increases the similarity to the opinion when vocabulary is held constant. Thus, in keeping with our theory, policy coalescence and repetition are associated with more similar opinions. The results regarding precedent, specifically for total cites and precedent vocabulary, are significant and follow the same trends as the general language of the corpora. Additionally, the number of briefs filed for a side is significantly related to more similar opinions. This finding is in keeping with our results in chapter 4 and prior research finding that the number of amicus filers is related to winning cases (Caldeira and Wright 1990b). Furthermore, the fact that the number of briefs is significant while controlling for the number of cosigners indicates that costly participation, as opposed to general involvement, influences the rules the Court announces.

Language, Citations, and Briefs
Log Word Count
Vocabulary (1000's)
Total Cites (100's)
Precedent Vocabulary (100's)
# of Briefs
Types of Information
Citations to Current Median
Technical Language
Future Language
Grade Level
Emotional Language
Attorney and Litigant Characteristics
Log # of Cosigners
Log # of Attys
Log Median Filer Exp.
Log Median Attorney Exp.
# of Former Clerks
# of Former SGs
Current SG
# of Briefs Invited by the Court
Litigation Environment
Petitioner's Side
Ideological Alignment
Log Word Count LC Opinion
Amicus Activity in Lower Court
# of Oral Arg. Questions to Side
Term

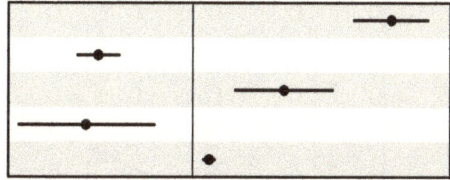

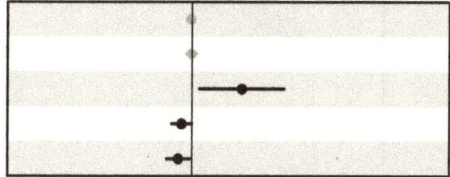

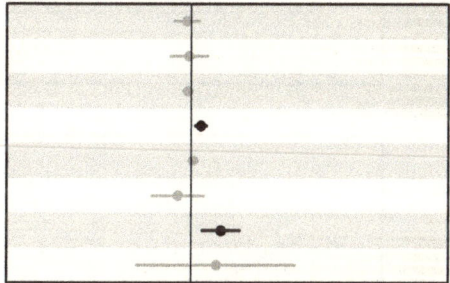

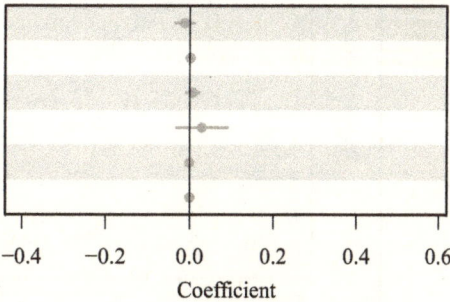

−0.4   −0.2   0.0   0.2   0.4   0.6
Coefficient

Figure 6.1. Cosine similarity by case side. Fractional logit estimates (and associated 95 percent confidence intervals) of the effect of amount and type of information, attorney and litigant characteristics, and a range of control variables on the similarity between the text of the opinion and the collective briefs filed on behalf of one side. Estimates and confidence intervals in gray (instead of black) indicate that the confidence interval includes zero.

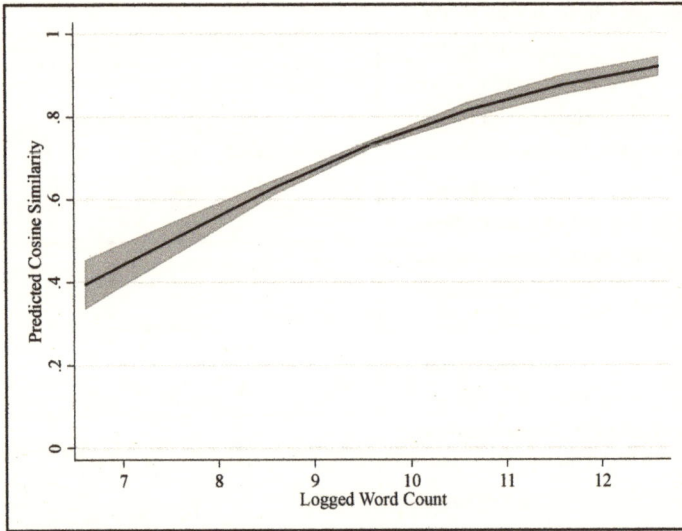

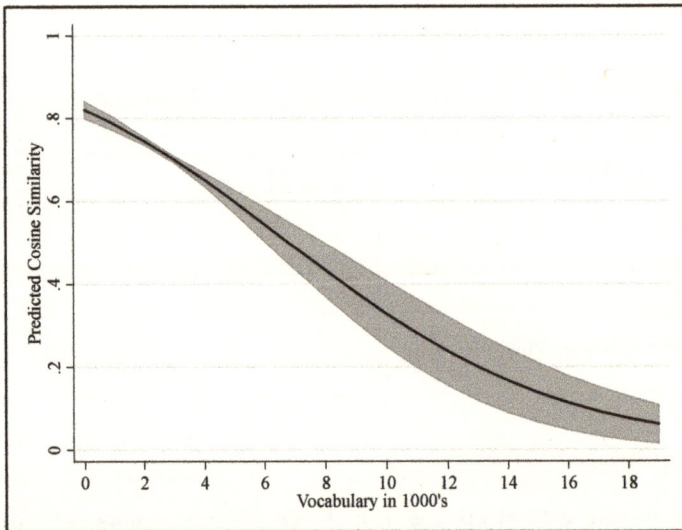

Figure 6.2. Predicted cosine similarity over the range of log
word count and vocabulary (1000s): Predicted cosine similarity
between the opinion and briefs assembled for a side over
the range of log word count (top) and vocabulary (1000s)
(bottom). All other variables are held to their central values in
keeping with figure 6.3.

Next, we consider how the types of information found in the collective briefs influence the content of the majority opinion. First, we find that "love letters" to the median in the form of citations to their former opinions did not have a statistically significant effect. The percentage of types of technical language was also not significant. We do, however, find that higher percentages of future language relate to overall document similarity. Additionally, higher grade levels in the underlying briefs for a side negatively correlate with similarity to the majority opinion. An increase in the percentage of emotional language is significantly associated with a decrease in resemblance to the opinion. These findings are in keeping with our theory.

Moving from the texts to the characteristics of the attorneys and litigants behind the briefs, we find many interesting relationships with the Court's decisions. First, there is no evidence that the number of cosigners or attorneys on a side is associated with similarity to the majority opinion. We also do not find a significant effect for the median experience of filers; the median experience of the attorneys behind the briefs, however, is a significant factor in increasing similarity. The presence of former clerks is not significant at the case-side level. In addition, while we do not find that the presence of past solicitors general is associated with higher document similarity, the support of the current solicitor general significantly increases similarity with the opinion. This illustrates the importance of political conditions and the United States as a participant.

Finally, we considered the litigation environment in which the case was located. None of our variables related to these factors are statistically significant when considering the collective features per side.

To provide information regarding the substantive effects of the variables, we also report the differences in predicted cosine similarity from this analysis in figure 6.3. A standard deviation in similarity for this aggregation of data is 0.13. Thus, while our largest effects of moving from a low to high value are around two-thirds of a standard deviation, some of the effects are much smaller. Specifically, moving from the twenty-fifth percentile values for the "Log Word Count" (which maps to approximately 7,640 words) to the seventy-fifth percentile (corresponding to approximately 19,750 words) results in an increase of predicted similarity of 0.092. The equivalent change in "Document Vocabulary (1000s)" (moving from a vocabulary of 1,940 words to 3,710) results in a decrease in similarity of −0.08. On the other hand, the relative size of the effect of

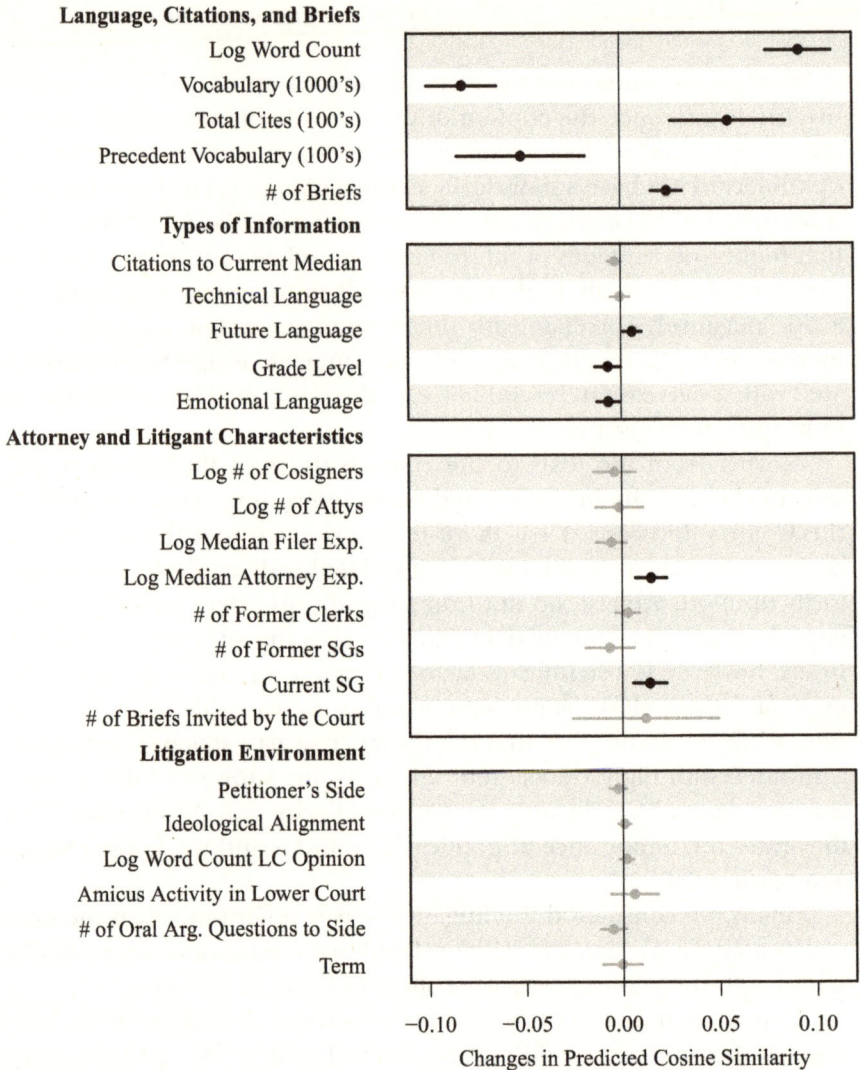

Language, Citations, and Briefs
Log Word Count
Vocabulary (1000's)
Total Cites (100's)
Precedent Vocabulary (100's)
# of Briefs
Types of Information
Citations to Current Median
Technical Language
Future Language
Grade Level
Emotional Language
Attorney and Litigant Characteristics
Log # of Cosigners
Log # of Attys
Log Median Filer Exp.
Log Median Attorney Exp.
# of Former Clerks
# of Former SGs
Current SG
# of Briefs Invited by the Court
Litigation Environment
Petitioner's Side
Ideological Alignment
Log Word Count LC Opinion
Amicus Activity in Lower Court
# of Oral Arg. Questions to Side
Term

−0.10   −0.05   0.00   0.05   0.10

Changes in Predicted Cosine Similarity

Figure 6.3. Changes in predicted cosine similarity by case side. Estimates (and associated 95 percent confidence intervals) of the change in the predicted cosine similarity between all briefs on a side and the majority opinion generated by moving each variable from a low to high value while holding all other variables at their median. Most continuous variables are moved from their twenty-fifth to seventy-fifth percentile values. The only exceptions are former solicitors general and number of briefs invited by the court, which are moved from zero to one along with the binary variables. Estimates and confidence intervals in gray (instead of black) indicate that the confidence interval includes zero.

the median experience of the attorneys behind the briefs is rather small for most cases: moving the "Log Median Attorney Experience" from the twenty-fifth percentile (1.39) to seventy-fifth percentile (4.48) results in a 0.015 increase (a little more than a tenth of a standard deviation) in predicted cosine similarity.

Case Analysis

Now, we turn to our analysis at the case level to consider the extent to which differences within cases matter. Since our second outcome variable, "Difference in Cosine Similarity," is a continuous measure (albeit bounded between negative one and one), we use linear regression to assess the relationships between the outcome variable and the explanatory and control variables. The regression analysis can be found in figure 6.4.[5]

As with the case-side analysis, we find that relatively longer corpora (petitioners compared to respondents) are associated with comparatively greater similarity to the opinion. Yet, corpora with relatively larger vocabularies are negatively associated with such similarity. Again, these findings indicate that policy coalescence and psychological factors related to repetition likely play an important role in shaping policy making at the Court. Neither the relative difference in total cites or precedent vocabulary is significant when considering the difference in cosine similarity between the sides. The number of briefs, however, is significant and positive, indicating that there is strength in numbers with regards to costly participation in obtaining an opinion whose language reflects the information one's side provided.

The results concerning the types of information vary from those in the previous case-side analysis. Unlike in the case-side model, we find evidence that where a side enjoys an advantage with respect to technical language, it will have more relative influence over the opinion language. Differences in emotional language, on the other hand, do not have significant effects at this level. The results are consistent with those for the case-side model regarding the differences in language focused on the future and grade level. The side that talks about the future more and uses a more accessible writing style fares better.

Next, attorney and litigant characteristics also reveal some differences with the case-side analysis. Unlike at the case-side level, the differ-

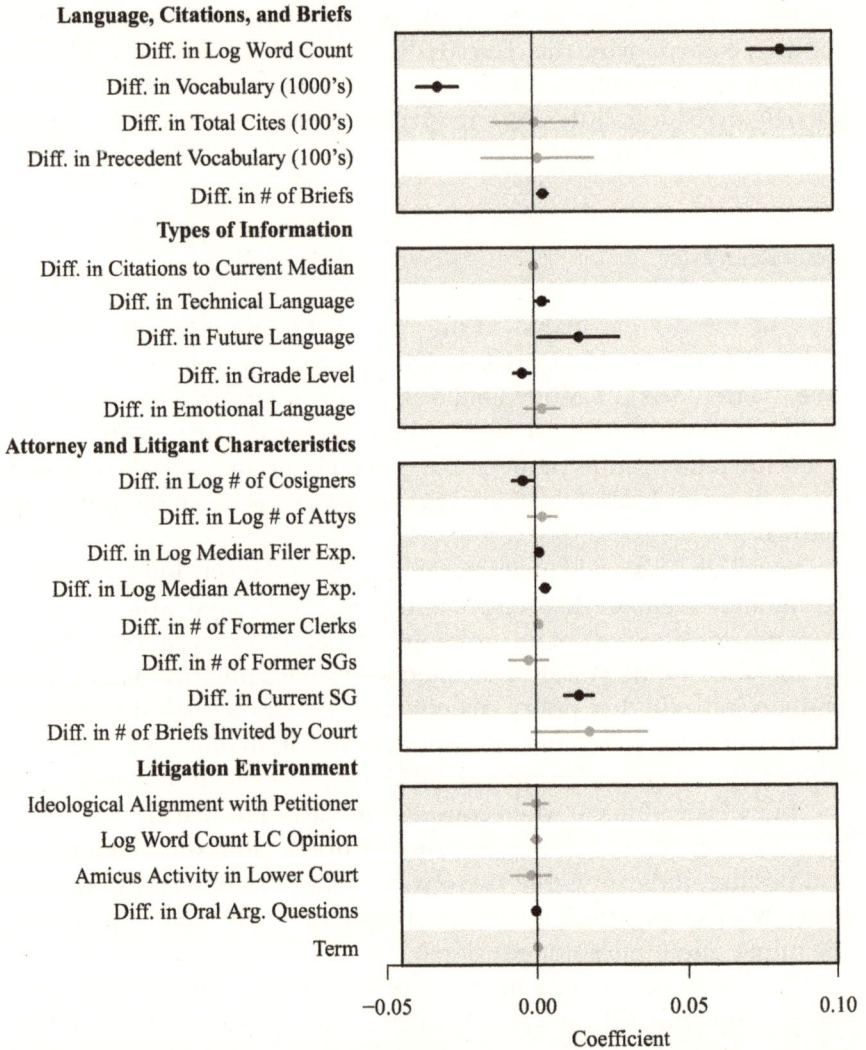

Language, Citations, and Briefs
Diff. in Log Word Count
Diff. in Vocabulary (1000's)
Diff. in Total Cites (100's)
Diff. in Precedent Vocabulary (100's)
Diff. in # of Briefs
Types of Information
Diff. in Citations to Current Median
Diff. in Technical Language
Diff. in Future Language
Diff. in Grade Level
Diff. in Emotional Language
Attorney and Litigant Characteristics
Diff. in Log # of Cosigners
Diff. in Log # of Attys
Diff. in Log Median Filer Exp.
Diff. in Log Median Attorney Exp.
Diff. in # of Former Clerks
Diff. in # of Former SGs
Diff. in Current SG
Diff. in # of Briefs Invited by Court
Litigation Environment
Ideological Alignment with Petitioner
Log Word Count LC Opinion
Amicus Activity in Lower Court
Diff. in Oral Arg. Questions
Term

Coefficient

Figure 6.4. Differences in cosine similarity by case. Linear regression estimates (and associated 95 percent confidence intervals) of the effect of differences in the amount and type of information, attorney and litigant characteristics, and a range of control variables between the two sides on differences in the similarity between the text of the opinion and the collective briefs. Estimates and confidence intervals in gray (instead of black) indicate that the confidence interval includes zero.

ence in the log of the number of cosigners for a case is significant and negative. Additionally, the difference in log median experience by filer is positive and significant. The remaining results are consistent with the case-side model. The difference in the log of the number of attorneys is not statistically significant whereas the difference in the log of the median attorney experience is positive and significant. As before, the differences in former clerks and solicitors general and an amicus brief invited by the Court are not significant. Finally, where the petitioner's side has the backing of the current solicitor general, the opinion is significantly more likely to resemble the petitioner's briefs. The continued importance of the "Current SG" indicates that a relative advantage in political power influences opinion content. Additionally, the results regarding litigation environment mirror the case-side analysis for the most part, except that the difference in the number of questions posed to each side at oral argument is statistically significant.

We again provide the changes in predicted differences in cosine similarity to allow for an understanding of the substantive size of the effects in figure 6.5. The standard deviation for the difference in similarity at the case level is 0.076. Our largest difference in predicted similarity moving from the twenty-fifth percentile value to the seventy-fifth percentile, for the "Difference in Log Word Count," is near a full standard deviation (0.071). Likewise, moving from a difference in vocabulary of where the petitioner has 570 fewer words than the respondent to a case in which the petitioner has 910 more words results in a change of difference in similarity of –0.046 (over half a standard deviation). There is also a slight increase in relative similarity with the opinion where the median filer for a side has more experience than the other side. In contrast, some effects are very small in substantive terms. The difference between a petitioner being asked fourteen fewer questions than the respondent in oral arguments to being asked fifteen more results in a difference of –0.008 in predicted change in similarity, or a little over a tenth of a standard deviation.

Conclusions

Founded on the understanding that individuals make decisions based on multiple sources of information, our approach of considering all the evidence assembled in favor of a side in Supreme Court litigation

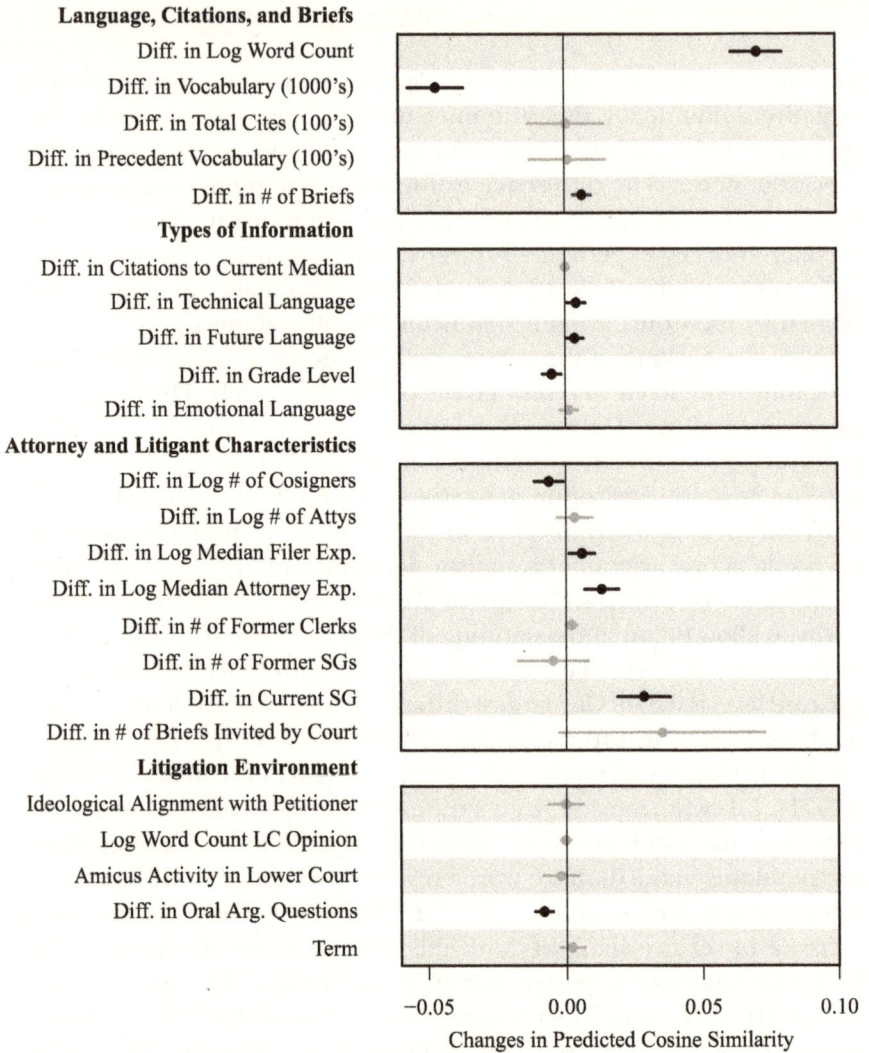

Language, Citations, and Briefs
Diff. in Log Word Count
Diff. in Vocabulary (1000's)
Diff. in Total Cites (100's)
Diff. in Precedent Vocabulary (100's)
Diff. in # of Briefs

Types of Information
Diff. in Citations to Current Median
Diff. in Technical Language
Diff. in Future Language
Diff. in Grade Level
Diff. in Emotional Language

Attorney and Litigant Characteristics
Diff. in Log # of Cosigners
Diff. in Log # of Attys
Diff. in Log Median Filer Exp.
Diff. in Log Median Attorney Exp.
Diff. in # of Former Clerks
Diff. in # of Former SGs
Diff. in Current SG
Diff. in # of Briefs Invited by Court

Litigation Environment
Ideological Alignment with Petitioner
Log Word Count LC Opinion
Amicus Activity in Lower Court
Diff. in Oral Arg. Questions
Term

−0.05   0.00   0.05   0.10
Changes in Predicted Cosine Similarity

Figure 6.5. Changes in predicted differences in cosine similarity by case. Estimates (and associated 95 percent confidence intervals) of the change in the predicted difference in cosine similarity generated by moving each variable from a low to high value while holding all other variables at their median. The difference variables for former clerks and solicitors general, the current solicitor general, and invited briefs are moved from negative one to one. The binary variable for amicus activity in the lower court is moved from zero to one. All other variables are moved from their twenty-fifth to seventy-fifth percentile values. Estimates and confidence intervals in gray (instead of black) indicate that the confidence interval includes zero.

helps advance our understanding of such decision-making. Our results confirm the role of repetition by showing that it is beneficial at the levels of both the case-side and case level in shaping opinions. We also find indications that costly participation matters in shaping opinions, as evidenced by consistent findings that the number of briefs matters even while controlling for the number of cosigners. Next, we provide mixed evidence regarding the influence of types of information: when considering the relationship between the text assembled for a side and the opinion, we find evidence that the Court is influenced, albeit modestly, by information that is oriented toward future implications from policy while also being dissuaded by emotional language and writing that is more difficult to read; the latter effect is not apparent in the differences model estimated at the case level, where we find evidence that the side with relatively more technical information, future information, and accessible language in the collective briefs enjoys greater similarity with the decision compared to the opposing side.

Additionally, we find evidence, although modest in effect sizes, that collective resources matter in shaping the language that defines the law announced by the Court. Attorney experience significantly correlated with more similar decisions in both analyses. This stands in contrast to the lack of findings regarding the number of attorneys. Also, the participation of the current solicitor general is significant and positive across the board. When it comes to the attorneys, it is quality that matters as opposed to quantity. Furthermore, in the differences model, greater filer experience was also associated with more opinion overlap. These results collectively reinforce a view of the Court as caring about interest groups and policy coalescence among such groups. In the previous two chapters, we found that former clerks have an advantage in terms of case outcomes, case votes, and having their amicus briefs influence the majority opinion. However, when examining influence over the opinion at the case level, in either absolute or relative terms, there is no evidence of former clerks shaping legal policy to a greater extent than other attorneys. While one should be very careful not to accept the null hypothesis or compare coefficients across differing models, the estimate for the influence of former clerks at a collective level is very close to zero (0.005) and with relatively low uncertainty (the standard error is also 0.005). This suggests that despite the huge signing bonuses law firms pay to hire Supreme Court clerks, there are limits and nuance to the benefits former clerks can provide to a firm's high court practice. This finding is consistent with Black and Owens's (2020) study that showed the size of a clerk's impact on votes was conditioned by when and for whom they clerked.

As with chapter 5, the results indicate that the Court does likely operate in a somewhat democratic way, as it is influenced by the extent to which groups are participating and agree and offer information regarding the impact of potential policies. For those who are concerned that this participation may not reflect the broader citizenry, these results, in conjunction with prior research indicating that participation tends to look reasonably pluralistic (Collins 2018), may offer some comfort: while we find resources matter, the effects are relatively small. However, we do find that costly participation, as measured by the filing of individual briefs, influences legal policy, while there is no evidence that general participation does. Thus, the haves are likely to come out ahead but in relatively modest ways.

Conclusion

As Clayton Harris's case made its way to the Supreme Court, the parties and a myriad of interested groups and individuals weighed in with a wealth of information via briefs. This information included legal arguments, data regarding the potential impact of the decision, emotional pleas, and beyond. In some instances, such as the Supreme Court briefs in favor of Florida, the information was fairly consistent. In those submissions, the briefers argued that the dog sniff passed constitutional muster based on training. At other points, such as the focus of some of the amicus briefs for Harris, some briefers were more likely to make unique points. In one example, the filer discussed the implications of a ruling for airport screenings. The fact that the two sides varied in the information they presented should be of no surprise given the difference in resources, including experience, enjoyed by the two sides. That case illustrates the complexity and importance of the amount of information in briefs, including total, novel, and shared material and the types of information. It also suggests the implications of differential resources being brought to bear.

We sought to go far beyond one case, to consider how these factors and more help explain the production and consumption of information at the Supreme Court. Our goal has been to explore these elements by developing theories that integrate the existing literature with insights from practice guides and in-depth interviews of individuals engaged in the trenches of Supreme Court briefing, both as writers and readers. We tested those theories using a large, comprehensive, and nuanced data set that leverages computational linguistics. This large-scale empirical investigation enables us to shed new light on both the construction and impact of briefs. In this concluding section, we provide an overview of this work in three parts. First, we outline how different factors shape the production and consumption of briefs. We provide an integrated view regarding how the roles of quantity and types of information, attorney and litigant characteristics and resources, and the litigation context matter regarding what information reaches the Supreme Court and what the justices do with it. Next, we discuss the most crucial elements of how this work has contributed to our big picture understanding of the role information and resources play in the Supreme Court. First, our research sheds new light on the relationship between how information is provided and consumed. Second, it also reveals that information operates differently in terms of influencing who wins and what policy is announced. Third, we offer new evidence that the resource advantage enjoyed by some parties likely stems from both the ability of their experienced attorneys to craft excellent briefs and their reputations with the justices. Fourth, we show how briefs provide vital information regarding policy coalescence among important groups and individuals to the Court. The next section describes the opportunities for future research on this topic, including limitations of our work and the resultant exciting new avenues of investigation for which we have paved the way. Finally, we offer some concluding thoughts.

Factors Shaping the Production and Consumption of Briefs

By considering both the creation and impact of the information in briefs, we can consider the roles of key concepts throughout multiple facets of Supreme Court litigation. Specifically, we assess the extent to which the identity of the briefers and what they provide matter. In doing so, we can provide a more nuanced and comprehensive picture of both Supreme Court litigation and informational lobbying, even where effect sizes tend to be small. We now turn to the four fundamental concepts: quantity of information, types of information, attorney and litigant characteristics and resources, and litigation context.

Quantity of Information

Naturally, briefs contain differing amounts of information. In chapter 2, we uncovered several factors that explain the sources of such variation. Characteristics of both attorneys and filers are important components. We found robust evidence that larger teams of attorneys, more experienced attorneys, and former clerks tend to include a greater amount and range of information in their briefs. Along similar lines, amicus briefs cosigned by a greater number of entities and those with more previous experience in the Supreme Court also contain a broader range of information. Further, we found that less information is included in briefs advocating for reversal and those submitted by filers who are more closely aligned with the Court ideologically: in both such cases, the brief-ers enjoy a tactical advantage. In the absence of such favored positions, parties and amici reach for a wider range of information to sway the Court.

In chapters 4 through 6, we examined how the quantity of informa-tion in briefs affects the Supreme Court's work product in a variety of ways. The side that simply includes the most words in their collective briefing gets more justices to vote for them and wins more cases. When it comes to influencing the content of majority opinions, the amount of information also matters, but the direction of influence depends on whether that information is repetitive or unique. When a brief includes more language found in other filings, the Court's opinion more closely resembles the brief. The same is true where amicus briefs contained shared citations. Conversely, when briefs stand out and look very differ-ent from the rest of the documents in the case, they have less influence in shaping the opinion. The same pattern appears at the aggregate level as well. It is the side that exhibits policy coalescence across briefs that has more influence over the opinion. In short, policies that enjoy shared support among briefers are etched into law, a finding that is consistent with institutional and psychological theory.

Even after accounting for the amount of information, the number of briefs still emerges as significant in some contexts. For example, there is less cohesion between party and amicus briefs when there are more fil-ings on a side. In cases where there is a wealth of amicus briefs bolstering the party brief, a different type of strategy appears to be afoot. Based on interviews, it is likely that attorneys are employing a divide-and-conquer approach in such cases or perhaps coordinating less with fringe groups. We also find that each individual party brief has a smaller impact on the text of the opinion in cases where there are more briefs. This pattern is a logical product of an increasing number of briefs because there are more options available for the justices to consult and, ultimately, rely upon. Finally, the side with more briefs is both more likely to win and exerts more influence over majority opinion content. These findings indicate that justices can be persuaded by the sheer number of those willing to invest extensive resources in creating a brief. Notably, more entities signing on to the briefs does not have a significant effect on winning and the side with more overall filers is actually less similar to the opinion. It is the number of briefs (which require substantial investment) rather than the total number of affected entities who join the fray, that carries persuasive weight.

Types of Information

In examining the effects of information, we looked at five different types. The side that includes more strategic information (in the form of citations to the current median justice) is more likely to win. Types of information related to policy making were also influential in certain instances. The side that uses more technical language of the kind found in Brandeis briefs is more likely to influence the majority opinion. Additionally, both individually and in the aggregate, briefs that discuss the future more have a greater influence over the opinion. This is in keeping with concerns regarding policy coalescence.

While the other two types of information show no evidence of shaping justice votes or case outcomes, they each have some impact on opinion formation. The side where the briefs are written in a more accessible way has a greater impact on the majority opinion. This suggests that while the complexity of writing may only matter at the margins, the simple, straightforward writing style recommended by legal writing experts can confer an advantage. When it comes to emotionally charged language, individual amicus briefs that avoid such language play a larger role in shaping the opinion. Along the same lines, a collection of briefs for one side that uses less emotional language also influences the opinion more. These findings comport with advice from legal writing experts to avoid unnecessary emotionality. Finally, the side with more technical information present in its briefs achieves greater similarity to the opinion. Overall, types of information played a much larger role in explaining opinion content than votes or case outcomes. This is in keeping with one of our interviewees' observations that the influence of briefs is primarily felt in the text of the opinion.

Attorney and Litigant Characteristics and Resources

As is true in many contexts, resources confer an advantage in Supreme Court litigation. This manifests in a variety of ways. We have uncovered considerable evidence that resources impact the way briefs are produced and consumed. First, we explore the impact of the number of filers and attorneys that sign each brief. Due to the time-intensive nature of extracting these numbers, previous work has focused primarily on the number of briefs. We provide the first extensive look at how the number of participants shapes what goes into briefs and litigation results. Amicus briefs with more filers contain more information and are more emotional while amicus briefs with more attorneys are written with a larger amount of information as well as more complex text, more strategic citations, more technical information, and less emotional language. Party briefs with more attorneys also contain more information and more strategic and technical information. Although the numbers of filers and attorneys affect the content of briefs in myriad ways, there is little evidence of the volume of participants affecting the case results. The only significant effect that the number of filers or attorneys had in chapters 4 through 6 is that the side with more overall cosigners than their opponents has a smaller affect on the text of the majority opinion.

Of course, not all filers and attorneys are equally well-equipped to succeed. We also considered the effect of how often the filers and attorneys had previously participated in filing briefs in the Supreme Court. As expected, repeat players are different than a one-shot participant in the high court. Experience can be golden. This is especially true when it comes to affecting the Court's policy. But it also shapes the way briefs are constructed. For example, more experienced filers produce amicus briefs with more total information, strategic citations, and technical information, and focus on the future and litigant briefs that are both more accessible and emotional. Briefs written by more experienced attorneys have more information overall, strategic citations, future-oriented discussion, and emotionality. The experience of filers and attorneys also drives the linguistic similarity between briefs but in different ways. For filers, there is less similarity between party and amicus briefs for a side when the parties have more experience and more when the amici have more experience. These results indicate that coordination strategies vary based on the different goals of parties and amici. However, attorney experience on the part of both parties and amici increases similarity between a party and amicus brief. Firsthand familiarity with the Supreme Court plays an important factor in the consumption of briefs as well as their production. More experienced attorneys lead to more positive outcomes on every measure of the Court's output we examine. While there is no evidence that filer experience has an impact on the probability of securing justices' votes or winning cases, the side with more experienced filers than their opponents does have a greater impact on the opinion.

Finally, we explored the role of attorney characteristics that should indicate greater ability to persuade the Court: former Supreme Court clerkships, previous experience as the solicitor general, and the current solicitor general. Former clerks write briefs with more information overall and more future-oriented and complex information. Their amicus briefs also have more strategic citations and technical language. Somewhat surprisingly, briefs written by both former and current solicitors general do not look considerably different from those written by other attorneys. The current solicitor general does write clearer amicus briefs, but the remaining few significant effects are not in the expected direction. Both current and former solicitors general write party briefs with less information, and former solicitors general write amicus briefs with fewer strategic citations and party briefs with less technical information.

Attorney qualifications also shape coordination, but it is amicus attorneys who emerge as important to this dynamic. Amicus briefs are more similar to the party brief when the legal team for the amicus includes more clerks, more former solicitors general, or the current solicitor general. Lastly, we turn to the case results. Former clerks get more votes and win more cases, and their amicus briefs have more influence over the majority opinion. However, there is no evidence of former solicitors general conferring an advantage over any type of Court output. Conversely, at every turn, the current solicitor general has the consistent positive effect we expect. The institutional role of the United States government is a powerful force in the Court. The side lucky enough to include the current solicitor general is more likely to secure justice votes, win the case, and shape the majority opinion.

Litigation Environment

Throughout our analyses, we controlled for various features of the litigation environment. Although those factors were not our primary focus, it is worth noting how they shape Supreme Court litigation. First, we were careful to account for the petitioner's side of the case in light of the Supreme Court's well-known tendency to reverse rather than affirm cases. Petitioners are inherently asking the Court to change the status quo. Because the Court tends to affect change in the matters it decides, petitioners enter the arena at an advantage. Interestingly, this position appears to affect the way litigants write their briefs. Compared to respondent briefs, petitioner briefs contain less overall information, less future-oriented and emotional language, more technical language, and more complicated syntactic structure. Amicus briefs filed on behalf of the petitioner have less overall information but otherwise no significant differences emerge when compared to amicus briefs filed on behalf of respondents. Furthermore, there is evidence that the coordination process is different for the two sides, with more similarity occurring between party and amicus briefs on the petitioner's side. Finally, as expected, both party and amicus briefs submitted on the petitioner's side are more similar to the majority opinion.

Judicial ideology is indubitably a fundamental element of Supreme Court decision-making, and we find that it matters in various ways through our analyses. The ideological alignment between the briefs and the median justice shapes how attorneys write. Both party and amicus briefs contain less overall information and more focus on the future when they are more closely aligned with the median. Amici aligned with the pivotal justice write in more simple, straightforward terms. However, there is no evidence that ideological proximity shapes the way parties and amici collaborate to coordinate the content of their briefs. Ideology has the expected effect on who wins and loses and how justices vote. However, when we examine how briefs shape opinion content in chapters 5 and 6, there is no evidence that the relationships between brief content and majority opinions are affected by ideological alignment with the median. This is not terribly surprising considering that many opinions are signed by a subset of the full Court.

Supreme Court cases vary in terms of legal complexity and salience to the public. Thus, these factors could confound our results if we do not include them based on the importance of the public to the Court. Measuring both of these features in a way that is not influenced by the briefs themselves is challenging. We turn to the lower court litigation to gain some traction on accounting for such variability. First, we argue that lengthy lower court opinions indicate tricky and complicated legal questions. Second, we leverage amicus participation in the lower court (which is fairly uncommon) as an indicator of exceptional salience. These variables are only statistically significant sporadically across our models. The litigant briefs have more information and less technical information and similarity to amicus briefs in more complicated cases. Particularly salient cases generate briefs that have more information overall and less focus on the future. These two variables affect the Court outputs in a couple of ways. In complex cases, the petitioner is less likely to garner individual justice votes and in more salient cases the petitioner is less likely to win. Finally, there is less overlap between each individual brief and the majority opinion in more complex and prominent cases.

Since our analyses span multiple decades, we control for the term to account for changing trends over time. And we find evidence for several such trends. Over the years, amicus briefs have shrunk in terms of overall content. This may be related to the proliferation of the number of amicus briefs. While the overall numbers have increased, each individual brief contains less information. The number of strategic citations has decreased in both party and amicus briefs with each passing year. This may be due to sophisticated briefers getting a sense about the results we show empirically in chapters 4 through 6: strategic citations are largely ineffective, and even where they are statistically significant, the substantive size of the effect is negligible. Submissions have increased in the complexity of the writing and those filed by litigants have increased in emotion and technical information while discussing the future less. We also find a trend in coordination. Over time, the overlap between party and amicus briefs has declined. The Court's tendency to favor the petitioner has only intensified with the decades. Finally, the overlap between the majority opinion and amicus opinions has decreased. That is likely also related to the trend of an increasing number of such briefs.

Major Contributions

Among our many findings, four overall takeaways stand out as particularly important contributions to how we understand the process of influencing the Supreme Court and policy makers generally. The first is that factors known to influence Court outputs also shape the way briefs are produced. We provide the first comprehensive empirical analyses of both how briefs are composed individually and how briefs reflect coordination between parties and amici. The resources and experience of both filers and attorneys play a role in these processes in complex and nuanced ways. For example, amicus briefs from more experienced filers contain more information overall, more strategic citations to the median justice, and a higher concentration of technical information and future-tense verbs. When it comes to coordination, this factor plays different roles for parties and amici. When the amicus filers have more experience, there is a greater amount of cohesion with the text of the party brief while the opposite is true regarding party filers.

Our second major takeaway is that the information within briefs, in terms of both amount and content, primarily influences the majority opinion's content rather than who wins and loses. This finding is hardly surprising since information is nuanced by its very nature, and opinions contain far more subtlety than the binary determination of whether to affirm or reverse the lower court. While the outcome of who wins the case matters to the litigants and has an important link to the opinion's content, it is the details in that opinion that generate the legal policy that governs people's lives. For example, if in *Mapp v. Ohio* the Supreme Court had ruled in favor of Dollree Mapp on the grounds that the Ohio obscenity law violated the First Amendment (the argument her attorney pursued in her brief), that case would have had a very different impact than their ruling that the Fourth Amendment mandates the use of the exclusionary rule (an argument from the ACLU's amicus brief).[1] Opinions matter. And, we provide evidence that the amount and type of information in briefs, both individually and collectively, impact majority opinions.

The third major contribution is expanding knowledge of how resources can provide an advantage in the Supreme Court. Understandable data limitations have previously hindered disentangling the various mechanisms that might drive the often-observed resource advantage. We devoted the time and effort necessary to both quantify the level of resources in more detail than previous work and quantify the amount and content of information in briefs. These data enabled us to uncover the reality that resources provide two types of advantage. First, filers with more extensive resources can produce briefs with more and better-presented information. Those types of briefs wield greater influence over the content of majority opinions. However, there is a second conduit of influence as well. Greater resources lead to better results in the Supreme Court even after controlling for the briefs' content. Filers with lots of money can hire big-name litigators with Supreme Court experience. Such members of the elite Supreme Court bar craft better briefs. But the justices also know they can trust such attorneys since repeat players in the Supreme Court environment can't afford to get caught misleading the Court. The evidence that both of these mechanisms are in play suggests that even a brilliantly crafted brief submitted by those unfamiliar in the halls of the Supreme Court cannot fully compete with the elite attorneys and filers well known to the justices.

Finally, our results underscore the importance of costly signals and policy coalescence, in addition to psychological factors, in Supreme Court litigation. We show that affected groups theory provides an incomplete picture. There is some limited indication the justices rely on briefs to signal public opinion in the way proposed by that theory. But, the number of groups who sign briefs does not have much impact in our models. If the Court was using briefs as a way to simply estimate public opinion, we would expect that marshaling large numbers of filers to sign on to amicus briefs would have an effect. The side with a greater number of briefs does have an impact on both outcomes and opinion content, which suggests that justices care about costly signals of support to gauge the direction of public opinion and the salience of a topic. Generating a brief takes substantial resources while signing on to someone else's brief is little more than cheap talk. Consequently, justices are using briefs as a more refined measure of the opinions of important players rather than a mere general assessment.

Our results highlight the importance of information in policy making beyond the assertion that information is helpful. The side with more words gets more individual votes and wins more cases. The sheer bulk of information can help justices reduce their uncertainty about how their preferences will map on to policy outcomes. There is even more extensive evidence that the amount and type of information within briefs shapes the content of majority opinions. Policy coalescence communicated through shared information is very important in opinion formation. This indicates that not all information helps justices reduce their uncertainty. Unique information is of dubious value and does not communicate popular support. This makes sense given the increasing amount of information justices are provided within each case. They can use the prevalence of an argument as a cue or shortcut to evaluate its credibility. In short, the repetition of information becomes its own type of information for the Court. We see further evidence of this dynamic when we evaluate the impact of the briefs collectively for each side. The side that uses more shared information has more influence over the majority opinion while the side that uses more unusual information has less influence. Another finding that supports the importance of information in policy making is that both individually and collectively, briefs that focus more on the future play a larger role in shaping the opinion. All of these findings indicate that the information provided in briefs helps justices resolve cases and write opinions by reducing their uncertainty about what impact their actions will ultimately have.

Going Forward

While this book provides many insights regarding Supreme Court litigation and briefing, including information about informational lobbying, resource advantages, and structural features, no research can answer every question perfectly. This book leaves some questions unanswered and raises new ones. Thus, we end with a discussion of future areas of research that can build further on our work.[2] Our theoretical development and empirical analyses, both qualitative and quantitative, help illuminate new important areas for inquiry, including more nuanced aspects of policy coalescence, the role of attorney experience and reputation, and the varying types of information. We necessarily rely on proxies for several crucial concepts that future scholars may well be able to build upon. For example, the textual overlap between briefs is only one way that coordination may manifest. Measuring the type of technical information provided in Brandeis briefs is a challenging task. We look forward to seeing advances in how new and improved computational linguistic techniques can be deployed to measure this concept even better. Raw numbers of attorneys hired masks considerable variation in those attorneys beyond the features we measure. We are excited to see these issues explored further, both in our research and the work of others.

Additionally, in chapter 3, we discussed reasons to believe that different parties and amicus are pursuing differing goals that might influence their briefing and coordination strategies. We did not find all of the differences that we expected, but this may be a result of the way we conceptualize the goals of parties and amicus. This is another area where future research can build on this book in conjunction with other prior work (see appendix A). Which types of filers are more interested in outcomes or legal doctrines and what influence do those goals have on the way experience shapes the information they provide to the Court? Does it influence the extent to which such filers engage in producing unique or shared information and collaboration? Future work may also seek to explore coordination among amici themselves. While we focused on the coordination between parties and amici, there is every reason to expect that amici discuss cases among themselves as well.

Furthermore, what we have learned about briefs highlights other questions that are now ripe for investigation. Several interviewees discussed how strategies and dynamics regarding briefs at the certiorari stage differ from those at the merit stage (see appendix A). Further research regarding the briefing strategies at the cert stage would be fruitful, especially in light of the information provided in this book, which would allow for comparisons. This would also further our understanding of how differing goals (i.e., seeking review regarding attempting to secure a favorable outcome or doctrine), influence the tactics of Supreme Court litigants and interest groups.

Additionally, a host of quality research investigates the impact of oral arguments (Black, Johnson, and Wedeking 2012; Johnson, Wahlbeck, and Spriggs 2006). Just as we integrated related literatures on litigant and amicus briefs and information and resources, there is a need for research that explores the combined impact of briefs and oral arguments. Data-collection challenges have rendered this a considerable challenge. Both our theoretical integration of work related to briefs and the availability of our data will pave the way for such work. Furthermore, we provide firsthand accounts related to oral arguments from our interviews.

Likewise, the potential for a special role for states within Supreme Court litigation is another area where even more research is warranted. One interviewee raised interesting issues regarding states and state attorneys general and solicitors general (see appendix A). Research about such figures and entities continues to grow and can be bolstered by the theories, data, and findings we provide.

Final Thoughts

Ultimately, we care about these documents—Supreme Court opinions and briefs that inform them—due to the extensive real-world consequences that they have for people's lives. What started as a bad day for Clayton Harris ended in a decision that resolved inconsistent approaches to the federal constitutional standards for dog searches in the United States. The highest court in the land blessed an approach that relied on training rather than evidence of reliability in the field. This decision was widely reported in media aimed at law enforcement, as it had serious implications for the future use of dogs in searches (Rutledge 2013).[3] Thus, it had ramifications for how the police departments that employ tens of thousands of dogs (Lou 2015) approach searches and, thus, who is arrested, charged, and convicted. The efficacy of dogs in these types of searches is still a matter of controversy (Wolfson 2019), but current use seems quite secure based on the decision in *Florida v. Harris.*

While we do not have specific numbers, there are likely many individuals who have served time after this decision who would not have if the Court had ruled in favor of Harris and affirmed the Florida Supreme Court's decision. There are almost certainly many more individuals who have had their property searched using dogs who might not otherwise be considered up to snuff based on the relatively high false positive rate with dog alerts (Wolfson 2019). Furthermore, the whole of society is affected by how law is enforced and who is convicted. And, this is but one example based on a single case among the thousands that we studied.

Appendix A
Interviews

Interview Methods

To identify attorneys who had experience before the US Supreme Court, we used two main sources: (1) attorneys who signed briefs filed in a small sample of Supreme Court cases from a single term in the 2010s (the year is not specifically identified to help ensure the anonymity of the interview subjects), and (2) a snowball approach of speaking to attorneys within the author's professional network and individuals who received letters. We sent out ninety-seven inquiries—ninety-four through the briefs and three directly from contacts. In one case, the individual we sent a letter to put us into contact with other attorneys working in the area. We also obtained interviews with individuals who practiced in front of the Court by contacting former clerks. Six interviewees with attorney experience came directly from the solicitation of attorneys from the briefs, four through a snowball approach (three from contacts and one from letters), and five were also former clerks. Among the attorneys, there was variation as to the number of appearances in front of the Court, years of practice, the types of cases that the attorneys had participated in (both civil and criminal practice were represented), as well as variation in demographic characteristics.

We obtained the names of Supreme Court clerks from Wikipedia. We trimmed the list to those clerks who served between 1999 and 2017. Next, we located contact information for those former clerks from internet searches for publicly available information, including law firm and law school websites, etc. We sent out three waves of requests in spring and summer of 2018 for a total of 562 requests to randomly sampled former clerks. We ultimately interviewed eight former clerks. There was variation as to demographic characteristics, the justices represented, and the party of the appointing president for the represented justices.

Anonymity was promised to the interviewees. Specifically, the terms of the interviews were set that interviewees would not be identified other than based on the type of participant they were (e.g., attorney). Thus, we have worked to obscure specific examples provided by the participants that would identify specific cases in which they were involved; for example, the names of specific statutes and terms within those statutes that needed to be defined. Furthermore, to protect the interviewees and clients, the participants were not asked about specific cases. The interviews were not recorded other than handwritten notes by Morgan Hazelton. Thus, the quoted material tends to include shorter quotes based on the constraints of such a system. One interviewee also sent additional written comments after the interview, which allowed for longer quotations from that material.

Interview Questions

Attorney—Amicus Brief

General
- Please tell me about what it is like to write an amicus brief for the Supreme Court.
- What are your main goals in writing the brief?
- What makes a good amicus brief? A bad one?
- What are the major sources of influence over the briefs you write? Lower court opinions? Opponent's brief(s)? Precedent? Justices?
- What do you think would surprise most people to learn about the process of writing a brief?

Information
- How do you see the amicus's role regarding bringing information to the Court?
- What type of information, if any, do you try to provide to the Court? Facts? Scientific knowledge? Precedent? Arguments? Etc.?
- When are you likely to repeat information?
- When are you likely to provide unique information?

Coalition
- How much coordination is there among the amici and parties?
- To what extent do amici strategize with each other and/or parties regarding the arguments they make? What are the strategies?

Practice

- What advice would you give other attorneys about writing these briefs?
- What mistakes do you see other brief writers making?

Attorney—Party Brief

General

- Please tell me about what it is like to write a brief for the Supreme Court.
- What are your main goals in writing the brief?
- What makes a good brief? A bad one?
- What are the major sources of influence over the briefs you write? Lower court opinions? Opponent's brief(s)? Precedent? Justices?
- What do you think would surprise most people to learn about the process of writing a brief to the Supreme Court?

Audience

- Who are you writing to? To what extent are you writing to the Court? To specific members of the Court? To the public? To the client? To the members of any other group?

Information

- How do you see the party's role regarding bringing information to the Court?
- What type of information, if any, do you try to provide to the Court? Facts? Scientific knowledge? Precedent? Arguments? Etc.?
- When are you likely to repeat information?
- When are you likely to provide unique information?

Coalition

- How much coordination is there among the amici and parties?
- To what extent do parties strategize with amici regarding the arguments they make? What are the strategies?

Practice
- What advice would you give other attorneys about writing these briefs?
- What mistakes do you see other brief writers making?

Clerk

General
- Please tell me about what it is like to write an amicus brief for the Supreme Court.
- What are your main goals in writing the brief?
- What makes a good amicus brief? A bad one?
- What are the major sources of influence over the briefs you write? Lower court opinions? Opponent's brief(s)? Precedent? Justices?
- What do you think would surprise most people to learn about the process of writing a brief to the Supreme Court?

Audience
- Who are you writing to? To what extent are you writing to the Court? To specific members of the Court? To the public? To the client? To the members of any other group?

Information
- How do you see the amicus's role regarding bringing information to the Court? What type of information, if any, do you try to provide to the Court? Facts? Scientific knowledge? Precedent? Arguments? Etc.?
- When are you likely to repeat information?
- When are you likely to provide unique information?

Coalition
- How much coordination is there among the amici and parties?
- To what extent do amici strategize with each other and/or parties regarding the arguments they make? What are the strategies?

Practice
- What advice would you give other attorneys about writing these briefs?
- What mistakes do you see other brief writers making?

Interview Statements Suggesting Avenues for Future Research

Differing Goals

Attorney P noted that I should ask the difference between "petitioner and respondent briefs." Petitioners and respondents have different goals and "context matters." They noted that petitioners lost and respondents won but they were ultimately "unsure how different." "Facts are most important in both." Petitioners are positioned to argue the lower court was wrong while the respondent will say it was right. But they did note that it is a "different experience."

Certiorari

Interviewees offered a number of interesting insights regarding briefing for cert. Attorney R noted when drafting briefs at the certiorari stage, it is important to know the "standards for taking cases" and referred to the Court's rules. One should "provide enough incentive for supporting justices" in amicus briefs at the cert stage: "[You] don't want cert on cases that will go the other way on merits." So, "don't file" in such cases unless there is another issue that can be won: "Former clerks and experienced attorneys are good at identifying cert issues." This includes "what kind of analysis." They also noted the existence of strategic denials (Attorney J). Former Clerk N noted that the party briefs for cert can "be spotty." While "some understand the goals of the Court" with regards to issues related to the Constitution or circuit splits, "some don't." The ones who don't get it focus on "[how] the lower court got it wrong" and ask the Court to act in an error correction capacity. They described this mass of briefs as the "scrum." Attorney A did note that "it is more obvious at the cert petition stage who to target." Specifically, if dealing with new clerks in October, "you need to hit them between the eyes." Attorney and Former Clerk H described dealing with briefs related to certiorari—each amicus brief would get a "very short write up. Around a sentence each unless it was very special." Clerks would group some amicus briefs together in these memos.

States

One interviewee offered interesting perspectives regarding states before the Court. Attorney F noted that attorneys general meet and the justices speak with them. States are "heard as sovereigns" so there is "a lot of attention to" their positions. They also noted that states increasingly have their own solicitors general and have moved away from law firms as part of expressing the "voice of a sovereign." This also parallels the creation of a center for attorneys general with many resources; they praised the wealth of information and programs available. State solicitors general tend to the "state's authority" and care about such power, even when it is another state that is directly affected. They believe the solicitors general are "where the action is" and inform the attorney general. They described them as being similar to clerks to justices. They thought that attorney general groups that divide by partisanship are a mistake because it is unhelpful to the larger cause.

Media

There are also avenues to consider media coverage. Attorney Q noted that the "general public generally doesn't understand" issues and the "media misconstrues" them. Specifically, they described that the adversarial nature of the legal system is "misunderstood," and excerpts from cases are often "not in context" with "the media pull[ing from] only one [side] sometimes." This leads to the public misunderstanding and thinking the presented arguments are correct.

Printing Services

Attorney A pointed out that the Supreme Court is unusual in that there are brief printing services dedicated solely to preparing Supreme Court briefs. According to the attorney, they do a lot to help shape the briefs in terms of procedural matters and are a hidden resource.

Order at Conference

Another potential future research area involves the order of justices speaking at conference. Former Clerk K believed that the order in which the justices speak in conference is likely to matter: "Who is most senior matters." When the line-up changes, it is a "totally different court." The conference is set up so that the chief justice speaks first and then, second, the most senior justice. Here the arguments are "framed up." When the second to speak varies, it matters. They believed that process matters to decision-making.

Advice and General Mistakes

Attorney P thinks it is a mistake to "tell . . . the Court [that deciding the case] is easy." Among the mistakes that Attorney and Former Clerk I has witnessed are "trying to tell the justices [how to arrive at] the ultimate decision." Additionally, several advocates and former clerks mentioned the importance of clear and well-edited briefs. Some amicus briefs are "sloppy," according to Attorney and Former Clerk I. Attorney and Former Clerk L described what makes a good brief as "context dependent." The bare minimums include that it is clearly written and correctly formatted—in other words, legal writing "101." Attorney Q similarly noted that in federal appellate cases generally cite form matters—readers (clerks) "look to see if correct as a signal of diligence and carefulness." Q advised advocates to "do your homework"—there is "nothing as important as [careful] review [of the] record, case law, and [other aspects of the case]." Such review helps produce an "excellent product." Attorney J believed one needs to "recognize procedural pitfalls." Were the issues preserved? Is it harmless error? On the theme of clarity, Attorney R said that in briefing, one should "signal before you turn." In other words, let the reader know when making a new argument. They also suggested attorneys read *Make No Law* by Anthony Lewis. Attorney P noted that attorneys often don't produce "clear and succinct" questions presented. This is a mistake because "the clearer the points, the easier it is to deal with." Attorneys should be careful with "word crafting." Similarly, Attorney Q said that attorneys should make their headings "understandable at first glance."

Use of the Record

Attorney and Former Clerk B thought there would be more variability regarding use of the record among amici.

Senior Justice

Furthermore, one attorney described targeting the senior justice in a likely majority. Attorney D discussed prioritizing the senior justice in the likely majority due to issues related to opinion assignments. They specifically noted Justice Burger voting in strategic ways to be able to assign opinions. They also noted the difference between Justice Roberts as being "doctrinaire" and filling an "institutional role" as opposed to a more political approach from someone such as Burger. They noted knowing these aspects is "important inside baseball" and they "might pander" if the situation called for it.

Academic Work

A few interviewees noted the importance of scholarly work specifically. Attorney and Former Clerk B noted that the Court was hungry for the types of information that tend to be in peer-reviewed publications. Attorney A who has practiced before the Court also noted that briefs from academics are particularly helpful. Justice Roberts has questioned the role of legal academic work (Garner 2010, 37).

Caring Justices

Attorney and Former Clerk B noted that "no federal judges are lazy" and that "justices work hard." They felt that practitioners sometimes forget that the cases are "serious" to the justices. When the attorneys forget this, they tend to spend time "belaboring points that are readily apparent." There is "a line between effective [and obvious]." It is a matter of "art, not science." But, generally one should "assume the tribunal cares."

Appendix B
Data Collection, Scope, and Processing

Data Collection Process

We collected the briefs through a multistage process. Our focus was on party and amicus briefs related to the merits, so we excluded documents related to certiorari, joint appendices, and other extraneous documents. We began by collecting all briefs available via Westlaw and then filled in gaps with LexisNexis. While Lexis generally has a smaller number of briefs overall, we did find a meaningful number of such briefs that were not available from Westlaw.[1] Subsequent examination revealed that before the 1984 term, there are intermittent substantial gaps in the availability of merits briefs from these electronic sources. For example, a couple of hundred briefs appear to be missing from 1974 and approximatively seven hundred appear to be missing from 1982. Consequently, we ran all of our analyses and data summaries using the data from 1984 to 2015. The data from the earlier briefs going back to 1970 are used to calculate the previous experience of filers and attorneys.

Inclusion of Briefs that Are Not Available Electronically

Even after the 1983 term, further comparison of the number of amicus briefs in our data with the numbers provided in the Friends of the Supreme Court (FOSC) Database (Collins 2008), along with occasional missing party briefs, suggested that our data were still not comprehensive. For the terms from 1988 to 2005, we examined the hard copy briefs available in the archives at the Cornell Law Library and electronically scanned all briefs missing from our data. This task involved comparing our list of briefs (using the name of the entity filing the brief) with all available hard copy briefs for the docket number of every case in which we either (a) had no main petitioner brief and/or no respondent brief or (b) we had fewer amicus briefs than the number listed in the FOSC database.

Our archival work to obtain as many missing briefs as possible was limited to the 1988 to 2005 terms for a variety of reasons. First, the FOSC database only covers through the 2005 term and this resource was critical to our strategy of identifying potential gaps in the data. One of the main challenges is knowing what is missing, and there is no simple way to tell which amicus briefs we didn't have. We went back as many years as feasible to gain a sufficient number of missing briefs to be able to assess the impact of relying on electronically available briefs. During the process it became evident that extending the project earlier in time would make a labor-intensive task increasingly more difficult, as there are substantially more briefs missing further back in time. Finally, upon collecting the hard copies of missing briefs for the aforementioned span of time, a wide variety of analyses indicated that the inclusion of such briefs did not alter the results. Consequently, while we continue to use the additional briefs we collected from the archives, we did not continue to pursue the prohibitively resource-intensive work that would have been required to extend those data collection efforts forward and backward in time. Overall, 90 percent of our briefs came from Westlaw, another 6 percent from LexisNexis, and 4 percent from the Cornell archives.

Accounting for Negations

The cosine similarity scores we use in chapters 3, 5, and 6 and the term frequency, inverse document frequency (tf-idf) scores we use in chapter 5 are both "bag of words" measures. This means that the order of words is not taken into account by either measure. Instead, the overall similarity of the individual words used is the basis of estimating the similarity between two sets of words or documents. This provides much-needed computational efficiency. However, one type of context in the English language that is particularly important in assessing meaning is whether a word is preceded by a negation word (Jia, Yu and Meng 2009). Negations are words that operate to change the meaning of a statement to essentially the exact opposite. For example, the statements "the argument has merit" and "the argument has zero merit" have diametrically opposed meanings because of the insertion of the negation "zero." Because measures using tf-idf scores do not account for the order of words, without modification these two statements would appear to have very closely related meanings. We address this problem by combining all negation words with the following word in order to create a new "word" that is analyzed separately.[2] Using the forgoing example, our measure analyzes *merit* and *zeromerit* as two distinct words to capture the fact that they express opposite ideas. The tf-idf scores will still pick up the common subject between the two statements, but the object will no longer be treated as matching. As a result, two opposing statements about the same topic will be more similar than two statements about totally different topics, but they will still be considerably less similar than two statements that express the same opinion about the same topic. As further illustration, the statements *the store has apples* and *the store has no apples* will have the same level of similarity as the statements *the store has apples* and *the store has oranges*.

1. Since briefs do not have unique identifiers such as case reporter citations that are common to both databases, we eliminated Lexis briefs present in the Westlaw collection by the simple expedient of using the cosine similarity scores described in chapter 3 (since identical documents have a cosine score of one).
2. The negations we collapse in this manner include "no," "not," "neither," "nor," "zero," "without," and "sans" (Pennebaker, Booth and Francis 2007).

Appendix C
Regression Tables

Models from Chapter 2

Table A.1. Quantity of Information

	Quantity of Information	
	Parties	**Amici**
Filer Type (Baseline Is Interest Group)		
Individual	−0.049	−0.425*
	(0.492)	(0.215)
Business	−0.500	−1.438*
	(0.514)	(0.287)
Subnational Government	−0.772	−2.295*
	(0.515)	(0.215)
National Government	−1.969*	0.681*
	(0.857)	(0.334)
Log No. of Cosigners	−0.924	1.098*
	(0.851)	(0.094)
Log No. of Attorneys	3.513*	0.283*
	(0.324)	(0.121)
Log Max. Filer Exp.	−0.097	0.174*
	(0.070)	(0.043)
Log Max. Attorney Exp.	0.678*	0.656*
	(0.091)	(0.052)
No. of Former Clerks	0.332*	1.084*
	(0.136)	(0.087)
No. of Former SGs	−1.571*	−0.290
	(0.601)	(0.445)
Current SG	−2.856*	0.434
	(0.759)	(0.411)
Court Invited Brief		3.457*
		(1.085)
Petitioner's Side	−1.753*	−1.312*
	(0.190)	(0.127)

(continued on the next page)

Table A.1. *Continued*

	Quantity of Information	
	Parties	**Amici**
Ideological Alignment	−0.667*	−0.215*
	(0.151)	(0.102)
Log Word Count LC Opinion	0.566*	0.076
	(0.098)	(0.086)
Amicus Activity in Lower Court	1.770*	0.730*
	(0.356)	(0.188)
Term	−0.008	−0.058*
	(0.017)	(0.010)
Intercept	14.564	107.893*
	(33.070)	(20.073)
N	6,096	16,186
R²	0.12	0.12
BIC	44220.9	109415.0

OLS regression estimates of the effect of resources, experience, expertise, and a range of control variables on the quantity of information in a brief. The reported standard errors are robust standard errors that are clustered on the case and * denotes a *p*-value less than 0.05.

Table A.2. Strategic Information

	Strategic Citation	
	Parties	**Amici**
Filer Type (Baseline Is Interest Group)		
Individual	0.383	0.029
	(0.313)	(0.103)
Business	−0.762*	−0.438*
	(0.312)	(0.121)
Subnational Government	0.153	−0.314*
	(0.347)	(0.105)
National Government	−1.256*	−0.169
	(0.473)	(0.164)
Log No. of Cosigners	−0.988*	0.027
	(0.367)	(0.040)
Log No. of Attorneys	0.717*	0.153*
	(0.198)	(0.066)
Log Max. Filer Exp.	0.001	0.099*
	(0.046)	(0.023)

Log Max. Attorney Exp.	0.279*	0.177*
	(0.059)	(0.026)
No. of Former Clerks	−0.171	0.200*
	(0.098)	(0.065)
No. of Former SGs	-0.902	−0.785*
	(0.466)	(0.261)
Current SG	−0.101	0.19
	(0.412)	(0.283)
Court Invited Brief		0.105
		(0.441)
Petitioner's Side	−0.115	−0.027
	(0.102)	(0.069)
Ideological Alignment	0.031	0.003
	(0.081)	(0.058)
Log Word Count LC Opinion	0.063	−0.034
	(0.067)	(0.052)
Amicus Activity in Lower Court	0.524	0.126
	(0.268)	(0.152)
Term	−0.057*	−0.056*
	(0.011)	(0.008)
Intercept	115.941*	113.616*
	(22.679)	(15.999)
N	6,096	16,186
R²	0.02	0.05
BIC	39190.2	87709.2

OLS regression estimates of the effect of resources, experience, expertise, and a range of control variables on the number of citations in a brief to a precedent written by the current median justice. The reported standard errors are robust standard errors that are clustered on the case and * denotes a p-value less than 0.05.

Table A.3. Legislative Facts

	Technical Language		Future Tense Verbs	
	Parties	**Amici**	**Parties**	**Amici**
Filer Type (Baseline Is Interest Group)				
Individual	−0.244*	0.069	0.014	0.027*
	(0.095)	(0.060)	(0.013)	(0.010)
Business	0.162	0.352*	0.006	0.081*
	(0.104)	(0.083)	(0.013)	(0.012)

(continued on the next page)

Table A.3. *Continued*

	Technical Language		Future Tense Verbs	
	Parties	**Amici**	**Parties**	**Amici**
Subnational	−0.588*	-0.225*	-0.016	0.002
Government	(0.090)	(0.046)	(0.015)	(0.009)
National Government	0.852*	0.297*	0.009	−0.023
	(0.194)	(0.085)	(0.022)	(0.012)
Log No. of Cosigners	0.397*	-0.056*	−0.009	−0.020*
	(0.175)	(0.019)	(0.018)	(0.004)
Log No. of Attorneys	0.359*	0.211*	−0.018*	−0.009
	(0.060)	(0.029)	(0.008)	(0.005)
Log Max. Filer Exp.	−0.012	0.067*	-0.002	0.009*
	(0.015)	(0.010)	(0.002)	(0.002)
Log Max. Attorney	0.01	0.009	0.007*	0.004*
Exp.	(0.019)	(0.012)	(0.002)	(0.002)
No. of Former Clerks	0.047	0.120*	0.009*	0.015*
	(0.030)	(0.021)	(0.004)	(0.004)
No. of Former SGs	−0.320*	0.087	−0.013	0.003
	(0.139)	(0.111)	(0.017)	(0.023)
Current SG	0.239	−0.019	−0.004	−0.017
	(0.186)	(0.117)	(0.019)	(0.016)
Court Invited Brief		0.221		0.004
		(0.217)		(0.039)
Petitioner's Side	0.079*	0.002	−0.027*	−0.006
	(0.031)	(0.035)	(0.005)	(0.007)
Ideological Alignment	−0.013	-0.011	0.010*	0.021*
	(0.025)	(0.024)	(0.004)	(0.005)
Log Word Count	−0.054*	−0.035	−0.002	−0.001
LC Opinion	(0.022)	(0.021)	(0.003)	(0.004)
Amicus Activity in	−0.031	−0.095	−0.022*	−0.044*
Lower Court	(0.076)	(0.059)	(0.010)	(0.009)
Term	0.030*	0.021*	−0.001	−0.002*
	(0.004)	(0.003)	(0.000)	(0.000)
Intercept	−52.618*	−34.039*	2.310*	5.290*
	(7.688)	(5.699)	(0.808)	(0.898)
N	6,096	16,186	6,096	16,186
R²	0.14	0.06	0.01	0.03
BIC	24554.8	61790.1	-709.2	6203.2

OLS regression estimates of the effect of resources, experience, expertise, and a range of control variables on technical and future-oriented language. The reported standard errors are robust standard errors that are clustered on the case and * denotes a *p*-value less than 0.05.

Table A.4. Presentation Style

	Emotional Language		Reading Grade Level	
	Parties	Amici	Parties	Amici
Filer Type (Baseline Is Interest Group)				
Individual	0.215*	−0.034	−0.369*	−0.122*
	(0.044)	(0.033)	(0.065)	(0.046)
Business	0.051	−0.171*	−0.151*	0.145*
	(0.047)	(0.042)	(0.069)	(0.059)
Subnational Government	0.008	−0.294*	−0.232*	−0.097*
	(0.044)	(0.029)	(0.070)	(0.042)
National Government	−0.257*	−0.350*	0.18	0.023
	(0.070)	(0.037)	(0.103)	(0.062)
Log No. of Cosigners	−0.164	0.082*	0.022	−0.011
	(0.089)	(0.012)	(0.092)	(0.018)
Log No. of Attorneys	−0.014	−0.032*	−0.064	0.089*
	(0.028)	(0.016)	(0.038)	(0.022)
Log Max. Filer Exp.	0.029*	−0.009	−0.029*	−0.003
	(0.007)	(0.006)	(0.009)	(0.008)
Log Max. Attorney Exp.	0.019*	0.029*	0.015	−0.022*
	(0.009)	(0.007)	(0.012)	(0.010)
No. of Former Clerks	−0.009	0.002	0.064*	0.060*
	(0.013)	(0.011)	(0.019)	(0.015)
No. of Former SGs	−0.053	0.049	0.153	0.144
	(0.059)	(0.078)	(0.084)	(0.091)
Current SG	−0.042	−0.068	−0.018	−0.235*
	(0.068)	(0.051)	(0.093)	(0.074)
Court Invited Brief		0.003		−0.055
		(0.131)		(0.177)
Petitioner's Side	−0.027*	0.029	0.073*	0.047
	(0.012)	(0.020)	(0.024)	(0.029)
Ideological Alignment	0.016	0.024	0.013	−0.077*
	(0.009)	(0.016)	(0.018)	(0.023)
Log Word Count LC Opinion	0.002	−0.017	0.003	0.02
	(0.010)	(0.016)	(0.012)	(0.017)
Amicus Activity in Lower Court	−0.056	−0.044	0.044	−0.063
	(0.036)	(0.042)	(0.044)	(0.048)
Term	0.005*	0.003	0.059*	0.063*
	(0.002)	(0.002)	(0.002)	(0.002)
Intercept	−6.808*	−2.999	−101.066*	−108.891*
	(3.345)	(3.947)	(4.367)	(4.512)

(continued on the next page)

Table A.4. *Continued*

	Emotional Language		Reading Grade Level	
	Parties	**Amici**	**Parties**	**Amici**
N	6,096	16,186	6,096	16,186
R²	0.03	0.03	0.23	0.16
BIC	15109.7	43606.4	18917.2	55799.5

OLS regression estimates of the effect of resources, experience, expertise, and a range of control variables on emotional language and reading grade level. The reported standard errors are robust standard errors that are clustered on the case and * denotes a *p*-value less than 0.05.

Models from Chapter 3

Table A.5. Cosine Similarity between Briefs

	Coef.	**S.E.**
Log Max. Attorney Exp., Party	0.018*	(0.007)
Log Max. Attorney Exp., Amicus	0.016*	(0.004)
No. of Former Clerks, Party	−0.011	(0.012)
No. of Former Clerks, Amicus	0.071*	(0.007)
No. of Former SGs, Party	0.018	(0.041)
No. of Former SGs, Amicus	0.166*	(0.050)
Log Prev. Attorney Collaboration	−0.018	(0.021)
Log Max. Filer Exp., Party	−0.012*	(0.006)
Log Max. Filer Exp., Amicus	0.052*	(0.004)
Interest Group Amicus	−0.043*	(0.013)
Current SG, Party	−0.077	(0.041)
Current SG, Amicus	0.209*	(0.030)
Court Invited Amicus Brief	0.050	(0.089)
Log No. of Amicus Cosigners	−0.006	(0.007)
No. of Ally Briefs	−0.008*	(0.002)
Petitioner's Side	0.169*	(0.016)
Ideological Alignment	−0.010	(0.011)
Log Word Count LC Opinion	−0.020*	(0.008)
Amicus Activity in Lower Court	−0.033	(0.023)
Term	−0.011*	(0.001)
Intercept	22.864*	(2.537)
N	19,674	
AIC	18158.9	
BIC	18324.5	

Fractional logit estimates of the effect of party and amicus characteristics and a range of control variables on the cosine similarity between the text of each litigant brief and each amicus brief filed on that litigant's behalf. The reported standard errors are robust standard errors that are clustered on the case and * denotes a p-value less than 0.05.

Models from Chapter 4

Table A.6. Modeling Votes and Case Outcomes

	Votes		Outcomes	
	Coef.	(SE)	Coef.	(SE)
Language, Citations, and Briefs				
Difference in Log Word Count	0.266*	(0.081)	0.408*	(0.117)
Difference in Vocabulary (1000's)	0.011	(0.047)	−0.057	(0.072)
Difference in Total Cites (100's)	−0.230*	(0.094)	−0.234	(0.148)
Difference in Precedent Vocabulary (100s)	0.270*	(0.123)	0.166	(0.192)
Difference in No. of Briefs	−0.002	(0.010)	0.036*	(0.018)
Types of Information				
Difference in Citations to Current Median	0.001	(0.001)	0.006*	(0.003)
Difference in Technical Language	0.018	(0.017)	0.023	(0.024)
Difference in Future Language	0.098	(0.099)	0.017	(0.140)
Difference in Grade Level	−0.029	(0.022)	−0.028	(0.029)
Difference in Emotional Language	−0.044	(0.044)	−0.041	(0.061)
Attorney and Litigant Characteristics				
Difference in Log No. of Cosigners	−0.02	(0.025)	0.013	(0.036)
Difference in Log No. of Attorneys	0	(0.035)	−0.036	(0.050)
Difference in Log Median Filer Exp.	0.01	(0.008)	0.012	(0.011)
Difference in Log Median Attorney Exp.	0.023*	(0.012)	0.049*	(0.016)
Difference in No. of Former Clerks	0.018*	(0.007)	0.022	(0.011)
Difference in No. of Former SGs	−0.122*	(0.046)	−0.121	(0.068)
Difference in Current SG	0.260*	(0.035)	0.306*	(0.051)
Difference in Briefs Invited by Court	−0.134	(0.150)	−0.253	(0.198)

(continued on the next page)

Table A.6. *Continued*

	Votes		Outcomes	
	Coef.	(SE)	Coef.	(SE)
Litigation Environment				
Ideological Alignment	0.183*	(0.006)	0.090*	(0.040)
Log Word Count LC Opinion	−0.031*	(0.012)	−0.015	(0.017)
Amicus Activity in Lower Court	−0.081	(0.047)	−0.132*	(0.067)
Difference in Oral Arg.				
Questions	−0.011*	(0.001)	−0.013*	(0.001)
Term	0.014*	(0.002)	0.016*	(0.003)
Intercept	−27.387*	(4.640)	−31.821*	(6.684)
N	21,627	2,439		
AIC	25418.5	2872.2		
BIC	25610	3011.4		

Probit regression estimates of the effect of amount and type of information, attorney and litigant characteristics, and a range of control variables on the probability of the petitioner securing justices' votes and case outcomes. The reported standard errors for the votes model are robust standard errors that are clustered on the case and * denotes a p-value less than 0.05.

Models from Chapter 5

Table A.7. Cosine Similarity between Each Brief and the Majority Opinion

	Party Briefs		Amicus Briefs	
	Coef.	(SE)	Coef.	(SE)
Language, Citations, and Briefs				
Overall Novelty (Words)	−3.099*	(0.509)	−2.467*	(0.215)
Overall Novelty (Cites)	−0.459*	(0.168)	−0.126*	(0.044)
Unique Words (1000s)	−0.216*	(0.045)	−0.485*	(0.062)
Unique Cites (100s)	−0.074	(0.073)	−0.240*	(0.086)
Shared Words (1000s)	0.001*	(0.000)	0.002*	(0.000)
Shared Cites (100s)	−0.006	(0.033)	0.160*	(0.046)
Similarity to Lower Court				
Opinion	0.828*	(0.085)	1.965*	(0.088)
No. of Briefs	−0.007*	(0.001)	−0.002	(0.001)

Types of Information

Citations to Current Median	−0.002	(0.002)	−0.005	(0.003)
Technical Language	−0.006	(0.005)	0.003	(0.005)
Future Language	0.090*	(0.036)	0.084*	(0.024)
Grade Level	0.005	(0.008)	0.006	(0.006)
Emotional Language	−0.017	(0.011)	−0.025*	(0.010)

Attorney and Litigant Characteristics

Log No. of Cosigners	−0.012	(0.042)	−0.001	(0.006)
Log No. of Attorneys	0.023	(0.020)	−0.012	(0.009)
Log Max. Filer Exp.	0.006	(0.004)	0.014*	(0.003)
Log Max. Attorney Exp.	0.019*	(0.006)	0.011*	(0.004)
No. of Former Clerks	0.003	(0.010)	0.017*	(0.007)
No. of Former SGs	−0.027	(0.051)	−0.019	(0.041)
Current SG	0.061*	(0.028)	0.130*	(0.028)
Court Invited Brief			0.148	(0.076)

Litigation Environment

Petitioner's Side	0.051*	(0.008)	0.036*	(0.012)
Ideological Alignment	−0.005	(0.006)	−0.001	(0.008)
Log Word Count LC Opinion	−0.072*	(0.009)	−0.106*	(0.009)
Amicus Activity in Lower Court	−0.047*	(0.024)	−0.077*	(0.025)
No. of Oral Arg. Questions to Side	−0.001*	(0.000)	0.000	(0.000)
Term	-0.001	(0.001)	−0.004*	(0.001)
Intercept	2.306	(2.885)	8.932*	(2.715)
N	5,258	12,200		
AIC	4666.7	11006.4		
BIC	4844	11213.9		

Fractional logit estimates of the effect of amount and type of information, attorney and litigant characteristics, and a range of control variables on the cosine similarity between the text of each brief and the majority opinion. The reported standard errors are robust standard errors that are clustered on the case and * denotes a p-value less than 0.05.

Models from Chapter 6

Table A.8. Case-Side Overlap between All Briefs and Majority Opinion

	Coef.	(S.E.)
Language, Citations, and Briefs		
Log Word Count	0.477*	(0.046)
Document Vocabulary (1000s)	−0.224*	(0.025)
Total Cites (100s)	0.218*	(0.060)
Precedent Vocabulary (100s)	−0.253*	(0.083)
No. of Briefs	0.039*	(0.007)
Types of Information		
Citations to Current Median	−0.001	(0.001)
Technical Language	−0.001	(0.007)
Future Language	0.119*	(0.052)
Grade Level	−0.024*	(0.012)
Emotional Language	−0.032*	(0.014)
Attorney and Litigant Characteristics		
Log No. of Cosigners	−0.01	(0.015)
Log No. of Attorneys	−0.005	(0.023)
Log Median Filer Exp.	−0.007	(0.005)
Log Median Attorney Exp.	0.024*	(0.007)
No. of Former Clerks	0.005	(0.005)
No. of Former SGs	−0.032	(0.031)
Current SG	0.071*	(0.022)
Court Invited Briefs	0.06	(0.097)
Litigation Environment		
Petitioner's Side	−0.012	(0.011)
Ideological Alignment	0.002	(0.005)
Log Word Count LC Opinion	0.007	(0.008)
Amicus Activity in Lower Court	0.029	(0.031)
Oral Argument Questions	−0.001	(0.001)
Term	0.000	(0.002)
Intercept	−2.299	(3.531)
N	4,912	
AIC	4114.0	
BIC	4276.5	

Fractional logit estimates of the effect of amount and type of information, attorney and litigant characteristics, and a range of control variables on the cosine similarity between the cumulative text of all briefs submitted on behalf of one side in a case and the majority opinion. The reported standard errors are robust standard errors that are clustered on the case and * denotes a p-value less than 0.05.

Table A.9. Case-Level Analysis of Relative Cosine Similarity to Majority Opinion

	Coef.	(SE)
Language, Citations, and Briefs		
Difference in Log Word Count	0.083*	(0.006)
Difference in Vocabulary (1000s)	−0.031*	(0.003)
Difference in Total Cites (100s)	0.001	(0.007)
Difference in Precedent Vocabulary (100s)	0.002	(0.009)
Difference in No. of Briefs	0.003*	(0.001)
Types of Information		
Difference in Citations to Current Median	0.000	(0.000)
Difference in Technical Language	0.003*	(0.001)
Difference in Future Language	0.015*	(0.007)
Difference in Grade Level	−0.004*	(0.001)
Difference in Emotional Language	0.002	(0.003)
Attorney and Litigant Characteristics		
Difference in Log No. of Cosigners	−0.004*	(0.002)
Difference in Log No. of Attorneys	0.002	(0.002)
Difference in Log Median Filer Exp.	0.001*	(0.001)
Difference in Log Median Attorney Exp.	0.003*	(0.001)
Difference in No. of Former Clerks	0.001	(0.001)
Difference in No. of Former SGs	−0.002	(0.003)
Difference in Current SG	0.014*	(0.002)
Difference in Court Invited Briefs	0.018	(0.010)
Litigation Environment		
Ideological Alignment with Petitioner	0.000	(0.002)
Log Word Count LC Opinion	0.000	(0.001)
Amicus Activity in Lower Court	−0.002	(0.003)
Difference in Oral Arg. Questions	−0.000*	(0.000)
Term	0.000	(0.000)
Intercept	−0.283	(0.323)
N	2,439	
R^2	0.27	
BIC	−6199.5	

OLS regression estimates of the effect of differences in the amount and type of information, attorney and litigant characteristics, and a range of control variables between the two sides on differences in the similarity between the text of the opinion and the collective briefs. The * denotes a *p*-value less than 0.05.

Notes

Introduction

1. *Florida v. Harris*, 568 U.S. 237 (2013).

2. The information regarding *Florida v. Harris* was obtained from court filings and opinions in the case. Specifically, the following opinions and orders were consulted: *Florida v. Harris*, 568 U.S. 237 (2013); *Harris v. State*, 71 So. 3d 756 (Fla. 2011); and *Harris v. State*, 989 S0.2d 1214 (Fl. App. 1 Dist. 2008). Additionally, we read all fourteen party and amicus briefs filed with the Supreme Court of the United States. A full list of the briefs is available in the docket from the Supreme Court of the United States, "Proceedings and Orders," accessed March 6, 2022, https://www.supremecourt.gov/docketfiles/11-817.htm.

3. Br. Pet'r 2, *Florida v. Harris*, No. 11–817 (U.S.).

4. Br. Pet'r 4, *Florida v. Harris*, No. 11–817 (U.S.); Jt. Appx., *Florida v. Harris*, No. 11–817, p. 68 (U.S.).

5. Such guides take the forms of books, articles, blogs, and webpages.

6. Dan Klau, "Briefs Are (Way) More Important Than Oral Argument," *Appealingly Brief* (blog), May 3, 2013, https://appealinglybrief.com/2013/05/03/briefs-are-way-more-important-thanoral-argument/.

7. All interviews were carried out and analyzed by Morgan Hazelton. Saint Louis University, internal review board #29160. The details regarding the methods related to the interviews are available in appendix A. The interviews were open-ended, but lists of general topics that guided the discussions are in appendix A.

Chapter 1. Briefs and the People Who Produce Them

1. See Hawthorn Mineart, (2011), "Word Count for Famous Novels (Organized)," Commonplacebook.com, November 22, http://commonplacebook.com/art/books/word-count-for-famous-novels/.

2. Specifically, we use the SMOG reading index (McLaughlin 1969), which we discuss in more detail later in this chapter.

3. Throughout the book, we use data going back to 1970 to calculate experience measures for filers and amici. See appendix B for further discussion and a description of the data collection process.

4. Supreme Court Rule 33.1(g) dictates a color-coding scheme whereby

each type of brief must have a cover of a particular color. Amicus briefs have green covers.

5. All such trends discussed in this chapter report the linear relationship between the variable under discussion and term.

6. Our measure of the word count in each brief (and all other measures derived from the content of briefs) are generated after excluding all preliminary material (such as tables of contents and authorities) and any appendices. The joint appendices submitted collectively by the parties are similarly excluded from our analysis.

7. The Supreme Court reduced the word limit for main party briefs in 2019. The historical Supreme Court Rules with the length limits that are applicable throughout our data are available at Supreme Court of the United States, "Historical Rules of the Supreme Court," accessed September 19, 2021, https://www.supremecourt.gov/ctrules/scannedrules.aspx. Attorney R noted that the "rules have changed regarding word limits" and parties "don't always have enough space." In their estimation, this is where amicus briefs are important.

8. The replication files available on the authors' websites include code for these analyses and all other robustness checks mentioned in the text.

9. The standard deviation is 3,628 words for litigant briefs and 2,327 words for amicus briefs.

10. As a practical matter, the form of citations to Supreme Court precedent is limited and the universe of such citations is known, which enables us to extract them reliably from the text of briefs.

11. From 2000 forward, there is an estimated decrease of 0.9 cites per amicus brief ($p < 0.001$) and a decrease of 1.1 cites per litigant brief ($p < 0.001$) per term.

12. Specifically, we use the SMOG index (McLaughlin 1969). SMOG is an acronym for simple measure of gobbeldygook. The average grade level using this measure is 17.2. This falls in the middle of the averages for the Coleman-Liau Index (14.8), Flesch-Kincaid Grade Level (15.9), the Gunning Fog Index (19.9), and the Automated Readability Index (20.3).

13. We compiled these numbers using the Linguistic Inquiry and Word Count (LIWC) software. More detail regarding this measure is provided in chapter 2.

14. For similar classification schemes, see Black and Boyd 2010; Collins 2008; and Szmer and Ginn 2014.

15. In order to provide as thorough a picture as possible, we examine all attorneys who sign the brief rather than looking only at the first listed or the counsel of record. While the counsel of record may lead the brief-writing efforts, their participation can vary widely all the way down to simply signing the brief (Gonen 1996; Szmer, Johnson, and Sarver 2007). Supreme Court Rule 9 dictates that the counsel of record must be a member of the Supreme Court bar.

So, for any instance in which a brief-writing team is led by an attorney who is not a member of the Supreme Court bar, the counsel of record may not reflect maximum involvement in crafting the brief.

16. While it would be ideal to account for work experience within the Office of the Solicitor General beyond simply holding the top job, such data are not readily available.

Chapter 2. Crafting a Brief

1. The replication files available at the authors' websites include code that generates all summary statistics related to our example cases referenced throughout this book.

2. There are some exceptions to the pattern (Haynie 1994), but the majority of the large amount of research devoted to exploring Galanter's theory reveals the expected relationship.

3. We can test the current solicitor general hypothesis alongside the filer type hypothesis because the solicitor general does not sign every brief involving the federal government. In our data, the solicitor general signed 69 percent of briefs filed by the federal government.

4. This approach is comparable to how other scholars have built similar measures (Haynie and Sill 2007; Flemming and Krutz 2002; Szmer and Ginn 2014; Szmer, Johnson, and Sarver 2007). Data constraints have even led some scholars to develop experience measures limited to the years analyzed (McGuire 1995).

5. We exclude petitioner reply briefs. Reply briefs are both much shorter than other briefs and strongly influenced by the content of the respondent's brief to which they are directed.

6. Individuals who are named in their capacity as representing an organization are coded based on the organization they represent (Haire and Moyer 2007; McCormick 1993; Songer, Sheehan, and Haire 1999; Songer and Sheehan 1992).

7. Since our data set contains over twenty-three thousand distinct filing entities, seeking additional information on each would be impracticable.

8. For example, the difference between having one attorney or two should have a bigger impact than the difference between having twenty or twenty-one attorneys.

9. Using the maximum is not a universal approach. Some studies simply use the experience of the lead counsel based on the assumption they are the most experienced (Hanretty 2014; Hansford 2004; Haynie and Sill 2007). Our approach follows a similar logic while relying on the data, rather than assumption, to identify the most experienced member of the litigation team. Other

scholars measure the total amount of experience for all filers and all attorneys on the brief (Szmer, Johnson, and Sarver 2007), but that would necessarily correlate with the number of filers/attorneys, which we are measuring separately. Finally, we could simply use the average experience rather than the maximum. However, similar to McGuire (1995, 191, fn. 3), we find that both approaches produce results that are very similar.

10. Available at "Lists of Law Clerks of the Supreme Court of the United States," Wikipedia, accessed November 21, 2021, https://en.wikipedia.org/wiki/List_of_law_clerks_of_the_Supreme_Court_of_the_United_States. We confirmed the comprehensive scope of this source by comparing it to the data available from Peppers (2006) for the overlapping years.

11. The most common invitee at both the cert and merits stage is the office of the solicitor general; and some scholars focus on such invitations exclusively (Black and Owens 2011; Pacelle Jr. 2005). Because we are examining all briefs in a broad fashion (and are separately accounting for the role of both the federal government generally and the solicitor general specifically) we control for any invitation to brief.

12. We use a standard measure of Supreme Court ideology, Martin-Quinn scores (Martin and Quinn 2002). When the filer is seeking a conservative outcome, the variable "Ideological Alignment" is the median Martin-Quinn score of the Court, because higher Martin-Quinn scores denote greater conservatism. When the filer is advocating a liberal outcome, "Ideological Alignment" is the Martin-Quinn score of the Court median multiplied by negative one.

13. We compiled a count of all citations by writing Python code to extract all references to Supreme Court cases from the text of each brief using regular expressions.

14. The counts of total words and unique words are logged throughout our analyses, including compiling this combined metric of quantity of information. All four indicators load onto a single factor, with loadings greater than 0.82, and analysis of a Scree plot provides evidence that quantity of information is a unidimensional concept.

15. All discussion of statistical significance throughout the book is at a 0.05 alpha level.

16. While the median justice is not always the pivotal voter, they are the most common pivotal voter (Enns and Koch 2013), which makes our approach a reasonable approximation.

17. *Muller v. Oregon*, 208 U.S. 412 (1908).

18. *Brown v. Board*, 347 U.S. 483 (1954); *Brown v. Entertainment Merchants Association*, 564 U.S. 786 (2005).

19. In some areas of law, especially tort law, causation is an important legal concept in its own right. However, tort cases rarely involve federal law, and even

if some use of causal language is related to mainstream legal analysis, we still expect higher levels to be associated with more use of technical information.

20. The regression tables are provided in appendix C and include the R^2 for each model.

21. We use a somewhat modified version of the original LIWC 2007 dictionary in order to account for variations in linguistic usage in the legal context.

22. All of the same statistically significant relationships that are found in the models below also emerge if we instead use a composite measure of readability formulated using the Flesch-Kincaid Grade Level, the Coleman Liau Index, the Gunning Fog Index, SMOG, the Automated Readability Index, the Dale-Chall Score, and words per sentence. The code to run these alternative models (along with all other robustness checks mentioned throughout the book) is included in the replication files.

23. SMOG is an acronym for simple measure of gobbeldygook.

24. The analysis of our filer-type hypothesis is not included in the table due to the fact that its complex nature does not lend itself well to succinct summarization.

25. We have examined the effects of adding filer type variables to our models where applicable in later chapters, and the decision to exclude them is not driving our substantive findings.

Chapter 3. Coordinating and Coalescing: Investigating Information Sharing between Briefs

1. While briefing at the Supreme Court resembles other forms of lobbying and related information provision, Supreme Court justices do not stand for reelection, accept donations, or have private conversations about cases with interested groups (Hazelton, Hinkle, and Spriggs 2019). Furthermore, access to the courts is relatively free and open compared to the other branches (Collins 2008; Hazelton, Hinkle, and Spriggs 2019). Thus, analysis of Supreme Court briefing is free of potential confounders that exist with other forms of lobbying (Hazelton, Hinkle, and Spriggs 2019).

2. There is also evidence that changes in the nature of government have led to an increase in groups working together; namely, the growth in the size and complexity of the government (Hula 1999). In this regard, Supreme Court litigation looks quite different. Rather than growing in size and complexity, the Court has maintained its current size of nine justices for one-hundred and fifty years (Judicial Circuits Act of 1866). Additionally, over time the Court has reduced its docket size while effectively gaining nearly absolute docket control (McGuire 2004).

3. Such information provision can take many forms, including repetition (Hazelton, Hinkle, and Spriggs 2019).

4. Several attorneys broached such variation across stages of litigation and the specifics of a case. For example, Attorney A noted that briefs regarding certiorari and on the merits serve different goals. Briefs at the certiorari stage are about getting the Court interested in taking the case whereas briefing on the merits speaks to policy-making concerns. In this vein, Attorney and Former Clerk H described the cert stage as being about "vehicle issue[s]" while the merits are where you "fully develop" arguments. They reported being "less even-handed at the cert stage" and "may change tack" at the merits stage. Attorney P similarly explained that the goals for a brief "depend on type." Specifically, there are differences in the goals for briefs for cert and merits, with less strategy being required for merits briefs. In that vein, Attorney C said that "case and issue dictate a lot" in determining what makes a good brief. There are "different goals and approaches" depending on the case. Former Clerk G reiterated this point: a good brief "differs by party." Additionally, Attorney R noted that the ultimate goal is "to persuade the Court [through] rhetorical means" and that "approaches vary." They went so far as to say that it is "all about persuasion regarding facts and law" and "not fairness." But they also said this was truer in Constitutional cases rather than statutory ones.

5. *Snyder v. Phelps*, 562 U.S. 443 (2011).

6. Such blocking may not be successful, as the Supreme Court can allow such briefing if the potential amicus requests it (Supreme Court Rule 37.2[b]).

7. Furthermore, none of the responding justices were in favor of restricting amicus participation.

8. This primary framework was set forth by one attorney and was supplemented with additional information from other interviews. At least half of the interviewees mentioned each of the three main areas that are listed. Furthermore, these areas can certainly overlap.

9. *City of Hays, Kansas v. Vogt*, 138 S.Ct. 1683 (2018).

10. This is the type of sharing that cosine similarity is very well suited to detect, as we detail later.

11. Further information regarding cosine similarity, including the relevant equations, can be found in Manning, Raghavan, and Schütze (2008); and Hazelton, Hinkle, and Spriggs (2019).

12. Br. Pet'r, 31, fn. 6, *Florida v. Harris*, No. 11–817 (U.S.).

13. Br. US, 13, fn. 4, *Florida v. Harris*, No. 11–817 (U.S.).

14. This is a fairly high score for a paragraph-to-paragraph analysis due to the smaller amount of text involved. It should be noted that this is not the unit of analysis we are using for our full-scale empirical analysis. Instead, we compare at the document level, which allows for an even richer understanding of the texts in the corpus.

15. The difference in cosine similarity scores by side was 0.19, but this difference is not statistically significant likely due to the small number of observations.

16. Br. Resp., 10, *Florida v. Harris*, No. 11-817 (U.S.).

17. Br. Inst. for Just., 19, *Florida v. Harris*, No. 11-817 (U.S.).

18. We calculate this number using an extension of our data set that contains briefs going back to 1970.

19. As we noted in chapter 2, another possibility would be to use average attorney experience. However, as in our chapter 2 analyses, using the average number of briefs signed in lieu of maximum experience does not alter any of our substantive conclusions.

20. Our data set includes not just the attorney of record or the first listed attorney but every attorney who signed each brief.

21. It is also plausible that attorneys who clerked for the same justice during the same term would also be better positioned to coordinate their efforts. This would be broadly consistent with Black and Owens's (2020) finding that former clerks have the most influence over the vote of the justice for whom they clerked. However, this factor is too rare to account for in our model.

22. Some scholars attribute this success to the expertise of the attorneys in that office (e.g., Spriggs and Wahlbeck 1997). Relatedly, as described in chapter 2, one interviewee (Attorney and Former Clerk H), who emphasized the uniqueness of the solicitor general, felt that the solicitor general's credibility was a crucial feature in the unusual position they held with the Court (see also Larsen and Devins 2016). However, others attribute it to the fact that the solicitor general represents a key player in the political system: the United States government (Epstein and Knight 1998). Still, others note how political/partisan issues shape solicitor general success (Bailey, Kamoie, and Maltzman 2005).

23. For example, McGuire (1994, 826) noted that lawyers for petitioners were keenly interested in soliciting the support from the United States (as well as other "Supreme Court heavyweights"). One interviewee (P) also noted that parties work exceptionally hard to recruit the solicitor general to file a brief on their behalf due to the power of such a brief.

24. All binary variables, previous attorney collaboration, former clerks, former solicitors general, and invited briefs are moved from zero to one.

Chapter 4. The Win/Loss Column: Influencing Case Outcomes

1. In the time frame of our empirical analyses, there are only two cases that the Supreme Court database does not code as a clear win or loss for the petitioner. Fewer than 2 percent of justices' votes are not coded as clearly being in favor of one side or the other. We exclude such observations from our models.

2. Estimates for the cost to file an amicus brief range from $25,000 to $50,000 per brief (Totenberg 2015).

3. *Webster v. Reproductive Health Services*, 492 U.S. 490 (1989).

4. Among other things, brief writers should probably avoid using arcane terms like "fripperies."

5. Excluding a measure to compare filer type does not impact our empirical results. Robustness checks show largely the same results with the inclusion of such a measure and, as anticipated, the difference in status measure is not statistically significant.

6. These are far from exhaustive indicators of attorney expertise. For example, members of the office of the solicitor general are also likely to have benefited from similar insights as the solicitor general themselves. However, the two measures we use are ones for which data is readily available.

7. Some similar research uses separate variables for petitioner and respondent for each quantity of interest (Black, Owens, et al. 2016). We use difference measures because they are more directly linked to our theoretical expectations and because they provide for a more parsimonious model. Using the alternative approach reveals substantially similar patterns.

8. For convenience, the number of unique words on each side is normalized by one thousand, and the number of unique cases cited on each side is normalized by one hundred.

9. The total number of words and cites is necessarily related to the number of unique words and cites. However, there is sufficient variation in the data to separately model each of these concepts while holding the other constant. For example, the difference in word count is still significant even if we exclude the vocabulary variable.

10. In this chapter (and in chapter 6, which has the same unit of analysis), we use the median to summarize experience because we are summarizing across multiple briefs. While there is coordination across briefs, as we show in chapter 3, a team of attorneys working together to draft a single brief is quite different from distinct sets of attorneys drafting distinct documents. In the former case, the most experienced attorney can take charge in a way that is not possible in the latter situation. For this reason, we use the maximum experience where the brief is the unit of analysis and we use the median experience where the case or case side is the unit of analysis.

11. Oral argument came up in our interviews as well. Attorney R was dubious that oral arguments are a place that one can win a case.

12. We obtained data on the number of questions posed to each side at oral arguments from two sources. We used replication data from Epstein, Landes, and Posner (2013) for 1984 to 2007 and from Gleason (2020) for 2008 to 2015. These sources do not have data for some of our cases. However, alternative analyses show that all models for chapters 4, 5, and 6 have substantially similar

results when we exclude the oral argument question variable and use the entirety of our data set.

13. The regression results are available in table form in appendix C, table A.

14. While the number of briefs and word count are related, they are not as highly correlated as one might expect. The difference measures in our models for logged word count and number of briefs are correlated at $r = 0.69$.

15. For comparison, moving "Ideological Alignment" from its twenty-fifth to seventy-fifth percentile value increases the petitioner's probability of winning the case by 0.06.

*Chapter 5. Standing Out or Speaking Together: How Individual
Briefs Shape Opinion Content*

1. The importance of the outcomes themselves likely matter to parties and amici in varying ways (Collins 2008; Marvell 1978; Wofford 2020).

2. Here, we are referring to similarity as measured by cosine similarity.

3. The briefs have the following cosine similarity scores: Florida—0.68; Harris—0.65; US—0.65; Rutherford Institute (on behalf of Harris), National Police Canine Association and *Police K-9 Magazine* (for Florida), and Virginia and the other states (also for Florida) around 0.5; and four amici supporting Harris—the NACDL et al.—0.48, the Fourth Amendment scholars—0.39, Electronic Privacy Information Center (EPIC)—0.25, and the Institute for Justice—0.18. The briefs are easily accessible via SCOTUSBlog, "Florida v. Harris," accessed January 17, 2022, https://www.scotusblog.com/case-files/cases/florida-v-harris/, for substantive comparison.

4. There are, of course, other sources of information, including oral argument (Johnson 2004).

5. The concepts of minority and majority information are not identical to novel and shared information (Hazelton, Hinkle, and Spriggs 2019, 147, fn. 6). Instead, minority information is, by definition, promoted by less than half of the presenters. In comparison, only one speaker provides novel information. Novel information cannot be majority information by definition; rather, it is either minority information or information exerted by half of the speakers if there are only two. Thus, though varying in the degree to which speakers articulate it, novel information is related to the concept of minority information.

6. The importance of legal facts in legal writing was highlighted by several interviewees. In addition to the statements described in chapters 2 and 3, Attorney R was adamant about the importance of facts: one needs the "right facts and law to persuade . . . . Facts are very stubborn and important." Furthermore, "Specific facts are important." They pointed to the Masterpiece Cakeshop case as an example of the importance of specific facts. There, the Court resolved

the case based on the hostility of the commission rather than the First Amendment.

7. We look to the party's main brief, excluding the reply, to allow for a more natural comparison regarding the information provided.

8. *Romer v. Evans*, 517 US 620 (1996).

9. We used WCopyfind.4.1.5 using the same settings as Collins, Corley, and Hamner (2013).

10. As discussed in chapter 1, legal citations have special meaning in building legal arguments in the US common-law system. Therefore, they are a natural place to consider the influence of language in briefs.

11. All citations to Supreme Court precedents were stripped from the briefs and lower court opinions and separately analyzed when measuring the contributions of such cites.

12. The party and solicitor general briefs fell between 0.05 and 0.07, while the other amicus briefs had scores between 0.07 and 0.11.

13. While causation is a key legal concept in some areas of law, we still anticipate that higher levels of discussion of such concepts are associated with more technical information.

14. We use an abridged version of the original LIWC dictionaries to account for linguistic usage in the legal context.

15. Staci Zaretsky, 2018, "$400K Is Now the Official Market Rate for Supreme Court Clerk Bonuses," *Above the Law* (blog), November 15, https://abovethelaw .com/2018/11/400k-is-now-the-official-market-rate-for-supreme-court-clerk -bonuses/.

16. One aspect of the litigation that we purposely do not include in our models is how the justices voted. A brief filed on the side that wins a case should clearly exert more influence over the opinion text than one from the losing side, and this is the case in our data. However, it is inappropriate to include posttreatment variables in a regression model, and votes and opinion drafting take place in an iterative process in which they may well influence each other. While votes that do not change may be cast before opinion drafting in some cases, we do know there is back and forth behind the scenes as justices change votes and modify opinion text during the process of opinion drafting (Maltzman, Spriggs, and Wahlbeck 2000). Due to this concern regarding bias, we have chosen to not use the case outcome as an explanatory variable lest we try to explain something (opinion text) with a data point (votes) that might have been generated after the thing we are trying to explain. Such an approach could induce bias in our analyses. However, including variables for whether the side advocated by a brief won and how many votes were cast in their favor leads to substantive conclusions that are largely the same as those we present here.

17. The regression results may be found in table form in appendix C, table A7.

18. In fact, an alternative measure using the median of the majority is statistically significant (while little else in the models changes). Nevertheless, we use the median of the full Court to avoid the potential bias that would flow from opinion content shaping who is ultimately in the majority.

Chapter 6. Shaping the Law Together: Collectively Influencing Opinion Content

1. Due to the tendency of word counts to be right skewed, we use this standard technique to transform the raw counts.

2. Due to the unique position of the Supreme Court, only prior decisions from the Court arguably have precedential effect (Schauer 2007).

3. To illustrate this reasoning, consider a group of ten attorneys working together to write a brief. The most experienced can make sure the end product is consistent with their level of knowledge. However, if ten attorneys write ten separate briefs, the collective influence of those ten briefs is better described by the usual approach of employing a measure of central tendency because the attorney with maximal experience can only directly influence their work product, not everyone else's.

4. The regression results may be found in table form in appendix C, table A8.

5. The table form of regression results may be found in appendix C, table A9.

Conclusion

1. *Mapp v. Ohio*, 367 U.S. 643 (1961).

2. In the interest of transparency and encouraging future research, we have also included interview statements related to potential areas of research that didn't make it into the book in appendix A.3. This includes areas not discussed in the Conclusion.

3. As did another Florida dog search case decided that term—*Florida v. Jardines*, 569 U.S. 1 (2013), where the Court disallowed the warrantless use of a dog to sniff the porch of a home.

Bibliography

Abramowicz, Michael, and Thomas B. Colby. 2009. "Notice-and-Comment Judicial Decisionmaking." *University of Chicago Law Review* 76 (3): 965–1036.

Afflerbach, Peter, and Byeong-Young Cho. 2009. "Identifying and Describing Constructively Responsive Comprehension Strategies in New and Traditional Forms of Reading." In *Handbook of Research on Reading Comprehension*, ed. Susan E. Israel and Gerald G. Duffy, 69–90. New York: Routledge.

Albiston, Catherine. 1999. "The Rule of Law and the Litigation Process: The Paradox of Losing by Winning." *Law & Society Review* 33 (4): 869–910.

Aldisert, Ruggero J. 1989. "Precedent: What It Is and What It Isn't: When Do We Kiss It and When Do We Kill It." *Pepperdine Law Review* 17 (3): 605–636.

Anderson, Norman H. 1971. "Integration Theory and Attitude Change." *Psychological Review* 78 (3): 171–206.

Anmarkrud, Øistein, Ivar Bråten, and Helge I. Strømsø. 2014. "Multiple-Documents Literacy: Strategic Processing, Source Awareness, and Argumentation when Reading Multiple Conflicting Documents." *Learning and Individual Differences* 30:64–76.

Arnold, R. Douglas. 1992. *The Logic of Congressional Action*. New Haven, CT: Yale University Press.

Asch, Solomon E. 1951. "Effects of Group Pressure upon the Modification and Distortion of Judgments." In *Groups, Leadership and Men*, ed. Harold Guetzkow, 177–190. Pittsburgh, PA: Carnegie Press.

Atkins, Burton M. 1991. "Party Capability Theory as an Explanation for Intervention Behavior in the English Court of Appeal." *American Journal of Political Science* 35 (4): 881–903.

Austen-Smith, David. 1996. "Interest Groups: Money, Information and Influence." In *Perspectives on Public Choice: A Handbook*, ed. Dennis C. Muller, 296–321. Cambridge: Cambridge University Press.

Bailey, Michael A., Brian Kamoie, and Forrest Maltzman. 2005. "Signals from the Tenth Justice: The Political Role of the Solicitor General in Supreme Court Decision Making." *American Journal of Political Science* 49 (1): 72–85.

Barker, Lucius J. 1967. "Third Parties in Litigation: A Systemic View of the Judicial Function." *Journal of Politics* 29 (1): 41–69.

Barnes, Robert. 2007. "Justices Weigh Courts' Role in Detainee Cases." *Washington Post*, December 5, 2007.

Baron, Robert S., and S. Beth Bellman. 2007. "No Guts, No Glory: Courage,

Harassment and Minority Influence." *European Journal of Social Psychology* 37 (1): 101–124.

Baumgartner, Frank R., Jeffrey M. Berry, Marie Hojnacki, Beth L. Leech, and David C. Kimball. 2009. *Lobbying and Policy Change: Who Wins, Who Loses, and Why.* Chicago: University of Chicago Press.

Beazley, Mary Beth. 2010. *A Practical Guide to Appellate Advocacy.* New York: Aspen Publishers.

Behuniak-Long, Susan. 1990. "Friendly Fire: Amici Curiae and *Webster v. Reproductive Health Services.*" *Judicature* 74 (5): 261–270.

Belz, Emily. 2017. "High Court, High Costs." *World Magazine*, March 7, 2020, https://world.wng.org/2017/09/high_court_high_costs.

Bennett, Robert W. 2000. "Counter-Conversationalism and the Sense of Difficulty." *Northwestern University Law Review* 95 (3): 845–906.

Bennett, Winfield S., and Jonathan Slocum. 1985. "The LRC Machine Translation System." *Computational Linguistics* 11 (2–3): 111–121.

Berlo, David K., James B. Lemert, and Robert J. Mertz. 1969. "Dimensions for Evaluating the Acceptability of Message Sources." *Public Opinion Quarterly* 33 (4): 563–576.

Bils, Peter, Lawrence Rothenberg, and Bradley C. Smith. 2020. "The Amicus Game." *Journal of Politics* 82 (3): 1113–1126.

Black, Ryan C., and Christina L. Boyd. 2010. "U.S. Supreme Court Agenda Setting and the Role of Litigant Status." *Journal of Law, Economics & Organization* 28 (2): 1–27.

———, and Ryan J. Owens. 2011. "Solicitor General Influence and Agenda Setting on the US Supreme Court." *Political Research Quarterly* 64 (4): 765–778.

———, and Ryan J. Owens. 2012. *The Solicitor General and the United States Supreme Court: Executive Branch Influence and Judicial Decisions.* Cambridge: Cambridge University Press.

———, and Ryan J. Owens. 2020. "The Influence of Personalized Knowledge at the Supreme Court: How (Some) Former Law Clerks Have the Inside Track." *Political Research Quarterly* 74 (4):795–807.

———, Matthew E. K. Hall, Ryan J. Owens, and Eve M. Ringsmuth. 2016. "The Role of Emotional Language in Briefs Before the U.S. Supreme Court." *Journal of Law and Courts* 4 (2): 377–407.

———, Ryan J. Owens, Justin Wedeking, and Patrick C. Wohlfarth. 2016. *U.S. Supreme Court Opinions and Their Audiences.* Cambridge: Cambridge University Press.

———, Timothy R. Johnson, and Justin Wedeking. 2012. *Oral Arguments and Coalition Formation on the US Supreme Court: A Deliberate Dialogue.* Ann Arbor: University of Michigan Press.

Box-Steffensmeier, Janet M., Dino P. Christenson, and Matthew P. Hitt. 2013.

"Quality over Quantity: Amici Influence and Judicial Decision Making." *American Political Science Review* 107 (3): 446–460.

Braman, Eileen, and Thomas E. Nelson. 2007. "Mechanism of Motivated Reasoning? Analogical Perception in Discrimination Disputes." *American Journal of Political Science* 51 (4): 940–956.

Brandeis, Louis D. Brief for Oregon in *Muller v. Oregon*, 208 U.S. 412 (1908). https://louisville.edu/law/library/special-collections/the-louis-d.-brandeis-collection/the-brandeis-brief-in-its-entirety

Bruhl, Aaron-Andrew P., and Adam Feldman. 2017. "Separating Amicus Wheat from Chaff." *Georgetown Law Journal Online* 106:135–150.

Bryan, Amanda C., and Eve M. Ringsmuth. 2016. "Jeremiad or Weapon of Words." *Journal of Law and Courts* 3 (Spring): 159–185.

Buckler, Kevin G. 2015. "Supreme Court Outcomes in Criminal Justice Cases (1994–2012 Terms): An Examination of Status Differential and Amici Curiae Effects." *Criminal Justice Policy Review* 26 (8): 773–804.

Caldeira, Gregory A. 1987. "Public Opinion and the US Supreme Court: FDR's Court-Packing Plan." *American Political Science Review* 81 (4): 1139–1153.

———, and John R. Wright. 1990a. "Amici Curiae Before the Supreme Court: Who Participates, When, and How Much?" *Journal of Politics* 52 (3): 782–806.

———, and John R. Wright. 1990b. "The Discuss List: Agenda Building in the Supreme Court." *Law & Society Review* 24 (3): 807–836.

Canary, Daniel J., Brent G. Brossmann, and David R. Seibold. 1987. "Argument Structures in Decision-Making Groups." *Southern Speech Communication Journal* 53 (1): 18–37.

Canelo, Kayla S. 2022. "The Supreme Court, Ideology, and the Decision to Cite or Borrow from Amicus Curiae Briefs." *American Politics Research* 50 (2): 255-264.

Canon, Bradley C., and Bradley A. Johnson. 1998. *Judicial Policies: Implementation and Impact*. 2nd ed. Washington, DC: CQ Press.

Carpenter, Dale. 2012. *Flagrant Conduct: The Story of* Lawrence v. Texas. New York: W. W. Norton.

Carrubba, Clifford J., and Tom S. Clark. 2012. "Rule Creation in a Political Hierarchy." *American Political Science Review* 106 (3): 622–643.

Christensen, Leah M. 2008. "The Paradox of Legal Expertise: A Study of Experts and Novices Reading the Law." *BYU Education and Law Journal*, no. 1, 53—88.

Clark, Tom S., and Benjamin Lauderdale. 2010. "Locating Supreme Court Opinions in Doctrine Space." *American Journal of Political Science* 54 (4): 871–890.

Clawson, Rosalee A., and Eric Waltenburg. 2008. *Legacy and Legitimacy: Black Americans and the Supreme Court*. Philadelphia, PA: Temple University Press.

Collins, Paul M., Jr. 2004. "Friends of the Court: Examining the Influence of

Amicus Curiae Participation in US Supreme Court Litigation." *Law & Society Review* 38 (4): 807–832.

———. 2007. "Lobbyists Before the US Supreme Court: Investigating the Influence of Amicus Curiae Briefs." *Political Research Quarterly* 60 (1): 55–70.

———. 2008. *Friends of the Supreme Court: Interest Groups and Judicial Decision Making.* New York: Oxford University Press.

———. 2018. "The Use of Amicus Briefs." *Annual Review of Law and Social Science* 14 (1): 219–237.

———, and Lauren A. McCarthy. 2017. "Friends and Interveners: Interest Group Litigation in a Comparative Context." *Journal of Law and Courts* 5 (1): 55–80.

———, and Lisa A. Solowiej. 2007. "Interest Group Participation, Competition, and Conflict in the US Supreme Court." *Law & Social Inquiry* 32 (4): 955-984.

———, and Wendy L. Martinek. 2015. "Judges and Friends: The Influence of Amici Curiae on US Court of Appeals Judges." *American Politics Research* 43 (2): 255–282.

———, Pamela C. Corley, and Jesse Hamner. 2013. "Me Too: An Investigation of Repetition in US Supreme Court Amicus Curiae Briefs." *Judicature* 97 (5): 228-234.

———, Pamela C. Corley, and Jesse Hamner. 2015. "The Influence of Amicus Curiae Briefs on US Supreme Court Opinion Content." *Law & Society Review* 49 (4): 917–944.

Corley, Pamela C. 2008. "The Supreme Court and Opinion Content: The Influence of Parties' Briefs." *Political Research Quarterly* 61:468–478.

———, Amy Steigerwalt, and Artemus Ward. 2013. *The Puzzle of Unanimity: Explaining Consensus on the U.S. Supreme Court.* Stanford, CA: Stanford University Press.

———, and Justin Wedeking. 2014. "The (Dis) Advantage of Certainty: The Importance of Certainty in Language." *Law & Society Review* 48 (1): 35–62.

———, Paul M. Collins, and Bryan Calvin. 2011. "Lower Court Influence on US Supreme Court Opinion Content." *Journal of Politics* 73:31–44.

Crano, William D., and Radmila Prislin. 2006. "Attitudes and Persuasion." *Annual Review of Psychology* 57:345–374.

Dahl, Robert A. 1957. "Decision-Making in a Democracy: The Supreme Court as a National Policy Maker." *Journal of Public Law* 6:279–295.

Davis, Kenneth Culp. 1955. "Judicial Notice." *Columbia Law Review* 55 (7): 945–984.

Dewitz, Peter. 1995. "Reading Law-Three Suggestions for Legal Education." *University of Toledo Law Review* 27 (Spring): 657–673.

Downs, A. 1957. *An Economic Theory of Democracy.* New York: Harper.

DuBay, William H. 2004. *The Principles of Readability.* Costa Mesa, CA: Impact Information.

Dumas, Tao L., Stacia L. Haynie, and Dorothy Daboval. 2015. "Does Size Matter? The Influence of Law Firm Size on Litigant Success Rates." *Justice System Journal* 36 (4): 341–354.

Ebner, L. 2017. "Learning the High Art of Amicus Brief Writing." For the Defense, February, https://capitalappellate.com/wp-content/uploads/Learning-the-High-Art-of-Amicus-Brief-Writing.pdf.

Enns, Peter K., and Julianna Koch. 2013. "Public Opinion in the US States 1956 to 2010." *State Politics & Policy Quarterly* 13 (3): 349–372.

Epstein, Lee, and Eric A. Posner. 2016. "Supreme Court Justices' Loyalty to the President." *Journal of Legal Studies* 45, 2: 401–436.

———, and Jack Knight. 1998. *The Choices Justices Make.* Washington, DC: CQ Press.

———, and Jack Knight. 1999. "Mapping out the Strategic Terrain: The Informational Role of Amici Curiae." In *Supreme Court Decision-Making: New Institutionalist Approaches,* ed. Cornell W. Clayton and Howard Gillman, 225–228. Chicago: University of Chicago Press.

———, and Joseph F. Kobylka. 1992. *The Supreme Court and Legal Change: Abortion and the Death Penalty.* Chapel Hill: University of North Carolina Press.

———, Jeffrey A. Segal, and Timothy Johnson. 1996. "The Claim of Issue Creation on the US Supreme Court." *American Political Science Review* 90 (4): 845–852.

———, Valerie Hoekstra, Jeffrey A. Segal, and Harold J. Spaeth. 1998. "Do Political Preferences Change? A Longitudinal Study of U.S. Supreme Court Justices." *Journal of Politics* 60 (3): 801–818.

———, William M. Landes, and Richard A. Posner. 2010. "Inferring the Winning Party in the Supreme Court from the Pattern of Questioning at Oral Argument." *Journal of Legal Studies* 39 (2): 433–467.

———, William M. Landes, and Richard A. Posner. 2013. *The Behavior of Federal Judges.* Cambridge, MA: Harvard University Press.

Erb, Hans-Peter, Denis J. Hilton, Gerd Bohner, and Lucia Roffey. 2015. "The Minority Decision—A Risky Choice." *Journal of Experimental Social Psychology* 57 (March): 43–50.

Farganis, Dion. 2012. "Do Reasons Matter? The Impact of Opinion Content on Supreme Court Legitimacy." *Political Research Quarterly* 65 (1): 206–216.

Farole, Donald J., Jr. 1999. "Reexamining Litigant Success in State Supreme Courts." *Law & Society Review* 33 (4): 1043–1058.

Feldman, Adam. 2016. "Counting on Quality: The Effects of Merits Brief Quality on Supreme Court Decisions." *Denver Law Review* 94 (1): 43–70.

———. 2017a. "A Brief Assessment of Supreme Court Opinion Language, 1946–2013." *Mississippi Law Journal* 86 (1): 105–150.

———. 2017b. "Opinion Construction in the Roberts Court." *Law & Policy* 39 (2): 192–209.

Flanders, Chad. 2009. "Toward a Theory of Persuasive Authority." *Oklahoma Law Review* 62 (1): 55–88.

Flemming, R. B., and Glen S. Krutz. 2002. "Repeat Litigators and Agenda Setting on the Supreme Court of Canada." *Canadian Journal of Political Science* 35 (4): 811–833.

Fontham, Michael R. 1985. *Written and Oral Advocacy*. Hoboken, NJ: Wiley Law Publications.

Forman, David S. 2016. "7 Tips for Writing an Effective Amicus Brief." Law360, June, https://oshaliang.com/wp-content/uploads/2016/06/7-Tips-For-Writing-An-Effective-Amicus-Brief.pdf.

Friedman, Barry. 2009. *The Will of the People: How Public Opinion Has Influenced the Supreme Court and Shaped the Meaning of the Constitution*. New York: Farrar, Straus & Giroux.

Galanter, Marc. 1974. "Why the Haves Come out Ahead: Speculations on the Limits of Legal Change." *Law & Society Review* 9:95–160.

Garner, Bryan A. 2010. "Interviews with United States Supreme Court Justices." *Scribes Journal of Legal Writing* 13:1–62.

———. 2014. *The Winning Brief: 100 Tips for Persuasive Briefing in Trial and Appellate Courts*. 2nd ed. New York: Oxford University Press.

Gibson, James L., and Gregory A. Caldeira. 1992. "Blacks and the United States Supreme Court: Models of Diffuse Support." *Journal of Politics* 54 (4): 1120–1145.

Gleason, Shane A. 2020. "Beyond Mere Presence: Gender Norms in Oral Arguments at the US Supreme Court." *Political Research Quarterly* 73 (3): 596–608.

Gonen, Julianna Susan. 1996. "Reproductive Hazards Litigation: Gender and Labor Politics in the Third Branch." PhD diss., American University.

Greenhouse, Linda. 2008. "The Counter-Factual Court." *University of Louisville Law Review* 47 (1): 1–20.

Haire, Susan B., and Laura P. Moyer. 2007. "Advocacy through Briefs in the US Courts of Appeals." *Southern Illinois University Law Journal* 32 (3): 593–609.

———, Roger Hartley, and Stefanie A. Lindquist. 1999. "Attorney Expertise, Litigant Success, and Judicial Decisionmaking in the U.S. Courts of Appeals." *Law & Society Review* 33 (3): 667–685.

Hall, Matthew E. K. 2010. *The Nature of Supreme Court Power*. Cambridge: Cambridge University Press.

———. 2014. "The Semiconstrained Court: Public Opinion, the Separation of Powers, and the U.S. Supreme Court's Fear of Nonimplementation." *American Journal of Political Science* 58 (2): 352–366.

Hanretty, Chris. 2014. "Haves and Have-Nots Before the Law Lords." *Political Studies* 62 (3): 686–697.

Hansford, Thomas G. 2004. "Information Provision, Organizational Constraints, and the Decision to Submit an Amicus Curiae Brief in a U.S. Supreme Court Case." *Political Research Quarterly* 57 (2): 219–230.

———, and James F. Spriggs II. 2006. *The Politics of Precedent on the U.S. Supreme Court.* Princeton, NJ: Princeton University Press.

———, and Kristen Johnson. 2014. "The Supply of Amicus Curiae Briefs in the Market for Information at the US Supreme Court." *Justice System Journal* 35 (4): 362–382.

Harkins, Stephen G., and Richard E. Petty. 1981a. "Effects of Source Magnification of Cognitive Effort on Attitudes: An Information-Processing View." *Journal of Personality and Social Psychology* 40 (3): 401–413.

———, and Richard E. Petty. 1981b. "The Multiple Source Effect in Persuasion: The Effects of Distraction." *Personality and Social Psychology Bulletin* 7 (4): 627–635.

Harris, Scott S. 2019. "Memorandum to Those Intending to File an Amicus Curiae Brief in the Supreme Court of the United States." Supreme Court of the United States, October. https://www.supremecourt.gov/casehand /AmicusGuide2019.pdf.

Haynie, Stacia L. 1994. "Resource Inequalities and Litigation Outcomes in the Philippine Supreme Court." *Journal of Politics* 56 (3): 752–772.

———, and Kaitlyn L. Sill. 2007. "Experienced Advocates and Litigation Outcomes: Repeat Players in the South African Supreme Court of Appeal." *Political Research Quarterly* 60 (3): 443–453.

Hazelton, Morgan L. W., Rachael K. Hinkle, and James F. Spriggs II. 2017. "The Long and the Short of It: The Influence of Briefs on Outcomes in the Roberts Courts." *Washington University Journal of Law & Policy* 54:123–138.

———, Rachael K. Hinkle, and James F. Spriggs II. 2019. "The Influence of Unique Information in Briefs on Supreme Court Opinion Content." *Justice System Journal* 40 (2): 126–157.

Heaney, Michael T., and Philip Leifeld. 2018. "Contributions by Interest Groups to Lobbying Coalitions." *Journal of Politics* 80 (2): 494–509.

Hinkle, Rachael K. 2015a. "Into the Words: Using Statutory Text to Explore the Impact of Federal Courts on State Policy Diffusion." *American Journal of Political Science* 59 (4): 1002–1021.

———. 2015b. "Legal Constraint in the U.S. Courts of Appeals." *Journal of Politics* 77 (3): 721–735.

———. 2016. "Strategic Anticipation of En Banc Review in the US Courts of Appeals." *Law & Society Review* 50 (2): 383–414.

———. 2017. "Panel Effects and Opinion Crafting in the US Courts of Appeals." *Journal of Law and Courts* 5 (2): 313–336.

———, and Michael J. Nelson. 2017. "How to Lose Cases and Influence People." *Statistics, Politics and Policy* 8 (2): 195–221.

Hoekstra, Valerie J. 2000. "The Supreme Court and Local Public Opinion." *American Political Science Review* 94 (1): 89–100.

―――. 2003. *Public Reaction to Supreme Court Decisions.* Cambridge: Cambridge University Press.

Hojnacki, Marie, and David C. Kimball. 1998. "Organized Interests and the Decision of Whom to Lobby in Congress." *American Political Science Review* 92 (4): 775–790.

―――, David C. Kimball, Frank R. Baumgartner, Jeffrey M. Berry, and Beth L. Leech. 2012. "Studying Organizational Advocacy and Influence: Reexamining Interest Group Research." *Annual Review of Political Science* 15 (1): 379–399.

Holyoak, Keith J., and Dan Simon. 1999. "Bidirectional Reasoning in Decision Making by Constraint Satisfaction." *Journal of Experimental Psychology: General* 128 (1): 3–31.

Holyoke, Thomas T. 2009. "Interest Group Competition and Coalition Formation." *American Journal of Political Science* 53 (2): 360–375.

Hovland, Carl I., and Walter Weiss. 1951. "The Influence of Source Credibility on Communication Effectiveness." *Public Opinion Quarterly* 15 (4): 635–650.

Huber, John D., and Charles R. Shipan. 2002. *Deliberate Discretion? The Institutional Foundations of Bureaucratic Autonomy.* Cambridge: Cambridge University Press.

―――, Charles R. Shipan, and Madelaine Pfahler. 2001. "Legislatures and Statutory Control of Bureaucracy." *American Journal of Political Science* 45 (2): 330–345.

Hula, Kevin W. 1999. *Lobbying Together: Interest Group Coalitions in Legislative Politics.* Washington, DC: Georgetown University Press.

Jia, Lifeng, Clement Yu, and Weiyi Meng. 2009. "The Effect of Negation on Sentiment Analysis and Retrieval Effectiveness." In *Proceedings of the 18th ACM conference on Information and Knowledge Management,* 1827–1830. New York: Association for Computing Machinery.

Johnson, Timothy R. 2001. "Information, Oral Arguments, and Supreme Court Decision Making." *American Politics Research* 29 (4): 331–351.

―――. 2004. *Oral Arguments and Decision Making on the United States Supreme Court.* Albany: State University of New York Press.

―――, James F. Spriggs II, and Paul J. Wahlbeck. 2012. "The Origin and Development of Stare Decisis at the US Supreme Court." In *New Directions in Judicial Politics,* edited by Kevin T. McGuire, 167–185. New York: Routledge.

―――, Paul J. Wahlbeck, and James F. Spriggs II. 2006. "The Influence of Oral Arguments on the U.S. Supreme Court." *American Political Science Review* 100 (1): 99–113.

Junk, Wiebke Marie. 2019. "When Diversity Works: The Effects of Coalition

Composition on the Success of Lobbying Coalitions." *American Journal of Political Science* 63 (3): 660–674.

Katyal, Neal Kumar. 2006. *"Hamdan v. Rumsfeld:* The Legal Academy Goes to Practice." *Harvard Law Review* 120 (1): 65–124.

Kearney, Joseph D., and Thomas W. Merrill. 2000. "The Influence of Amicus Curiae Briefs on the Supreme Court." *University of Pennsylvania Law Review* 148 (3): 743–855.

Kim, Chulyoung. 2014. "Adversarial and Inquisitorial Procedures with Information Acquisition." *Journal of Law, Economics & Organization* 30 (4): 767–803.

Kole, Janet S. 2013. *A Brief Guide to Brief Writing.* Chicago: American Bar Association.

Kollross, Melinda S. 2021. "10 Tips for Securing Beneficial Amicus Support on Appeal." Clausen Miller, September 10, https://www.clausen.com/10-tips -for-securing-beneficial-amicus-support-on-appeal/.

Kramer, Larry D. 2004. *The People Themselves: Popular Constitutionalism and Judicial Review.* New York: Oxford University Press.

Krehbiel, Keith. 1992. *Information and Legislative Organization.* Ann Arbor: University of Michigan Press.

Krislov, Samuel. 1963. "The Amicus Curiae Brief: From Friendship to Advocacy." *Yale Law Journal* 72 (4): 694–721.

Kurby, Christopher A., M. Anne Britt, and Joseph P. Magliano. 2005. "The Role of Top-Down and Bottom-Up Processes in Between-Text Integration." *Reading Psychology* 26 (4–5): 335–362.

Kurtz, Donn M., and Mandy A. Simon. 2007. "The Education of the American Political Elite: 1949–2001." *Social Science Journal* 44 (3): 480–494.

Larsen, Allison Orr. 2014. "The Trouble with Amicus Facts." *Virginia Law Review* 100 (8): 1757–1818.

———, and Neal Devins. 2016. "The Amicus Machine." *Virginia Law Review* 102 (8): 1901–1968.

Lat, David. 2015. "Top Supreme Court Advocates Charge How Much per Hour?" Above the Law, August 10, https://abovethelaw.com/2015/08/top -supreme-court-advocates-charge-how-much-per-hour/.

Lazarus, Richard J. 2007. "Advocacy Matters before and within the Supreme Court: Transforming the Court by Transforming the Bar." *Georgetown Law Journal* 96 (5): 1487–1564.

Levin, Mark R. 2006. *Men in Black: How the Supreme Court Is Destroying America.* Washington, DC: Regnery Publishing.

Leyden, Kevin M. 1995. "Interest Group Resources and Testimony at Congressional Hearings." *Legislative Studies Quarterly* 20 (3): 431–439.

Long, Lance N., and William F. Christensen. 2011. "Does the Readability of Your Brief Affect Your Chance of Winning an Appeal." *Journal of Appellate Practice & Process* 12 (1): 145–162.

Lou, JoAnna. 2015. "Surprising Cause of Death for Police Dogs." The Bark, November, https://thebark.com/content/surprising-cause-death-police-dogs.

Lundeberg, Mary A. 1987. "Metacognitive Aspects of Reading Comprehension: Studying Understanding in Legal Case Analysis." *Reading Research Quarterly* 22 (4): 407–432.

Lynch, Kelly J. 2004. "Best Friends? Supreme Court Law Clerks on Effective Amicus Curiae Briefs." *Journal of Law and Public Policy* 20 (1): 33–46.

Mahoney, Christine, and Frank R. Baumgartner. 2015. "Partners in Advocacy: Lobbyists and Government Officials in Washington." *Journal of Politics* 77 (1): 202–215.

Maltzman, Forrest, James F. Spriggs, II and Paul J. Wahlbeck. 2000. *Crafting Law on the Supreme Court: The Collegial Game*. Cambridge: Cambridge University Press.

Manning, Christopher D., Prabhakar Raghavan, and Hinrich Schütze. 2008. *Introduction to Information Retrieval*. Cambridge: Cambridge University Press.

Manz, William H. 2002. "Citations in Supreme Court Opinions and Briefs: A Comparative Study." *Law Library Journal* 94 (2): 267–300.

Manzi, Lucia, and Matthew E. K. Hall. 2017. "Friends You Can Trust: A Signaling Theory of Interest Group Litigation Before the US Supreme Court." *Law & Society Review* 51 (3): 704–734.

Margolis, Ellie. 2000. "Beyond Brandeis: Exploring the Uses of Non-Legal Materials in Appellate Briefs." *University of San Francisco Law Review* 34 (2): 197–236.

Martin, Andrew D., and Kevin M. Quinn. 2002. "Dynamic Ideal Point Estimation via Markov Chain Monte Carlo for the U.S. Supreme Court, 1953–1999." *Political Analysis* 10 (2): 134–153.

Martin, Robin, Miles Hewstone, and Pearl Y. Martin. 2007. "Systematic and Heuristic Processing of Majority and Minority-Endorsed Messages: The Effects of Varying Outcome Relevance and Levels of Orientation on Attitude and Message Processing." *Personality and Social Psychology Bulletin* 33 (1): 43–56.

Marvell, Thomas. 1978. *Appellate Courts and Lawyers: Information-Gathering in the Adversary System*. Westport, CT: Greenwood Press.

Massaro, Dominic W., and Daniel Friedman. 1990. "Models of Integration Given Multiple Sources of Information." *Psychological Review* 97 (2): 134–153.

Mauro, Tony. 2019. "US Supreme Court Tells Lawyers: Write Tighter." *National Law Journal*, April 19, https://www.law.com/nationallawjournal/2019/04/19/u-s-supreme-court-tells-lawyers-write-tighter/?slreturn=20211023152317.

Mayer Brown. n.d. "Amicus Briefs in the Supreme Court." Accessed January 7, 2022, https://www.mayerbrown.com/en/perspectives-events/publications/no-date/amicus-briefs-in-the-supreme-court.

McAtee, Andrea, and Kevin T. McGuire. 2007. "Lawyers, Justices, and Issue

Salience: When and How Do Legal Arguments Affect the U.S. Supreme Court?" *Law & Society Review* 41 (2): 259–278.

McCloskey, Robert G., and Sanford Levinson. 2016. *The American Supreme Court*. Chicago: University of Chicago Press.

McCormick, Peter. 1993. "Party Capability Theory and Appellate Success in the Supreme Court of Canada, 1949–1992." *Canadian Journal of Political Science* 26 (3): 523–540.

McGimsey, Diane. 2016 "Expert Q&A on Best Practices for Amicus Briefing." *Practical Law*, August/September. https://www.sullcrom.com/files/upload /LIT_AugSep16_OfNote-Amicus.pdf.

McGuire, Kevin T. 1993. "Lawyers and the US Supreme Court: The Washington Community and Legal Elites." *American Journal of Political Science* 37 (2): 365–390.

———. 1994. "Amici Curiae and Strategies for Gaining Access to the Supreme Court." *Political Research Quarterly* 47 (4): 821–837.

———. 1995. "Repeat Players in the Supreme Court: The Role of Experienced Lawyers in Litigation Success." *Journal of Politics* 57 (1): 187–196.

———. 2004. "The Institutionalization of the US Supreme Court." *Political Analysis* 12 (2): 128–142.

———, and Barbara Palmer. 1996. "Issues, Agendas, and Decision Making on the Supreme Court." *American Political Science Review* 90 (4): 853–865.

———, and Gregory A. Caldeira. 1993. "Lawyers, Organized Interests, and the Law of Obscenity: Agenda Setting in the Supreme Court." *American Political Science Review* 87 (3): 717–726.

———, Georg Vanberg, and Alixandra B. Yanus. 2007. "Targeting the Median Justice: A Content Analysis of Legal Arguments and Judicial Opinions." Paper presented at the Annual Meeting of the Southern Political Science Association, New Orleans, https://mcguire.web.unc.edu/wp-content/uploads /sites/1749/2014/01/targeting_median.pdf.

———, Georg Vanberg, Charles E. Smith Jr., and Gregory A. Caldeira. 2009. "Measuring Policy Content on the US Supreme Court." *Journal of Politics* 71 (4): 1305–1321.

McKay, Amy. 2012. "Buying Policy? The Effects of Lobbyists' Resources on Their Policy Success." *Political Research Quarterly* 65 (4): 908–923.

McLaughlin, G. Harry. 1969. "SMOG Grading–A New Readability Formula." *Journal of Reading* 12 (8): 639–646.

Meyers, Renée A., Dale E. Brashers, and Jennifer Hanner. 2000. "Majority-Minority Influence: Identifying Argumentative Patterns and Predicting Argument-Outcome Links." *Journal of Communication* 50 (4): 3–30.

Miller, Banks, Linda Camp Keith, and Jennifer S. Holmes. 2015. "Leveling the Odds: The Effect of Quality Legal Representation in Cases of Asymmetrical Capability." *Law & Society Review* 49 (1): 209–239.

Miller, Michael D., and Timothy R. Levine. 2019. "Persuasion." In *An Integrated Approach to Communication Theory and Research*, ed. Don W. Stacks, Michael B. Salwen, and Kristen C. Eichhorn, 261–276. New York: Routledge

Millett, Patricia A. 2009. "We're Your Government and We're Here to Help: Obtaining Amicus Support from the Federal Government in Supreme Court Cases." *Journal of Appellate Practice & Process* 10 (1): 209–228.

Moe, Terry M. 1988. *The Organization of Interests: Incentives and the Internal Dynamics of Political Interest Groups*. Chicago: University of Chicago Press.

Monaghan, Henry P. 2019. "Jurisdiction Stripping circa 2020: What the Dialogue (Still) Has to Teach Us." *Duke Law Journal* 69 (1): 1–70.

Moscovici, Serge. 1980. "Toward a Theory of Conversion Behavior." *Advances in Experimental Social Psychology* 13:209–239.

Myers, Jerome L., and Edward J. O'Brien. 1998. "Accessing the Discourse Representation During Reading." *Discourse Processes* 26 (2–3): 131–157.

Nelson, David, and Susan Webb Yackee. 2012. "Lobbying Coalitions and Government Policy Change: An Analysis of Federal Agency Rulemaking." *Journal of Politics* 74 (2): 339–353.

Nelson, Michael J., and Rachael K. Hinkle. 2018. "Crafting the Law: How Opinion Content Influences Legal Development." *Justice System Journal* 39 (2): 97–122.

Nemeth, Charlan J. 1986. "Differential Contributions of Majority and Minority influence." *Psychological Review* 93 (1): 23–32.

———, Kathleen Mosier, and Cynthia Chiles. 1992. "When Convergent Thought Improves Performance: Majority Versus Minority Influence." *Personality and Social Psychology Bulletin* 18 (2): 139–144.

Nida, Eugene A. 1992. "Sociolinguistic Implications of Academic Writing." *Language in Society* 21 (3): 477–485.

Nownes, Anthony J. 2006. *Total Lobbying: What Lobbyists Want (And How They Try to Get It)*. Cambridge: Cambridge University Press.

O'Brien, Edward J., and Jerome L. Myers. 1999. "Text Comprehension: A View from the Bottom Up." In *Narrative Comprehension, Causality, and Coherence*, ed. Susan R. Goldman, Arthur C. Graesser, and Paul van den Broek, 35–54. New York: Routledge.

O'Connor, Karen, and John R. Hermann. 1994. "Clerk Connection: Appearances Before the Supreme Court by Former Law Clerks." *Judicature* 78 (5): 247–249.

O'Keefe, Daniel J. 2015. *Persuasion: Theory and Research*. Thousand Oaks, CA: Sage Publications.

Owens, Ryan J., and Patrick C. Wohlfarth. 2014. "State Solicitors General, Appellate Expertise, and State Success Before the US Supreme Court." *Law & Society Review* 48 (3): 657–685.

Pacelle, Richard L., Jr. 2005. "Amicus Curiae or Amicus Praesidentis-Reexamining the Role of the Solicitor General in Filing Amici." *Judicature* 89 (6): 317–325.

———, John M. Scheb, Hemant K. Sharma, and David H. Scott. 2018. "Assessing the Influence of Amicus Curiae Briefs on the Roberts Court." *Social Science Quarterly* 99 (4): 1253–1266.

Packer, Dominic J. 2011. "The Dissenter's Dilemma, and a Social Identity Solution." In *Rebels in Groups: Dissent, Deviance, Difference, and Defiance*, ed. Jolanda Jetten and Matthew J. Hornsey, 281–301. Malden, MA: Wiley-Blackwell.

Pennebaker, James W., Martha E. Francis, and Roger J. Booth. 2001. *Linguistic Inquiry and Word Count: LIWC 2001 Manual.* Vol. 71. Mahwah, NJ: Earlbaum.

———, Roger J. Booth, and Martha E. Francis. 2007. *Linguistic Inquiry and Word Count: LIWC2007.* Austin, TX: LIWC.net.

Peppers, Todd C. 2006. *Courtiers of the Marble Palace: The Rise and Influence of the Supreme Court Law Clerk.* Stanford, CA: Stanford University Press.

———, and Artemus Ward. 2012. *In Chambers: Stories of Supreme Court Law Clerks and Their Justices.* Charlottesville: University of Virginia Press.

———, and Christopher Zorn. 2008. "Law Clerk Influence on Supreme Court Decision Making: An Empirical Assessment." *DePaul Law Review* 58 (1): 51–78.

Perkins, Jared. 2018. "Why File? Organized Interests and Amicus Briefs in State Courts of Last Resort." *Justice System Journal* 39 (1): 39–53.

———, and Paul M. Collins. 2017. *Interest Groups and the Judiciary.* New York: Oxford University Press.

Pildes, Richard H. 2011. "Is the Supreme Court a 'Majoritarian' Institution?" *Supreme Court Review* 2010 (1): 103–158.

"Preparing for the MPT." 2022. National Conference of Bar Examiners. https://www.ncbex.org/exams/mpt/preparing/.

Rice, Douglas. 2020. *Lighting the Way: Federal Courts, Civil Rights, and Public Policy.* Charlottesville: University of Virginia Press.

Rosen, Jeffrey. 2006. *The Most Democratic Branch: How the Courts Serve America.* New York: Oxford University Press.

Rutledge, Devallis. 2013. "Dogs, Drugs, and the Fourth Amendment." *POLICE Magazine*, May. https://www.policemag.com/340949/dogs-drugs-and-the-fourth-amendment.

Salamone, Michael Frank. 2014. "Judicial Consensus and Public Opinion: Conditional Response to Supreme Court Majority Size." *Political Research Quarterly* 67 (2): 320–334.

———. 2018. *Perceptions of a Polarized Court: How Division among Justices Shapes the Supreme Court's Public Image.* Philadelphia, PA: Temple University Press.

Salzman, Ryan, Christopher J. Williams, and Bryan T. Calvin. 2011. "The Determinants of the Number of Amicus Briefs Filed Before the US Supreme Court, 1953–2001." *Justice System Journal* 32 (3): 293–313.

Samaha, Adam M., Michael Heise, and Gregory C. Sisk. 2020. "Inputs and Outputs on Appeal: An Empirical Study of Briefs, Big Law, and Case Complexity." *Journal of Empirical Legal Studies* 17 (3): 519–555.

Scalia, Antonin, and Bryan A. Garner. 2008. *Making your Case: The Art of Persuading Judges.* St. Paul, MN: Thomson/West.

Schauer, Frederick. 1987. "Precedent." *Stanford Law Review* 39 (3): 571–605.

———. 2007. "Has Precedent Ever Really Mattered in the Supreme Court." *Georgia State University Law Review* 24 (2): 381–402.

———. 2008. "Authority and Authorities." *Virginia Law Review* 94 (8): 1931–1961.

Scott, David Hooper. 2013. "Friendly Fire: Amicus Curiae Participation and Impact at the Roberts Court." PhD diss., University of Tennessee-Knoxville.

Segal, Jeffrey A., and Harold J. Spaeth. 2002. *The Supreme Court and the Attitudinal Model Revisited.* Cambridge: Cambridge University Press.

Shapiro, Stephen M., Kenneth Geller, Timothy S. Bishop, Edward A. Hartnett, and Dan Himmelfarb. 2019. *Supreme Court Practice: For Practice in the Supreme Court of the United States.* Arlington, VA: Bloomberg Law.

Shaw, Katherine. 2015. "Friends of the Court: Evaluating the Supreme Court's Amicus Invitations." *Cornell Law Review* 101 (6): 1533–1596.

Sheehan, Reginald S., and Kirk A. Randazzo. 2012. "Explaining Litigant Success in the High Court of Australia." *Australian Journal of Political Science* 47 (2): 239–255.

———, William Mishler, and Donald R. Songer. 1992. "Ideology, Status, and the Differential Success of Direct Parties Before the Supreme Court." *American Political Science Review* 86 (2): 464–471.

Simard, Linda Sandstrom. 2007. "An Empirical Study of Amici Curiae in Federal Court: A Fine Balance of Access, Efficiency, and Adversarialism." *Review of Litigation* 27 (4): 669–712.

Simon, Dan, and Keith J. Holyoak. 2002. "Structural Dynamics of Cognition: From Consistency Theories to Constraint Satisfaction." *Personality and Social Psychology Review* 6 (4): 283–294.

Simpson, Reagan W., and Mary R. Vasaly. 2015. *The Amicus Brief: Answering the Ten Most Important Questions about Amicus Practice.* 4th ed. Chicago: American Bar Association.

Sinsheimer, Ann, and David J. Herring. 2016. "Lawyers at Work: A Study of the Reading, Writing, and Communication Practices of Legal Professionals." *Legal Writing: Journal of the Legal Writing Institute* 21:63–128.

Smith, Paul M. 1997. "The Sometimes Troubled Relationship between Courts and Their Friends." *Litigation* 24 (4): 24–26.

Songer, Donald R., and Reginald S. Sheehan. 1992. "Who Wins on Appeal? Upperdogs and Underdogs in the United States Courts of Appeals." *American Journal of Political Science* 36 (1): 235–258.

———, and Reginald S. Sheehan. 1993. "Interest Group Success in the Courts: Amicus Participation in the Supreme Court." *Political Research Quarterly* 46 (2): 339–354.

———, Ashlyn Kuersten, and Erin Kaheny. 2000. "Why the Haves Don't Always Come Out Ahead: Repeat Players Meet Amici Curiae for the Disadvantaged." *Political Research Quarterly* 53 (3): 537–556.

———, Reginald S. Sheehan, and Susan B. Haire. 1999. "Do the Haves Come Out Ahead over Time-Applying Galanter's Framework to Decisions of the US Courts of Appeals, 1925–1988." *Law & Society Review* 33 (4): 811–832.

Spriggs, James F., II. 1996. "The Supreme Court and Federal Administrative Agencies: A Resource-Based Theory and Analysis of Judicial Impact." *American Journal of Political Science* 40 (4): 1122–1151.

———, and Paul J. Wahlbeck. 1997. "Amicus Curiae and the Role of Information at the Supreme Court." *Political Research Quarterly* 50 (2): 365–386.

Stasser, Garold, and William Titus. 1985. "Pooling of Unshared Information in Group Decision Making: Biased Information Sampling During Discussion." *Journal of Personality and Social Psychology* 48 (6): 1467–1478.

Sungaila, Mary-Christine. 1998. "Effective Amicus Practice Before the United States Supreme Court: A Case Study." *Southern California Review of Law & Women's Studies* 8 (2): 187–196.

Sunstein, Cass R. 1993. "On Analogical Reasoning." *Harvard Law Review* 106 (3): 741–791.

Szmer, John J. 2005. "Unequal Justice Under Law? The Effects of Party and Attorney Capability on United States Supreme Court Decision Making." PhD diss., University of South Carolina.

———, and Martha Humphries Ginn. 2014. "Examining the Effects of Information, Attorney Capability, and Amicus Participation on US Supreme Court Decision Making." *American Politics Research* 42 (3): 441–471.

———, Donald R. Songer, and Jennifer Bowie. 2016. "Party Capability and the US Courts of Appeals: Understanding Why the 'Haves' Win." *Journal of Law and Courts* 4 (1): 65–102.

———, Susan W. Johnson, and Tammy A. Sarver. 2007. "Does the Lawyer Matter? Influencing Outcomes on the Supreme Court of Canada." *Law & Society Review* 41 (2): 279–304.

Tiller, Emerson H., and Frank B. Cross. 2006. "What Is Legal Doctrine." *Northwestern University Law Review* 100 (1): 517–534.

Toelch, Ulf, and Raymond J. Dolan. 2015. "Informational and Normative Influences in Conformity from a Neurocomputational Perspective." *Trends in Cognitive Sciences* 19 (10): 579–589.

Totenberg, Nina. 2015. "Record Number of Amicus Briefs Filed in Same-Sex-Marriage Case." NPR, April. https://www.npr.org/sections/itsallpolitics

/2015/04/28/402628280/recordnumber-of-amicus-briefs-filed-in-same-sex
-marriage-cases.

Ura, Joseph Daniel, and Alison Higgins Merrill. 2017. "The Supreme Court and Public Opinion." In *The Oxford Handbook of US Judicial Behavior*, ed. Lee Epstein and Stefanie A. Lindquist, 432–437. New York: Oxford University Press.

US Supreme Court. 2019. *Rules of the Supreme Court of the United States.* April. https://www.supremecourt.gov/ctrules/2019RulesoftheCourt.pdf

Wahlbeck, Paul J. 1997. "The Life of the Law: Judicial Politics and Legal Change." *Journal of Politics* 59 (3): 778–802.

Wanner, C. 1975. "The Public Ordering of Private Relations-Part One: Initiating Civil Cases in Urban Trial Courts." *Law & Society Review* 8 (3): 421–440.

Ward, Artemus, and David L. Weiden. 2006. *Sorcerers' Apprentices: 100 Years of Law Clerks at the United States Supreme Court.* New York: NYU Press.

———, Christina Dwyer, and Kiranjit Gill. 2014. "Bonus Babies Escape Golden Handcuffs: How Money and Politics Has Transformed the Career Paths of Supreme Court Law Clerks." *Marquette Law Review* 98 (1): 227–260.

Wheeler, Stanton, Bliss Cartwright, Robert A. Kagan, and Lawrence M. Friedman. 1987. "Do the Haves Come out Ahead? Winning and Losing in State Supreme Courts, 1870–1970." *Law & Society Review* 21 (3): 403–445.

Wofford, Claire B. 2015. "Assessing the Anecdotes: Amicus Curiae, Legal Rules, and the US Supreme Court." *Justice System Journal* 36 (3): 274–294.

———. 2020. "Why Try? Comparing the Aims of Parties and Amici in US Supreme Court Litigation." *Justice System Journal* 41 (2): 81–97.

Wolfson, Andrew. 2019. "Failing the Sniff Test? Narcotics Searches Spurred by Drug Dogs Often Come up Empty." *Courier-Journal,* June 13.

Yackee, Jason Webb, and Susan Webb Yackee. 2006. "A Bias Towards Business? Assessing Interest Group Influence on the US Bureaucracy." *Journal of Politics* 68 (1): 128–139.

Zink, James R., James F. Spriggs, and John T. Scott. 2009. "Courting the Public: The Influence of Decision Attributes on Individuals' Views of Court Opinions." *Journal of Politics* 71 (3): 909–925.

Index